005518

PN
1031
.W516
1976

Wimsatt, William
Kurtz

Day of the leop-
ards

DATE DUE

NOV 21 '96			

LAKE TAHOE COMMUN
LEARNING RESOURCE

D1017123

DAY OF THE LEOPARDS

DAY OF THE LEOPARDS

ESSAYS IN DEFENSE OF POEMS

W. K. Wimsatt

NEW HAVEN AND LONDON
YALE UNIVERSITY PRESS
1976

LAKE TAHOE COMMUNITY COLLEGE
LEARNING RESOURCES CENTER

Copyright © 1976 by Yale University.
All rights reserved. This book may not be
reproduced, in whole or in part, in any form
(except by reviewers for the public press),
without written permission from the publishers.
Library of Congress catalog card number: 75-27762
International standard book number: 0-300-01960-2

Set in IBM Century type.
Printed in the United States of America by
The Alpine Press, South Braintree, Massachusetts

Published in Great Britain, Europe, and Africa by
Yale University Press, Ltd., London.
Distributed in Latin America by Kaiman & Polon,
Inc., New York City; in Australasia by Book & Film
Services, Artarmon, N.S.W., Australia;
in Japan by John Weatherhill, Inc., Tokyo.

For
Martin and Mary
Price

11/76 Pd 12.58

. . . he develops a morbid and unhealthy faculty of truth-telling, begins to verify all statements made in his presence, has no hesitation in contradicting people who are much younger than himself . . . .

—Oscar Wilde, *The Decay of Lying*

CONTENTS

PREFACE

A book of critical essays which I published in 1965—*Hateful Contraries*—had the good fortune to be described by one reviewer, David Lodge, of Birmingham, in terms which seemed to me perfectly just. "What he stands for," wrote Lodge, is a "theory of poetry which regards poems as complexes of publicly accessible meanings, and which, without invoking the chimera of 'scientific' methodology, seeks to bring criticism to a maximum degree of precision compatible with the essential indeterminacy of its materials."[1] Some of the essays of 1965 were polemical. Some of the present collection are no less so. All the essays in each collection (as well as those of my earlier *Verbal Icon*) can, I believe, be said to be opinionated—that is, to urge some opinion as strongly as I am able, without my believing, however, that I am offering scientific proof of anything. All in the present collection deserve, I believe, to be read in the perspective sketched so fairly by my reviewer of 1965.

The present book is divided into three main parts. The five essays included in Part I pursue a medley of theoretical topics—the hoary issue of "intentionalism," the variegated mythopoeia of Northrop Frye. . . . The visit to Laokoön (essay 3) carries with it a supplement in the shape of a brief linguistic and stylistic meditation. Part II of the book inserts into the main argumentative sequence a vertical or historical dimension—four essays on as many different topics of eighteenth-century English literature. Part III returns to theory in four essays centering on the contemporary problematic status of poems as whole objects. I find no embarrassment in having taken both sides of the debate. The essay entitled "Battering the Object" argues for the salvage and preservation of whole poems against various kinds of analysis and dissolution. On the other hand, the adjacent essay on "Organic Form" argues against the extremes of the organistic or holistic conception.

The first essay in the book, "Day of the Leopards," furnishes, I think aptly, the title of the whole. *The Verbal Icon, Hateful Contraries, Day of the Leopards.* That sequence of titles runs with a kind of plausibility, even an apparent inevitability. For the concrete poetic unity demands parts, and not only parts but diverse parts, or complexity. This latter is not just a concession to the empirical made by the unifying poetic virtue—it is a needed condition for the exercise of that virtue. "Without con-

---

1. *Modern Language Review* 51 (October 1966): 647.

traries is no progression," we know.[2] Disparity, irony, tension have their own poetic rights. And in this complex of rights lies all too ready an invitation to division, disruption, destruction— at least for those who take poetry as a kind of directive for action, or take certain kinds of action as a kind of poetry. This is an old lesson, as old at least as the tenth book of Plato's *Republic.* Anything short of such anarchy will in fact be dubbed by the modern refining and nagging critical conscience as "Platonism."[3] During the later 1960s, not only criticism but drama, fiction, poetry, and real life seemed to move (if we keep to polite terms) in a crescendo of anti-Platonism. That is putting it *very* politely. When institutions are crumbling, when chaos surges at the gates, art can only record the event it has perhaps helped to bring on—sometimes with an accent of guileless impotence, sometimes pathetically, wringing its hands. Art has no remedies.

2. See the reprint of my "Day of the Leopards," with the rebukes of three Promethean voices in *College English* 33 (May 1972): 877-89.
3. See Murray Krieger, *The Tragic Vision* (New York, 1960), pp. 242-45.

ACKNOWLEDGMENTS

The essays have appeared in the following places: "Day of the Leopards" in *Ventures: Magazine of the Yale Graduate School* 9 (Fall 1969); "Genesis: An Argument Resumed" in *The Disciplines of Criticism: Essays in Literary Theory, Interpretation, and History*, ed. Peter Demetz, Thomas Greene, and Lowry Nelson (Yale University Press, 1968); "Laokoön: An Oracle Reconsulted" in *Eighteenth Century Studies in Honor of Donald F. Hyde*, ed. W. H. Bond (The Grolier Club, 1970); "In Search of Verbal Mimesis" in *Graphesis: Perspectives in Literature and Philosophy*, ed. Marie Rose Logan, *Yale French Studies* 52 (1976); "Northrop Frye: Criticism as Myth" in *Northrop Frye in Modern Criticism*, ed. Murray Krieger (Columbia University Press, 1966); "Belinda Ludens" in *New Literary History* 4 (Winter 1973); "Imitation as Freedom: 1717–1798" in *New Literary History* 1 (Winter 1970); "In Praise of *Rasselas*: Four Notes Converging" in *Imagined Worlds: Essays on Some English Novels and Novelists in Honour of John Butt*, ed. Maynard Mack and Ian Gregor (Methuen & Co., 1968); "Johnson's *Dictionary*" in *New Light on Dr. Johnson*, ed. Frederick W. Hilles (Yale University Press, 1959); "Battering the Object" in *Contemporary Criticism*, ed. Malcolm Bradbury and David Palmer (Edward Arnold, 1970); "Organic Form: Some Questions about a Metaphor" in *Organic Form: The Life of an Idea*, ed. George Rousseau (Routledge and Kegan Paul, 1972); "'Jam Nunc Debentia Dici': Answers to a Questionnaire" in *Arion: A Journal of Humanities and the Classics* 9 (Summer & Autumn, 1970); "I. A. R.: What to Say about a Poem" in *I. A. Richards: Essays in His Honor*, ed. Reuben A. Brower, Helen Vendler, and John Hollander (copyright © 1973 by Oxford University Press, Inc.).

I wish to thank the editors of the magazines and the directors of the presses for their courtesy in extending permission for the republication of these materials.

Some of the titles have been altered from the originals.

Some of the essays have already had other printings: "Day of the Leopards" in *College English* 33 (May 1972); a French version of "Belinda Ludens" in *Poétique* 10 (1972); an Italian version of "Imitation as Freedom: 1717–1798" in *Strumenti Critici* 9 (June 1969) and a shorter English version in *Forms of Lyric*, ed. Reuben A. Brower (Columbia University Press, 1970); "Organic Form: Some Questions about a Metaphor" in *Romanticism: Vistas, Instances, Continuities*, ed. David

Thorburn and Geoffrey Hartman (Cornell University Press, 1973).

Some of these essays or drafts approaching them have been read before learned societies, clubs, or symposia. Some were written specifically for the occasions. I am grateful to all the audiences and to the chairmen. Let me name the Modern Language Association of America, the Yale English Department Lectures, the English Institute, the Tudor and Stuart Club at The Johns Hopkins University, the New England College English Association. The date of first delivery or publication is given at the end of each essay. I have not attempted to bring internal references up to date for the year 1975. In a few places I have added or rewritten a sentence or two.

I owe a great deal, in one way or another, to many friends—and especially to Harold Bloom, Galen Brandt, Frank Brady, David Earnest, Janet Gezari, Bartlett Giamatti, Ellen Graham, Richard Greene, Murray Krieger, Marie Rose Logan, George Lord, Maynard Mack, Louis Martz, Lowry Nelson, G. N. G. Orsini, Barbara Packer, Martin and Mary Price, Andrew Rosenheim, George Rousseau, Rulon Wells, and (most of all) to Margaret Wimsatt, my wife. These and others (whom beyond question I am now overlooking) have joined to create for me that valuable adjunct of critical power named by Michael Riffaterre the "super-reader."

W. K. W.

New Haven
November 1975

I

CONTRARIES

DAY OF THE LEOPARDS

> Leopards break into the temple and drink the
> sacrificial chalices dry; this occurs repeatedly,
> again and again; finally it can be reckoned on
> beforehand and becomes part of the
> ceremony.
>
> —Franz Kafka

Visible time, public outrage, move faster these days than one can write and publish. As late as December 30th, 1967, E. B. White, in a New Year's Eve reflection for the *New York Times*, could write: "The *faint*, acrid smell of anarchy got into the air when those to whom law is intrinsically distasteful took charge." The emphasis is mine. The only thing novel about the meditation I am about to offer is a diffident glance at what one might suppose to be one of the last citadels of contemporary calm, academic literary criticism. The examples I shall quote are now nearly all out of date. I retain them, partly because examples of any date will serve the idea upon which I am intent, and partly because I am willing to advertise the fact that I wrote and delivered a paper which was substantially the same as the present, not during the spring of the tortured year 1969, when I submit this to the present editors, but in the relatively halcyon moment of January and February 1968.[1]

The first and better part of my essay is in effect an anthology of excerpts—in three series, two from the academy, one from the louder outside world. It happens that the three passages of the first series are all taken from the writing of colleagues, professors of English at Yale. This happens not because I detect in these anything like a Yale school of thought. Even less because I quote in a spirit of rancor or denunciation or any other kind of superior feeling. Long ago Austin Warren in a *Kenyon Review* essay (Autumn 1943) pointed out some alarming implications of the doctrine of poetic "irony" then championed, for our generation in America, most efficiently by the politically "reactionary" school of New Critics. "The danger of such a philosophy is that, in its awareness, its inclusiveness, it shall turn finally sceptical, or regard ambiguity and complexity as final virtues." There is hardly one of us among those who recognized the

---

1. A first version of this paper was read before the First Annual Congress for the Arts, Religion, and Culture (ARC), at the Museum of Modern Art, in New York City, February 3, 1968; and a second version, before a meeting of the English Forum at Yale, discussing "The Future of Criticism," October 28, 1968.

exciting truth of the novel doctrine who has not in some degree, here or there, with more or less force or feebleness, intimated as much as the three writers I am about to quote. Few others have written with equal trenchancy and clarity. One reason for my selection of these representatives is simply that they happen to be among the best critics that I read. They are not to be grouped together as critics of one school or sort. This is a further testimony to the current orthodoxy of the idea I would illustrate.

   1. "A deep art is bound to carry some shock to the devout, just as it carries some shock to the conventional. The devout man is committed to an order not of this world, and the conventional man is committed to an order of this world. Deep art implies a destruction of order for the sake of reordering. There is something incorrigible and anarchic lurking in art. The devout and the conventional are right. It is dangerous."— R. P. Warren, Foreword to *Christian Faith and the Contemporary Arts*, ed. Finley Eversole, New York and Nashville, 1957.[2]

   2. "The realization is gradually won that society is always based on some form of social lie or vital myth. . . . Language, social structure and mental life are systems that must be cleared of blockages, pseudo-problems, or scleroses. . . . Profanation enters the inner sanctum, and becomes part of the holy. . . . Does not every society, every relationship, every system have its necessary and permitted profanations? . . . literature is a kind of loyal (though not always legal) opposition which opens the sacred to scrutiny, and so at once profanes and purifies it. . . . Great art is always flanked by its dark sisters, blasphemy and pornography."—Geoffrey Hartman,

---

   2. See *The American Scholar* 37 (Summer 1968): 482-96, a "Symposium" on "Violence in Literature," held at the New School for Social Research in the spring of 1968. The novelists R. P. Warren and William Styron joined a psychiatrist, Robert Coles, and an editor, Theodore Solotaroff. "I think we've gotten over—I hope we've gotten over—the notion we're going to get over violence" (Coles, 484). "I have been attracted by violence, and . . . all of my works contain violence, because we live in a violent century" (Styron, 485-86). "This is 'ritualized' violence. . . . He's indulging his appetite for violence through ritualization, and including yours" (Warren, 487-88). ". . . violence in literature today is very much related to a certain kind of stake we have in irrationality itself" (Solotaroff, 492). ". . . a kind of anarchic murder is in the air" (Styron, 494). "The writer is obligated to try to make sense in some way of this shocking fact of existence" (Warren, 494). ". . . the world is now beating the modern writer at his own game" (Solotaroff, 496).

"Structuralism: The Anglo-American Adventure," *Yale French Studies* 36-37 (1966): 152, 162, 167, 168.[3]

  3. "Some thoughts about *Bacchae*: . . . I was inspired to a new production of this play during the recent march on Washington when the hippies determined to levitate the Pentagon. There was a harrowing photo in the New York *Times* Book Section showing troops in front of the Pentagon with their bayonets drawn against the hippies. . . . The play is about a conflict between irrationality, ecstasy, hallucination, disorder, anarchy, chaos, drunkenness on the one hand, and order, rigidity, inflexibility, tradition, organization on the other. I don't think that Euripides means to argue for one or the other pattern of being. His argument generally in such plays is that you cannot ignore any aspect of life without being destroyed by it."—Robert Brustein, letter to André Gregory, December 3, 1968, in program of *Bacchae*, The Yale School of Drama Repertory Theatre, March 6-22, 1969.[4]

End of my first series of quotations. Those of my second series are taken not from the groves of academe, but from the journalism of the everyday, unrefined world. The juxtaposition is coarse. Outlandish and far-fetched? I do not think so—even though I argue no actual or even likely causal connection between any of these moments of the two worlds which I adduce —aside from the incidental inspiration of the academic by the outside alluded to in the third above. I adduce the outer world as an amplifier for the academic—to give a step-up to its resonance, perhaps to induce a momentary suspicion, or illusion, for literary criticism, that the guns are loaded.

  1. "She was sleeping with her roommate in the bedroom. They were awakened by a knock on the door . . . about 11 P.M. . . . How did the killer get inside in the first place? The Commander of the South Chicago District theorized that he entered through a rear window leading to the kitchen on the first floor. Why didn't the women fight back? Or did they?

  3. I owe my epigraph from Kafka to Professor Hartman's brilliant essay.
  4. Dean Brustein's views on order and authority may be further consulted in *Yale Alumni Magazine* 32 (April 1969), "Ferment in the Drama School," p. 28. "In a theater, as in a professional school, only one man can be responsible for the decisions affecting the development of many. . . . No theater has ever been run by committee or democratic participation, not even the Living Theatre, which still finds its leaders in Beck and Malina, and no theater worth its name ever will be. . . . it is intolerable to seek to change these decisions through forms of disruption. . . . Our job here is to create, not to destroy."

The coroner reported many signs of struggle. . . . 'I got to the top of the stairs and walked past a bathroom, where I found a second body,' Officer Kelly said. 'Three more were in a front bedroom . . . and there was blood every place.'"—*The New York Times*, July 15, 1966, p. 14.

2. "Five men remained behind bars at the New Haven State Jail today. . . ." "The organization planning the bombings had all the money and access to all the dynamite needed to carry out the scheme; The organization had all the 'scientists' and 'everybody' needed for the operation; The organization wanted to obtain as much plastic explosives as possible; The organization was willing to exchange sticks of dynamite for machine guns; The organization was not interested in 'plain people' but rather in the law and wanted to break its back; Police Headquarters would be blown 'sky high' and the [First New Haven and Second National] banks would be blown up simultaneously with the headquarters building; the plot would be carried out with the first big snowstorm when police would be tied up with traffic conditions."—*The New Haven Register*, December 27, 1967, p. 1; December 29, p. 1.

3. "It was 4:30 in the morning and the president of the university leaned against the wall of the room that had been his office. He passed a hand over his face.

'My God,' he said, 'how could human beings do a thing like this?'"—A. M. Rosenthal, "Combat and Compassion at Columbia," *The New York Times*, May 1, 1968, p. 1.

End of my second series of quotations. But let me subjoin the following, which I do not consider a part of either of the above series, yet a legitimate supplement to both. I am quoting a kind of broadsheet which these days is given away at the newsstands in New York.

"POETRY IS REVOLUTION. BROTHERS . . . ARISE! FREE YOURSELVES! ARM YOURSELVES! WORK TO LIBERATE THE CREATIVE SPIRIT IN ALL MEN. POETRY IS REVOLUTION. . . . 'Came running out of the drugstore window with an electric alarm clock. . . . COME ON MAN. I SAW A TAPE RECORDER BACK THERE.' These are the words of lovers. Of dancers, of dynamite singers. These are the songs if you have the music.—LeRoi Jones. . . . 'Poor the pen without the gun; poor the gun without the pen.' . . . DOES LEROI JONES ASK LESS OF US. . . . an application of the discovery implicit in every true creative act: the absolute

necessity for total social & cultural revolution now if poetry is
to go forward. . . ."—*Guerilla, Free Newspaper of the Streets*,
Volume Two, Number 1, New York City, 1968.

That is the last of the ugly quotations. Surely another idiom,
several other idioms, are available to us? For example, the fol-
lowing:

   1. "This anarchic purpose coincides with the revolutionary
purpose . . . but contradicts it. . . . Thus the 'law' of poetic
language—which consists in maintaining the world 'open'
through the sheer force of words . . . is finally incompatible
with political language, which consists in 'closing,' in de-
limiting the world through laws. . . ."
   "It is easier now to see how the confusion developed be-
tween poetic language and political language. In the pre-
revolutionary phase both seem to seek the same thing, to be
in agreement in the urgent need to destroy the old order; they
even go so far as to merge in the terrorist phase of revolution,
although this is never more than the illusion of a common
cause."—Jacques Ehrmann, "On Articulation," *Yale French
Studies* 39, *Literature and Revolution* (1967), pp. 22, 23.

   2. "The study of the relations which can exist—and which
have repeatedly been said to exist—between revolution and
poetry swirls almost immediately into contradictions and con-
fusions."
   "Poetry is negativity: even that poetry which appeared at
first to be the most effective derives its powers . . . from the
status of poetic language, which, in essence, stands diamet-
rically opposed to the language of action."
   "Unlike the demonstration, which is a dated historical event
and a non-reoccurring one (unless it is institutionalized and
thus defused), the poem survives. . . . the poem survives by
virtue of those features which render it politically powerless
and designate it as a poem: its utopias (metaphors and other
tropes), its disregard for the present, the density of its linguis-
tic structure."—Michel Beaujour, "Flight out of Time: Poetic
Language and the Revolution," *Yale French Studies* 39,
Literature and Revolution (1967), pp. 29, 33, 33–34.

One is grateful for the detachment and sophistication of these
writers. Nevertheless, the very agility of their salvaging opera-
tion, as well as the further contents of the solid volume of
Yale French Studies in which they appear (its wide range, in
three-fold relevance to the historically pregnant dates 1789,

1848, and 1917) testify to the embarrassments of a strong contemporary resemblance between the aesthetic of the academy and that of the raging streets.

II

A president of the United States was assassinated in Dallas by a single, deranged opportunist. No tangible evidence of an effective conspiracy has ever been adduced. But on the day before the event, handbill photographs of the President with the legend: "Wanted for Treason" had circulated in Dallas. Large portions of our major cities are destroyed of a summer—in fulfillment of prophecies uttered by liberal voices in the spring. Our campuses become places of privilege for a repertory of violence ranging from incivility through hoodlum trespass and vandalism to armed banditry. These are the platitudes of an escalating history of outrage. If the leopards break into the temple often enough, according to the parable by Kafka, in time their violence becomes accepted as a part of the rite. It may be comfortable to the autonomous moralist and prophet in us to think so. The Crucifixion is necessary for the perpetual re-enactment of the Last Supper. And before that the *Felix Culpa.* "It needs must be," says the Gospel of Saint Matthew, "that offences come." But the modern mind has little interest in the words that immediately follow. "Woe to the man by whom the offence cometh." Poets and critics of our age, aesthetes and philosophers, have pursued themes of disorder and destruction as if they thought there was some danger that left to themselves disorder and destruction might not have fair play. The leopards might go away and forget the temple. And then there would be no more poetry—no savor or drama left in the relation between life and ritual.

In every revolutionary trend, it seems likely that there comes a phase when the feedback from the ruder levels is very strong. A convenient shorthand for the rapport which I am intimating, the intoxication of the contemporary élite with destructive symbols, appeared in August 1967 when a diagram of the Molotoff cocktail, executed in loving detail, was printed on the cover of an issue of *The New York Review of Books.* At this moment in our history, it may be difficult to say which affects the other more strongly:—on the one hand, the art of negation produced by the advance guard of sophisticates, the endgame drama of absurdity, blackness, cruelty, destruction, the so-called "Living Theater," and the new "young poets" of the "guerilla" school;

and on the other hand, the debased folk art of the red-neck
Dallas flysheets, the tragic mythopoeist with the Mannlicher-
Carcano rifle, the Evergreen poets of the revolver, the brickbat,
and the cocktail.

A few centuries ago in England a courtly lover, soldier, and
poet attempted a "pitiful defence of poor poetry." He was pro-
voked in part by a harsh attack on poetry from one of the self-
appointed moral censors of the age. But Sidney undertook to
defend poetry on terms which *we* will readily understand to be
wrong:

> Nature never set forth the earth in so rich tapestry as divers
> poets have done; neither with pleasant rivers, fruitful trees,
> sweet-smelling flowers, nor whatever else may make the too-
> much-loved earth more lovely; her word is brazen, the poets
> only deliver a golden.

This we know will not do. Poor poetry will scarcely let us de-
fend her in those terms. Any more than outraged justice will be
appeased by a handout. Poetry, or at least our more sophisticated
theoretical account of poetry, claims the voice of prophecy and
demands, presumably, nothing less than justice. And justice
may well mean our heads. As we can offer no such defence as
Sidney's, so we can look for no deliverance through poetry
from our own secularism or barbarism—only for extinction.
"Imagination," as the Parisian students have put it, with an air
of metaphysical control, "is Revolution."[5] Poetry as pleasure,
poetry as play, poetry as escape, poetry as wish, poetry as
dream, poetry as myth, poetry as beauty, poetry as truth,
poetry as challenge, poetry as violence, poetry as pornography,
poetry as blasphemy, poetry as absurdity, poetry as nausea,

---

5. Parisian "structural" theory of the past twenty years has been greatly
agitated to confer on "poetry," "writing," true "literature," some kind of
impersonal and autonomous power of destruction and revolution. Thus
Roland Barthes, a Director of Studies at the Ecole Pratique des Hautes
Etudes: "Modernism begins with a search for a literature which is no
longer possible . . . for order . . . is always a murder in intention" (*Writ-
ing Degree Zero*, New York, 1968, pp. 38-39—translated from *Le Degré
Zéro de l'Ecriture*, 1953, a book derived in turn from published essays of
1947). David Paul Funt, an American philosopher who spent the years
1964-66 in France as a Fulbright fellow, summarizes: "Literature is by
nature abnormal . . . 'guilty, it ought finally to avow itself so.' The task of
literature today is the subversion of language, of the language which clothes
society, protects its virtue, hides its unclean parts" ("Newer Criticism and
Revolution," *The Hudson Review* 22 [Spring 1919]: 96, 138).

poetry as nothing, poetry as rape and murder—poetry as executioner or assassin, poetry as suicide. Poetry, like the university, as sanctuary for the intolerable. "Destroyer and preserver; hear, oh hear!" Nothing more naively contrary to his art could be conceived by any modern poet of the free world than to seem to intimate approval of any aspect of establishment. He is likely to be diffident too about betraying admiration for any parts of the universe, or for any such human virtues as patience, fortitude, or prudence. Let these be represented by the squares. The insurrection is not mainly for the sake of anything else—if indeed it *is* for the sake of anything else. The insurrection, we understand, *is* the reason and the aim. Every schoolboy has heard the rumor that in 64 A.D. Nero, having set fire to the city of Rome, found the scene a suitable backdrop for singing a poem of his own composition entitled "The Destruction of Troy." It is an ancient emblem—a fable, a myth if we like. It may deserve a more prominent place than it actually enjoys in the system of our contemporary myths—in a world where, as we all know, "the best lack all conviction, while the worst are full of passionate intensity."

1969

GENESIS:
AN ARGUMENT RESUMED

It would appear that literary studies, and especially theoretical studies, are subject to endless metamorphic cycles, and if they sometimes make progress, they can also suffer regress. Why not? Poems are, on one view, more or less imperfectly recorded acts of personal agents, and in literary study they are open to boundless speculation by further persons, whose activity, though sometimes partly scientific and historical, is always driven by an aim of individual intelligence. There is no theoretical or critical term set up for the purpose of clarifying or recommending a given perspective which is not susceptible of being seen and used in an opposite light. There is no rational and methodological concept, no attempted translucent universal, which is not capable of being transformed, and very quickly, into an opaque historical gimmick—as if some poems could be "beautiful" in some special Platonic sense (after a certain date), or as if symbolism had begun to appear in poetry about the time of Baudelaire or Mallarmé, just as blood began to circulate in human bodies about the time of William Harvey or dreams to have significance about the time of Freud. These reflections, verging on the melancholy, occur as I survey some recent writings on the critical problem of the artist's life story, his inspirations and his intentions, in relation to his work of art.

Whatever the truth in this debate, or the superior side (if there is one, and I still think there is), it must be evident that there are two antithetically opposed sides, and probably always will be, corresponding to two aspects of literature and to two kinds of persons who come to the study of literature. To speak broadly and to avoid the simplicity of one-word labels (or to defer the economy of such labels), let us say that an art work is something which emerges from the private, individual, dynamic, and intentionalistic realm of its maker's mind and personality; it is in a sense (and this is especially true of the verbal work of art) made of intentions or intentionalistic material. But at the same time, in the moment it emerges, it enters a public and in a certain clear sense an objective realm; it claims and gets attention

Two friends have specially contributed to this essay—Monroe Beardsley of course, who brought to my attention some of our critics in the journals and who read my early draft, and Donald Hirsch, whose differences from me, whether in conversation or in print (see below, n. 52), have the unusual character of being always illuminative. His essay of 1960 in *PMLA*, which I cite below and argue with (nn. 17, 20, and 52), is one of the best on the subject which I now attempt to reapproach.

from an audience; it invites and receives discussion, about its meaning and value, in an idiom of inter-subjectivity and conceptualization. If the art work has emerged at all from the artist's private world, it has emerged into some kind of universal world. The artist was not merely *trying* to do something worthy of notice in that world. He has done it. Artistic activity has produced a valued result. Some critics will wish to talk about just that result. Other critics, however, will not. These will be the critics who entertain an antithetic drive toward viewing the art work as mainly a token of its source, a manifestation of something behind it, that is, the consciousness or personality of the artist (or perhaps of the society in which he lived, or of himself as representative of that society). These critics, wishing to throb in unison with the mind of the artist, will wish to know all about that individual artist and as much as possible about his historic context. At the very least, they will wish to know not only the poem in question, but also all his other poems, his essays, letters, and diaries, his thoughts and feelings,[1] and not only those which occurred before the poem and might in any sense have caused it, but (in the more recent idiom) all those which came after it at any time and are thus a part of the whole personality of which the poem is an expression, the system of contexts of which it is a part.[2]

It was against a background of triumphantly prevalent genetic studies in various modes, and in an effort to give assistance in what seemed a badly needed program to rescue poems from the morass of their origins, that my friend Monroe Beardsley and I published in a *Dictionary of World Literature* (1944) an article entitled "Intention" and then, in response to a critique of that article, a further development of our argument in the *Sewanee Review* (1945), an essay entitled "The Intentional Fallacy." Mr. Beardsley followed these articles thirteen years later with some very lucid pages in his volume entitled *Aesthetics* (1958). It seemed to me then, and it still seems, that Mr. Beardsley and I succeeded in formulating a clear, reasonable, and viable statement of the thesis that the intention of a literary artist qua intention is neither a valid ground for arguing the presence of a quality or a meaning in a given instance of his literary work nor a valid criterion for judging the value of that work. "The objec-

1. I leave out his headaches and his gallstones, though there was a time when these too would have been important. For a rich and orderly assortment of artist's drives and motives, conscious and unconscious, during the creative process, see Monroe C. Beardsley, "On the Creation of Art," *JAAC* 23 (Spring 1965): 291–304.

2. See below, n. 13.

tive critic's first question, when he is confronted with a new aesthetic object," says Mr. Beardsley in 1958, "is not, What is this supposed to be? but, What have we got here?"

As I have already noted, however, literary students who love the poem's genesis have no trouble in answering such arguments and returning to that luxuriant pasture. It is enough to assert that biography has such and such joys of discovery and communion, and thus biography *is* relevant to the study of the poem.[3] Or to say that the poet's life itself, or even the style of face he wears, is a work of art parallel to his produced art works, and hence the poet's life *is* a thing of great interest to the literary student.[4] Or that the intention of the artist, revealed in the title of a work or some similar adjacent index, is often a clue which the artist himself seems to feel it prudent to supply to his public, or which the given viewer of a work finds it very helpful to notice, and hence the intention of the artist *is* sometimes "relevant" to the work.[5] One may even add that in some instances, like that of Mr. Beardsley's invention, the "cruller-shaped object of polished teak" said by the sculptor to symbolize "Human Destiny," the plight of the artist who wishes to convey that meaning will indeed be hopeless unless we grant him the privilege of telling us what he wishes. And therefore his intention is indeed relevant and valid.[6] Or, a critic may prefer to talk, not about the meaning of a poem, but about his own "responses" to it,

3. See, for instance, Alfred Owen Aldridge, "Biography in the Interpretation of Poetry," *College English* 25 (March 1964): 412-20: "I shall try to indicate a few reasons why biography serves to humanize poetry and therefore to heighten our enjoyment." "No purely esthetic criticism has ever stimulated the same public interest," the same "extraordinary sensation which has been caused by the recent announcement of A. L. Rowse's biographical study of Shakespeare—with its revelations" (p. 415). Or see John A. Meixner, "The Uses of Biography in Criticism," *College English* 27 (November 1966): 108-13; or Carlos Baker, "Speaking of Books: The Relevance of a Writer's Life," *New York Times Book Review* (August 20, 1967), pp. 2, 31.

4. Leslie A. Fiedler, *No! In Thunder: Essays on Myth and Literature* (Boston, 1960), pp. 312-18.

5. William H. Capitan, "The Artist's Intention," *Revue Internationale de Philosophie* 68-69 (1964): 331-32. Cf. Joseph Margolis, *The Language of Art & Art Criticism, Analytic Questions in Aesthetics* (Detroit, 1965), p. 99, on stage directions and musical notations. Margolis is a writer who cheerfully piles up examples that tell in favor of Wimsatt and Beardsley and even quotes passages from them with which he cannot disagree and then with equal cheer somersaults to a guarded conclusion that they "must be mistaken," that "intentional criticism has, to some extent at least, a recognizable and not inappropriate place in the aesthetic examination of art" (p. 103).

6. Capitan, p. 332.

which may be "conditioned" by his knowledge of the author's
intentions, as these create a kind of "field of force round the
work" or a "web of associations." If Housman says that he
meant no irony at all, that, it would appear, will settle the ques-
tion for this critic. If Eliot were to testify that he had never
heard of Andrew Marvell, that too would settle a question.
Such a critic's responses might apparently also be conditioned
by his knowing what Mr. Leavis thinks about a problem—though
what this may be, in the given instance, seems unhappily in
doubt.[7]

The argument about intention is then, in a sense, hopelessly
circular and reentering. There is no way to keep the simpler
kinds of intention-hunters from jumping on the vehicle of lit-
erary inquiry, and nobody I suppose really wishes the power to
legislate anything against them. But at the precise level of ab-
straction and definition at which Mr. Beardsley and I argued the
question, I do not see that any notable revision is required, or
even any very emphatic repetition. Let me try to make a useful
reentry into the debate by first noticing a few related, parallel,
or complementary terms and focuses of recent literary criticism,
perhaps some of them obstructions to a right view of literary
"intention."

The idea of poetic "impersonality" is, I believe, in the think-
ing of many students a close adjunct to, or required condition
for, the kind of criticism which hopes to escape the "inten-
tional fallacy." Much difficulty seems to arise here, however,
and this has probably been promoted to a large extent by the
writings early and late of a poet-critic who did as much as any
other single authority to establish in English studies of the mid-
century a climate favorable to objective inquiry—T. S. Eliot, of
course. In a review of his posthumously collected essays, *To
Criticize the Critic*, I have already discussed this matter in the
perspective of his later career.[8] It will be sufficient here to look
back for a moment at his seminal essay "Tradition and the
Individual Talent" (published during the fall and early winter of
1919 in the last two numbers of *The Egoist, An Individualist
Review*). This celebrated early essay, despite its forceful sugges-
tiveness, the smoothness and fullness of its definition of the

7. Dr. F. Cioffi, "Intention and Interpretation in Criticism" (from *Pro-
ceedings of the Aristotelian Society*, 1963-64), in *Collected Papers on
Aesthetics*, ed. Cyril Barrett, S.J. (Oxford, 1965), pp. 161–83, esp. 168,
170-71, 172, 174, 175, 179–81. See M. C. Beardsley's review of this
volume, with special attention to Cioffi, in *JAAC* 26 (Fall 1967): 144-46.
    8. *The Massachusetts Review* 7 (Summer 1966): 584-90.

poet's impersonality (or perhaps inevitably in achieving these qualities), was a highly ambiguous statement. Therein, no doubt, consisted something of its pregnancy. In this essay Eliot as poet and critic is saying two things about three ideas (man, poet, and poem) and saying them simultaneously. He is saying that a poet ought to depersonalize his raw experience, transcend the immediacy of the suffering man. At the same time, he is saying that the reader ought to read the poem impersonally, as an achieved expression, not personally, with attendant inquiries into the sufferings, the motives, the confusions of the man behind the poem. The idea "poet" as Eliot employs it in this essay is sometimes the antithesis of "man" and sometimes the antithesis of "poem." "The more perfect the artist, the more completely separate in him will be the man who suffers and the mind which creates." "Honest criticism and sensitive appreciation are directed not upon the poet but upon the poetry." The two meanings are inextricably interwoven in Eliot's rich and memorable sentences. But they are not one meaning, nor does either one entail the other. Eliot, at moments much later in his career, could be very clear about one half of his doctrine. "I prefer not to define, or to test, poetry by means of speculations about its origins; you cannot find a sure test for poetry, a test by which you may distinguish between poetry and mere good verse, by reference to its putative antecedents in the mind of the poet."[9] But this injunction against peeping into the poet's activity, if it is valid at all, must be equally valid whether that activity itself is, in the poet's own consciousness, personal or impersonal. In fact, the critical lesson is that from the poem itself we cannot really tell, and so far as we are critics interested in the poem itself, we do not care. Despite his double doctrine of impersonality, the notion of the poet has always been, for Eliot, deeply centered in that personal suffering man himself. "It is not in his personal emotions . . . that the poet is in any way remarkable or interesting. His particular emotions may be simple, crude, or flat." Poetry is an "escape" from personality. Yes, but of course "only those who have personality and emotions know what it means to want to escape from these things."[10]

The dubious notion of the poet's impersonal personality, deriving so pervasively in modern American criticism from the ideas of Eliot, has also been colored no doubt by Yeatsian occultist notions of the "self" and the "anti-self" or "mask"

9. *The Use of Poetry and the Use of Criticism* (London, 1933), p. 140.
10. All the words quoted are from "Tradition and the Individual Talent."

(the latter either "true" or "false").[11] Which is the poet in a given poem expressing? His real self? A true mask? A false mask? A fascinating question—and a safe one, so long as the inquirer is aware that the area of his inquiry is at the moment biography, perhaps a very refined version of this art, but still biography. Perhaps it will be sufficient to say here, without a long excursion, that the thesis that biographical evidence does not establish meaning *in* poems is not the equivalent of a thesis that poems cannot contribute their own kind of meaning, and a very rich and subtle kind, to the writing of biography.[12] For whatever does get into a poem presumably is put there by the poet and reflects *something* in the poet's personality and life. It is for the biographer, in his particular insight and skill, to say what is reflected and in what relation to other things in the poet's life. Nowadays we are increasingly promised, or shown, the inner life of the author mainly on the evidence of the dialectic sequence of his works.[13] If anybody wishes to challenge this as sound biographical method (I at least have no specific wish to do so), it ought to be clear that he does not do so on the same principle as that on which a critic may refuse to decide the meaning or value of a poem on external auctorial testimony or other biographical evidence. Affirmation of a cause and affirmation of an effect are different in their entailments. If a poet sees red, he may well either write or not write a red poem. If he writes a red poem, it would seem to be a sound enough inference, though in some instances little more than a truism, that he has in some sense seen red.

Patrick Cruttwell, in a richly illustrated and nicely modulated essay of 1959, "Makers and Persons,"[14] discriminates four degrees of "distance" between a "maker" (poet) and the "person" (man in whom the maker perforce quarries his stuff): (1) the

11. See Richard Ellmann, *The Identity of Yeats* (New York, 1954) and *Yeats: The Man and the Masks* (New York, 1948). The article by A. O. Aldridge cited above confuses the poet's view and the critic's view throughout and refers to much literature which also does. In Slavic countries formalist critics during the 1920s defined a poem as "a deflection, not a reflection, of experience" (p. 412).
12. "We ought to impute the thoughts and attitudes of the poem immediately to the dramatic *speaker*, and if to the author at all, only by an act of biographical inference" ("The Intentional Fallacy" [1945], paragraph 7).
13. See Leon Edel, *Literary Biography* (London, 1957); J. Hillis Miller, *The Disappearance of God: Five Nineteenth-Century Writers* (New York, 1965)—De Quincey, Browning, Emily Brontë, Arnold, Hopkins. But for Miller chronology is not important.
14. *The Hudson Review* 12 (Winter 1959-60): 487-507.

degree or way of "simple transcript" (genuine or partly faked—Boswell, Pepys, Rousseau, Byron in letters and journals, Montaigne); (2) the "masked" way—"the making of a self which pretends not to be, but encourages the reader to think it is," the real person of the writer (Sterne-Shandy-Yorick, Conrad-Marlow); (3) the way of "mythologized" self-presentation—"transportation of the person into symbolic figures, references" (The master of this obscure and mysterious way is Mr. Eliot); (4) the "dramatized" way—here "the distance is greatest between maker and person" (clearest in actual stage drama—the Greeks, Shakespeare, "the ages of great drama"). After presenting these distinctions, Mr. Cruttwell traces, very interestingly and I believe correctly, the rise of the modern cult of personality, the author as "exhibitionist," from about the time of Boswell's *Johnson* (1791) through episodes in the career of Byron and in Victorian literary biography. Modern poets themselves have sometimes protested against the invasion of their privacy—in vain, and wrongly. The floodgates of the personal interest, once opened, cannot be forced back. Art betrays its creators, and properly. They betray themselves, once the public and the literary scholars have been put on the right track.

In a closing short section on problems for contemporary critics, Mr. Cruttwell argues that it is time for critics to overcome any anti-biographical inhibitions which may have been induced by the ideas of "Eliot, Richards, Leavis and the Scrutineers" or by the "New Criticism" in America. Let the critics now permit themselves a renewed and healthy release in the satisfaction of the "curiosity" which poems must in fact surely arouse in them. Who is the critic, after all, who can say that his responses to poetry *are* pure? After we "have enjoyed" and have been "impressed" by a writer, by Wordsworth in his Lucy poems, for instance, then we undertake the "microscopic investigation." We want to know about Wordsworth's "incestuous feelings for Dorothy" and what he "intended" Lucy to "stand for." So, in spite of Mr. Cruttwell's effort to establish a *critical* direction for his essay, the argument swings round in fact to postcritical interests, moving *from* the recognized and presumably understood poem toward the "putative antecedents." Mr. Cruttwell has earlier noted that a certain "degeneration" in Sterne's management of his Tristram and Yorick masks may be explained by a parallel in Sterne's life. "His failure to hold his masks was a symptom of his person's insincerity and weakness. . . . He slid from one pose to the next, from bawdy to sobstuff and back again, not through choice but through weakness" (p. 491). But

Mr. Cruttwell can also have his argument the opposite way, on a later page (503), where he argues that Byron aspiring to escape from his true personality in *Childe Harold* wrote untruthfully and badly, but when he abandoned his aspiration to purity and simply "wrote out his mood as it came to him" in the "shameless self-parading of *Don Juan*," he "wrote at his best." The lesson of these two examples seems to be that the biographically oriented critic will find a correspondence between life and work an explanation of either goodness or badness in the work, as he happens to find the work itself good or bad. On another page (494), Mr. Cruttwell expatiates upon the futility of trying to find Eliot's personal or secret motive in the epigraph from Marston prefixed to *Burbank with a Baedeker*. Mr. Cruttwell is severe on Eliot for his two-faced stance of impersonal secretiveness yet constant invitation to the reader to speculate about personal reasons (in the absence of clear public ones). I think there is some justice in the complaint. I have dwelt long on Mr. Cruttwell's essay, however, not only because it seems to me probably the richest and most informative in the recent resurgence of biographically oriented "critical" arguments, but because in its own ambivalence or thwarted struggle to arrive at a "critical" direction, it is in fact a larger rewriting of Eliot's original and seminally confused essay of 1919.

A kind of critical metamorphosis to which I alluded in my opening paragraph is well illustrated in the recent history of the very useful term "persona" in American criticism. This term seems to have gained currency during the mid-century because it was a convenient way of referring to something *in the poem* which could be thought of as a counterpart of the *im*personality which was supposed either to reside in the author or, more accurately, to be a perspective adopted by the critic. This economical employment of the term "persona" (along with certain related or nearly equivalent terms such as "fiction," "ethos," "mask," or "muse") might be illustrated near its zenith in Maynard Mack's essay of 1951, "The Muse of Satire,"[15] distinguishing three "voices" (the *vir bonus*, the *ingénu*, and the heroic public defender) in the persona or speaker of Pope's formal verse satire. All three of these voices were to be taken *by a critic* dramatically, not biographically, rhetorically, not historically. Something like a sheer reversal from that kind of critical use of persona to a convenient reconfusion of questions about criticism and questions about biography may be witnessed in a very

15. *Yale Review* 41 (Autumn 1951): 80–92.

richly variegated essay of 1963 by Irvin Ehrenpreis, entitled "Personae."[16] An expression of grave concern that certain nameless "scholars" have been doing the wrong thing with persona (making it a "distinguishing property" or special kind of merit in Augustan poetry, rather than the universal and "inescapable part of language and communication" that it actually is) leads Mr. Ehrenpreis, not, as one might at first hope, to a purified image of the scholar-critic, but very quickly into an opposite sort of thing, an exceedingly dense involvement of poet and poem as man and mask, reality and "rhetorical pose." "One could never reveal the whole truth about oneself, even supposing that one knew it." "If there is any meaning in the concept of persona or mask, it must imply a difference between appearance and reality."

Like Mr. Cruttwell, whom we have cited above, and like most writers on W. B. Yeats, Mr. Ehrenpreis reminds us forcefully that, whatever the relation of persona to author, it is not a simple one either of likeness or of difference. Other recent writers, Maynard Mack in the essay already cited, and notably Wayne Booth in *The Rhetoric of Fiction* (1961),[17] have been stressing a somewhat different, if parallel, truth—that the relation of persona, internally, to other parts or aspects of the work, need not be simple. Persona is not in fact a sufficient conception for the *de*personalization of the poetic object as the critic attends to it. It is not as if the persona is always the simple focus for the expression of everything in the poem. Sometimes he betrays himself in contrast to some cooler or saner perspective. This is the kind of thing that happens obviously in a monodrama like Browning's *Soliloquy of a Spanish Cloister*, a miniature of the situation in a full-scale play or novel, where numerous personae

16. *Restoration and Eighteenth-Century Literature, Essays in Honor of Alan Dugald McKillop*, ed. Carroll Camden (Chicago, 1963), pp. 25–37.
17. See this large and interesting work passim, esp. Chap. 8, "Telling as Showing: Dramatized Narrators, Reliable and Unreliable." See too Allan Rodway and Brian Lee, "Coming to Terms," *Essays in Criticism* 14 (April 1964): 122; and E. D. Hirsch's very subtle and accurate distinction between "speaking subject" and "biographical person," as illustrated in the "secret awareness" of lying and the "truth-telling stance" ("Objective Interpretation," *PMLA* 75 [September 1960]: 478–79). See also some good paragraphs on the theme of person and poet in Harry Berger, Jr., "Cadmus Unchanged," a review of *Selected Letters of Robert Frost*, in *Yale Review* 54 (Winter 1965): 277–82. For a range of examples and insights from a different area, see Victor Erlich, "The Concept of the Poet as a Problem of Poetics," *Poetics: Proceedings of the 1960 Warsaw Conference on Poetics* (The Hague, 1961), pp. 707–17, and "Some Uses of Monologue in Prose Fiction: Narrative Manner and World View," *Stil- und Formprobleme in der Literatur* (Heidelberg, 1959), pp. 371–78.

contend within the ambit of an encircling and managing intelligence. Browning's *Soliloquy* is a steady sequence of not very delicate little antithetic jolts. "*Ave, Virgo!* Gr-r-r—you swine!" The ironies of Swift are a more plenary instance of such internal cunning. Mr. Ehrenpreis observes that in *A Modest Proposal* there are not two, but three mentalities or "styles"—that of the initially prominent "sensible projector" of the proposal, that of the "monster" looming behind him, and that of a directly speaking, bitter denunciator, all three of these, as we should expect in this essay, said to be styles of the author's own voice. (Here perhaps it is worth adding that while projector and monster are aspects of the same persona, the denouncer is part of a perspective, or, if one wishes, he is a second person, who has already manipulated the projector so as to reveal him as a monster.) But what I am trying to get back to here is the direction of argument. From the work to the author (when one wishes to be biographical) is not the same as from the author (outside the work) to the work. These directions remain opposites no matter how numerous and complicated a set of deflectors or baffles we set up between the two termini.

The fact is that we can, if we wish, learn with relative certainty from biographical evidence that some personae are close to or identical with the author and some are much different from him. Nobody would confuse the persona of Browning's *Soliloquy of a Spanish Cloister* with Browning himself. But almost everybody rushes to confuse the persona of Gray's *Elegy in a Country Churchyard* with Gray himself. In fact it can be shown on quite convincing biographical evidence that the melancholy poet who is the anonymous speaker of that poem is very close to the melancholy poet Thomas Gray—"me I; il Pensoroso." Nor is that correspondence, in biographical terms, an accident. The *Elegy* does seem to come out of the historic person Thomas Gray much more directly than many other poems come out of their authors. Nevertheless, the *Elegy* is not *about* the historic person Gray. The self-contemplative speaker remains anonymous. The poem itself, if it were anonymous, would be intact.

What, however, if the poem does happen to be a poem *about* that historic person the author, about himself, his friends, and his enemies? If the author of the *Epistle to Arbuthnot*, says Ehrenpreis, "were not the great poet of his age, if his relations with his parents were not well known to have been as he testifies, if Atticus and Sporus did not belong to public life, the force of the poem would dwindle" (p. 32). Yet with increase of information, let us notice, comes complexity—and doubt. The canny persona of Pope's satire bears scarcely the same simple relation to the gardener of Twickenham as the melancholy churchyard speaker seems to bear to the pensive fellow of the Cambridge college. Three distinct voices are assigned by Mr. Mack to that satiric persona. In what variously shaded relations to the man who is both behind the poem and the subject of the poem may be difficult to say. Pope could be scheming and mean, as well as friendly and noble. The main evidence for his piety to his father is in the poem. Perhaps we do not inquire too rigorously whether he was in fact so righteous, charitable, and simple as the poem would make him. If he was not, still "his make-up of being so is in itself a piece of greatness; and not to enjoy it is a piece of stupidity."[18] Perhaps we enjoy it the more for its being in part make-up. And we sense that this is so, or may well be so, in large part from internal evidence, from the perspective or management of the whole witty poem.

In accepting this kind of biographical claim, let us notice that it is a particular kind of claim, not of intention but of subject matter. Pope's sincerity or insincerity, his virtue or his meanness, his character and intention, as generators of the poem or as criteria of its merit, do not really come into question. The poet and his friends and enemies are present in the poem as historic figures, and furthermore as well-established historic figures in precisely the roles they play in the poem. Milton's sonnets 17, 22, and 23 and his other allusions to his blindness provide similar, easy, and unimpeachable examples. Here we enter the problem of the universality and significance of the protagonist—the stature of Samson the agonist compared to that of Hobson the carrier. Aristotle understood that it gives a certain kind of advantage if the man is important. After Milton and Pope, the world became increasingly convinced of the importance of every man. Still it is not true, it never has been true, that the simple meanings or wishes of any man, even of any important man, can generate or guarantee a significant poetic symbol.[19]

"It is not illusory appearances," says Ehrenpreis, "that the real person sets before us: it is the visible effluences, aspects, reflec-

18. H. W. Garrod, *Poetry and the Criticism of Life* (Cambridge, Mass., 1931), p. 83. Garrod refers to Arnold's "make-up" of being the greatest English critic.

19. See the excellent article, in effect about anonymous lyric personae, by Arthur K. Moore, "Lyric Voices and Ethical Proofs," *JAAC* 23 (Summer 1965): 429–39. "Lyrics are vouched for simply— . . . through intelligible relationships to activities, conditions, occasions, lives, ideologies, and states of consciousness into which interest enters" (pp. 429–30). See the same author's later "Lyric Personae and Prying Critics," *Southern Humanities Review* 1 (1967): 43–64.

tions—however indirect, of an inner being that cannot be defined apart from them. In order to understand any literary work, we must view it as a transaction between us and that inner being" (p. 31). "Only as a relationship between a real speaker and a real listener can meaning exist" (p. 37). Some years earlier, Father Walter Ong, in one of the best essays on the "personalist approach" that I know, *The Jinnee in the Well-Wrought Urn*, had written:

Man's deepest orientation is personal. . . . Each work of art that bids for attention in an act of contemplation is a surrogate for a person. In proportion as the work of art is capable of being taken in full seriousness, it moves further and further along an asymptote to the curve of personality.[20]

Perhaps it does. Yet the argument against intentional reading need not suppose, and does not suppose, that the monkeys in the British Museum will in the foreseeable future, or in any future at all, type out *Paradise Lost*.[21] "The words of a poem come out of a head, not out of a hat," as we quoted long ago from E. E. Stoll. James Thorpe has recently demonstrated how much some literary works actually owe to editors and other agents of transmission and even to such chance activity as that of a compositor, who may by mistake introduce a word that conceivably is better than the author's. Mr. Thorpe's philosophy of textual criticism says, however, that we should restore the author's own word, and I say the same thing, though perhaps more simply on grounds of plain convenience than he wishes to. He believes that to accept the compositor's happy slip would be to put the aesthetic object not in the realm of "art" (intended or designed work), but in that of the now popularly received object made by "chance" (a spilled can of paint, words selected by throwing dice, sounds of traffic recorded at a busy intersection).[22] But it is possible and, as he shows, frequently is the fact that a designed work is the design of more than one head. A second completes the work of the first. In this instance, it would be ourselves, the editors, who, in assessing and adopting the

20. *Essays in Criticism* 4 (July 1954): 315, 319. And see below, n. 52, *langue* and *parole* as expounded by Hirsch, "Objective Interpretation," pp. 473-75.
21. One of the monkeys employed in this experiment once got through the whole poem all right, as far as the last word of the last book, but then he slipped and wrote, instead of "day.," "lxdz.," and the whole version of course had to be scrapped.
22. "The Aesthetics of Textual Criticism," *PMLA* 80 (December 1965): 465-82, esp. 465-68, 475.

accidental intrusion, were the very junior collaborators in the original author's designed and intended work.

In our frequent focus on the history of modern literature as outlined by Mr. Cruttwell, with its heavy personal underpainting, its vigorous cult of personal authentication, let us not forget the massive foundations of the world's literature—the Book of Genesis, the *Iliad*, the *Odyssey*, the works of Virgil, Dante, Chaucer, Shakespeare—which survive for us either anonymously or with the merest wisps or shadows of biography attached. These works, it is to be assumed, no less than those of Milton, Johnson, Byron, Keats, Yeats, or Joyce, speak to us with the "inner being" of "real speakers." They speak as "surrogates" for persons.

It may promote clarity if at this point we try to map the structure of the argument we are engaged in according to the following types of statement which are our subject matter:

1. Historical, biographical: Thomas Gray was a melancholy poet, and he planned or meant or was likely to mean certain things.
2. Historical, poetic: The speaker of Gray's *Elegy* is a melancholy poet; he uses certain words and images and means certain things.
3. Methodological, explicitly evaluative: The resemblance, or correspondence, between the poet Gray and either the speaker or the perspective of the *Elegy* makes it a good poem or shows that it is good.
4. Methodological, interpretive: The character, mind, or habitual meanings of the poet Gray are a valid guide (or the best guide) to the meaning of the *Elegy*.

This arrangement introduces one distinction on which I have so far not laid any emphasis, that between statements of type 3 and those of type 4. Statements of type 3 (the explicitly evaluative) are more ambitious than those of type 4 (the simply interpretive), but I use this order because those of type 3 are on the whole less plausible, and I wish to dispose of them first. In our articles of 1944 and 1945 Mr. Beardsley and I did not labor this distinction. In his *Aesthetics* of 1958 Mr. Beardsley has separated the two issues very cleanly, in fact by a space of 428 pages, with I think, considerable increase of clarity for the whole discussion. At the same time, it is my own view (and this will emerge more clearly as I go on) that an argument about instances of type 4 (the interpretive) will very often, or even characteristically, bring in considerations of value.

Let me proceed to notice and comment upon certain graded instances of argument, first some relating to statements of type 3 (a, b, c), then some relating to type 4 (a, b, c, d, e, f). There is some value in a chart or a guided tour of a field of argument even when the cartographer or guide has to confess that he looks on many of the stopping points as only of historic interest. The point of maximum live concern for our debate, and the one toward which I am working, let me confess in advance, is 4f.

(3a) The poet wrote his poem with the aim of making money, of winning a prize, of pleasing a mistress, of impressing an employer or patron—or for some opposite or more ideal sort of reason. His work was either a "free" work in Kant's sense, or not free. "He achieved a result commensurate with such aims. Therefore. . . ." Such reasonings concern what some writers on our problem take pains to distinguish as secondary or ulterior intentions of the artist. We ought to be able to see these as obviously outside any real critical question. In like manner, we should find no trouble in putting to one side the common artistic aim of creating a masterpiece—or perhaps of not creating a masterpiece, but just of turning out a potboiler—or of having a "lark."[23] He intended only to appeal to popular sentiment; therefore we should not. . . ." (Or, to translate this kind of motive into the key of interpretive argument and thus get it out of the way: "We know that he thought of this as his masterpiece; therefore it. . . .")

(3b) The poem is or says what the poet himself was or thought or felt; it is hence good—or bad. We have been close to this framing of the argument in our whole discussion of persona. We have seen both kinds of conclusion (bad, for Sterne; good, for Byron) in Mr. Cruttwell's essay. This form of the argument runs very readily into talk about "sincerity" and "inspiration" and "authenticity," topics which Mr. Beardsley and I noted with some care in our essay of 1945. In his *Aesthetics* (p. 457) he lists "expression," "sincerity," and "intention" together, under the general head of the "genetic," but, rightly I believe, he sees "intention" as focusing most or all of what can be handled with any precision in this area.[24]

23. See Sidney Gendin's sensible short article, "The Artist's Intentions," *JAAC* 23 (Winter 1964): 195.

24. Another term which Mr. Beardsley (pp. 457, 490-91) puts in this genetic group is "originality," which, like "skill" (see 3c below), is a merit which seems assignable more readily to the author than to his work. During the neoclassic age, in arguments comparing Homer and Virgil, the latter was sometimes said to have written doubtless the more perfect poem; the former got a high mark for originality. A 1966 Fairlane is a better automobile than a Model-T Ford, but not as original.

(3c) The poet had a specific aim or plan in mind; he managed (whether inspirationally or rationally) to carry this out in the poem; thus he is a successful artist; his work is good art. This is the "Spingarn-Croce-Carlyle-Goethe" theory named by H. L. Mencken. We alluded to this theory in our article of 1944, and it was defended by Ananda K. Coomaraswamy in his critique of that article.[25] A successfully planned and executed murder was for Mr. Coomaraswamy no less a work of art than a poem or painting. Mr. Beardsley makes the helpful suggestion that here we may indeed be likely to assign a kind of merit, but it should be understood as referring to the artist himself (who was "skillful" enough to do what he aimed at doing) rather than to the work—which may be a murder, a robbery, a libel, a silly lampoon. It would scarcely be feasible to illustrate all the kinds of evidence (or supposed evidence) that may be adduced for an author's plan outside his poem. I do not know how many kinds there may be, each no doubt with somewhat special problems. Let me adduce a single example, representative I believe, if in part synthetic. Edgar Allan Poe's *Philosophy of Composition* professes to tell us how he proceeded in writing *The Raven*—a poem of a certain ideal length, presenting the most melancholy, moving, and poetic subject conceivable, the death of a beautiful woman, and making use of the most effective poetic device conceivable, a certain simple and sonorous refrain, repeated in various applications. There can be little question that *The Raven* does manifest Poe's professed intentions so far as they are specific and can be made manifest. But to argue (as some proponents of "intention" have seemed in general to argue) that, because we can here prove that the artist achieved his intentions, we know that *The Raven* is a good work of art would seem a fairly obvious kind of fatuity. A critical enterprise that would more seriously recommend itself would surely be the inquiry whether the proposed subject and technique were actually the most poetic conceivable. One kind of objection to such an argument from Poe's intention (or one explanation for giving it up) might be to say that Poe's *Philosophy of Composition* is not a valid guide to his intention in the poem because it is an ex post facto invention and a tongue-in-cheek tour de force. Perhaps so. But here we catch ourselves moving from intention to intention—when does the witness mean what he says?—and we may

---

25. See Beardsley, *Aesthetics* (1958), p. 489. Dr. Cioffi (p. 164) dismisses this form of intentionalistic argument with great unconcern. He is no doubt largely unaware of the contexts of literary scholarship and criticism which framed our articles of 1944 and 1945. On "skill," cf. Gendin, p. 195.

be left with the generally not very satisfactory principle that an external statement of intention by an author has to be examined to see if it was written before the poem or after. So externality is invested with externality, and testimonies written before the poem might well have suffered by change of intention while the poem was being written.

Another sort of argument in favor of intention as a criterion of value might say: Well, what is meant is precisely the fullness of the executed plan as seen in the poem itself. We can see the author's *skill* precisely in this. To which we might retort: Yes, precisely. We see a value of fullness, richness, design in the poem itself. *From this* we infer an artist and a skillful artist, and not the other way round. We do not compare the poem with any blueprint of the author's mind.

Let us turn then and consider some phases of the intentionalistic argument relating to statements of type 4 in our plan, those of interpretation—the author's mind outside the poem as a key to his meaning inside the poem.

(4a) A few of the recent writers on the term "intention" have pointed out, as indeed Mr. Beardsley and I were careful to point out in 1944, that interpretations apparently based upon an author's "intention" often in fact refer to an intention as it is found in, or inferred from, the work itself.[26] Obviously the argument about intention (or about the author's intention outside the work) is not directed against such instances—unless in an incidental and general plea for clarity in the use of critical terms. Such arguments may extend to *conflicts* of intention, or shifts of design, in a given work. They may give rise to such notions as that of a "secret meaning" (or even an unconscious meaning) to be distinguished from an "overt meaning." "Milton was of the Devil's party without knowing it." That is, Milton's *Paradise Lost*, in spite of certain contrary indications in it, on the whole makes Satan a hero. This argument can be enlarged by appeals to Milton's own rebellious personality, his political and religious prose writings. Yet it can be carried on too, and sufficiently, within the poem itself. Actually the poem itself seems to be the chief or only evidence which Blake, the author of the assertion just quoted, has in mind. Another classic instance is Tolstoy's judgment that Chekhov, in his story *Darling*, while trying to ridicule the womanliness of a woman, succeeded (like Balaam

26. See, for instance, John Kemp, "The Work of Art and the Artist's Intentions," *The British Journal of Aesthetics* 4 (April 1964): 150–51; Capitan, pp. 324–26; and Gendin, p. 193.

trying to curse the Israelites) only in pronouncing a blessing. Tolstoy had behind him a tradition of Russian book-reviewing which looked for covert and risky political meanings in nineteenth-century fiction.

(4b) In another variation of the same interpretive argument, the author's intention is sometimes said to have at least an "advisory" force.[27] This seems hardly a claim that ought to be debated. No doubt the author is likely to be a good guide. Yet it cannot be that on principle he is an infallible guide. As a commentator on his own works he enjoys no prescriptive, or creative, rights. If he says there is red in his poem, we will look carefully in the expectation of *finding* it.[28]

(4c) A somewhat similar sounding, but actually different, argument says that the intention of the artist (as learned in titles of works, epigraphs, and the like) may sometimes be said to fill in certain details or aspects of a work actually missing from the work but presumably needed for its understanding and appreciation.[29] In our article of 1945, Mr. Beardsley and I discussed something like this under the head of the modern poet's penchant for esoteric allusion, and we suggested that titles, epigraphs, and notes such as T. S. Eliot wrote for *The Waste Land*, were in fact loosely attached parts of poems or annexes of half-assimilated materials. As such they seemed to raise some questions about the achieved integrity of the poems. The notes to *The Waste Land* are not a manifest virtue, rather something we accept and submit to being teased by, in view of the probable depths of the poem itself, and latterly in view of Mr. Eliot's reputation.[30] Taken literally, the argument seems to imply some deficiency in the work of art itself, some need of adjunct or aid. On the assumption that the work of art is on the whole, or basically, worthwhile, nobody would wish to rule out such help—any more than to deny a crutch to a lame man, or an extra stone to a sagging arch. Only note that the crutch must fit the man; the stone must fit the arch, and in fact the stone becomes

27. Henry David Aiken, "The Aesthetic Relevance of Artists' Intentions," *The Journal of Philosophy* 52 (24 November 1955), reprinted in *Problems in Aesthetics*, ed. Morris Weitz (New York, 1959), pp. 299–300. Cf. Gendin, p. 194.
28. Kemp, p. 121, describes this situation very clearly.
29. Capitan, pp. 331–32.
30. See his extremely intentionalistic justification of these notes in a lecture on Dante in 1950: "I gave the references in my notes, in order to make the reader who recognizes the allusion, know that I meant him to recognize it, and know that he would have missed the point if he did not recognize it" (*To Criticize the Critic and Other Writings* [New York, 1965], p. 128).

part of the arch. These analogies seem closer to what is meant
by such special invocations of artist's intentions than, say, the
use of a strong glass to see a miniature painting or a strong light
in a gallery. The glass and the light can find only what is already
there.[31]

Certain external aids or annexes to poems, we have just as-
sumed, do fit or are appropriate to the poems in question. More
broadly, however, if we are to think of poems as having any
built-in character or structure of their own at all, then the in-
quiry must run the risk of encountering inappropriately offered
annexes, false clues, mistaken efforts of the energetic historian.

(4d) Certainly there are features of gross material or of struc-
ture in art works which not only do not call for the artist's in-
tention to help their interpretation but will even strongly defy
contradictory indications. If the artist makes a statue of granite,
then it is granite, and an affidavit that he thought he was work-
ing in marble or intended to work in marble or would rather
have worked in marble will not make any difference.[32] The
same principle will hold if the artist writes in English but hap-
pens to think he is writing in French. Or if he defies some code
of classic rules, though he happens to think he is observing them,
or vice versa. The former, or conservative, self-deception may be
illustrated in Corneille's retrospective defense of Le Cid. The
general principle for literary criticism was put precisely by
Samuel Johnson in his Preface to Shakespeare: "Whether Shake-
speare knew the unities and rejected them by design, or devi-
ated from them by happy ignorance, it is, I think, impossible to
decide and useless to inquire."[33]

(4e) Problems of local semantics may be more difficult. But
even here, the more explicit the conflicting auctorial testimony,
the more likely it is to seem comic in the degree of its exter-
nality and irrelevance. A member of the London Literary Club,
Anthony Chamier, better known as a statesman than as a
litterateur, once asked Oliver Goldsmith "What he meant by
slow, the last word in the first line of 'The Traveller,' 'Remote,

31. The claim for artist's intentions as auxiliaries to works of art will
no doubt mean somewhat different things for different kinds and instances
of art. See, for instance, Beardsley, pp. 20–29; Capitan, pp. 327–33; Erwin
Panofsky, "On Intentions," in Problems in Aesthetics, pp. 288–95, ex-
tracted from Panofsky's "History of Art as a Humanistic Discipline," in
The Meaning of the Humanities, ed. T. M. Greene (Princeton, 1940).

32. See Beardsley, p. 20, on painting and sculpture, "the simplest de-
scriptive level." Cf. Gendin, p. 194.

33. Preface to Shakespeare (1765), paragraph 59.

unfriended, melancholy, slow.' Did he mean tardiness of loco-
motion? Goldsmith, who would say something without con-
sideration, answered 'Yes.'" But Samuel Johnson happened to
be present and cut in, "No, Sir; you do not mean tardiness of
locomotion; you mean, that sluggishness of mind which comes
upon a man in solitude." "Chamier believed then" that Johnson
"had written the line as much as if he had seen" Johnson write
it.[34] It is worth adding that one editor of Goldsmith, Austin
Dobson, has observed, "It is quite possible that Goldsmith meant
no more than he said."[35] But an earlier commentator, John
Forster, says: "Who can doubt that he also meant slowness of
motion? The first point of the picture is *that*. The poet is moving
slowly, his tardiness of gait measuring the heaviness of heart,
the pensive spirit, the melancholy of which it is the outward ex-
pression and sign."[36] The point of the present exposition is that
Goldsmith, though undoubtedly in some sense closer to the gen-
erative intention of his own poem than the others, is not in vir-
tue of that fact a better critic or interpreter. If Forster seems
better than Dobson and better even than Johnson in this in-
stance, the grounds of his judgment and ours must lie in the ob-
servable force and relevance of the word "slow" in the *context*
of the first line of Goldsmith's pensive travelogue.

Mr. Beardsley has cited the nearly parallel instance of A. E.
Housman's angry attempt to deny the irony at expense of state
and church manifest in his poem for Queen Victoria's fiftieth
anniversary. "Get you the sons your fathers got, And God will
save the Queen." Here a statement made in retrospect and under
provocation, a kind of profession of loyalty to a sovereign,
stands in sharp contradiction not only to the cunning details of
the poem in question but to the well-known skeptical and cyn-
ical cast of the poet's canon.

The two instances just adduced may seem a parody of the in-
tentionalistic argument, but they are no more than a fair parody
of that argument as often formulated. Simple, even extreme,
examples have the advantage of revealing and clarifying prin-
ciples.

A classic instance of an author's serious intention, antecedent
to and simultaneous with the writing, yet doomed to defeat, is
Chekhov's desire (revealed in his letters) to have his *Seagull* and
Cherry Orchard produced as comedies—resulting only in Stani-

34. Boswell, *Life of Johnson*, 9 April 1778.
35. *Poetical Works of Goldsmith* (Oxford, 1939), p. 167.
36. *Goldsmith* (London, 1848), I: 369.

slavsky's successful and now well-established interpretation of them as tragedies—or at least as very cloudy "dramas."[37]

(4f) But let us now refine (or complicate) the argument a little with an example from the other end of a scale of explicitness in auctorial testimony—where no single explicit statement is adduced, but where the author's life and canon or some parts of them are urged as a surrounding and controlling context for the poem or some details of it. In our article of 1945, Mr. Beardsley and I wrote: "The meaning of words is the history of words, and the biography of an author, his use of a word, and the associations which the word has for *him*, are part of the word's history and meaning." But a critic who is habitually concerned with this kind of evidence, we added, will in the long run produce a far different sort of comment from that of the critic who is mainly concerned with the public linguistic and cultural elements of the poem.

We are now seeking a maximum or crucial instance where a poet's private or personal and habitual meaning (as inferred from external documents) clearly clashed with what he managed to realize in the public materials (linguistic and cultural) of his poem. Such instances are no doubt difficult to find, because poets by and large do manage to say what they mean. There is a sense in which, even when their words are "peculiar" or catachrestic, poets remain the "servants" of their language rather than its "masters."[38] In order to show a clear instance of the sort of conflict we are interested in, it may be necessary for the expositor himself to drive both sides of an interpretive difference, the intentionalistic and the nonintentionalistic—and thus perhaps to expose himself to the opportunism of the captious.

37. Beardsley, p. 24; Margolis, pp. 97, 189; David Magarshack, *Chekhov the Dramatist* (New York, 1960), pp. 188–89, *The Seagull*, p. 273, *The Cherry Orchard*. "*The Seagull* is usually interpreted on the stage as a tragedy (a misinterpretation Stanislavsky was the first to impose on the play), and yet Chekhov always referred to it as a comedy" (p. 188). "Practically every producer . . . in spite of Chekhov's unmistakable intentions, regards the play as a tragedy" (p. 189). We are here concerned in part with nuances of local meaning, in part also with whole dramatic structure and import. The example of Chekhov might well have been adduced above under 4d.

Margolis, p. 96, quotes the instance, no doubt unusual in the annals of literature, of Melville's acknowledgment that Hawthorne had revealed to him allegorical meanings in *Moby Dick* which he himself had not specifically "meant."

38. Cf. T. S. Eliot, "What Dante Means to Me" (1950), in *To Criticize The Critic*, p. 133. The terms are Eliot's. Though he would concede that "some great English poets . . . were privileged by their genius to abuse the English language," yet the poets who have best served their language are the greatest, Virgil, Dante, Shakespeare.

But the following may serve at least to define the issue. The materials are well known, but not the interpretive problem as I shall urge it. William Blake wrote in a sketchbook:

An ancient Proverb

Remove away that blackning church
Remove away that marriage hearse
Remove away that man of blood
You'll quite remove the ancient curse[39]

These lines remained in the sketchbook, where they deserved to remain. They are a raw expression of certain soreheaded antinomian attitudes which are beyond doubt a part of Blake's biography at the period when he was writing the *Songs of Experience*. Blake also wrote in the same sketchbook a draft for his "song" *London*, which he worked over with much struggle, adding only as an afterthought, in several successive versions, the last black stanza.

I wander thro' each charter'd street,
Near where the charter'd Thames does flow,
And mark in every face I meet
Marks of weakness, marks of woe.

In every cry of every Man,
In every Infant's cry of fear,
In every voice, in every ban,
The mind-forg'd manacles I hear:

How the Chimney-sweeper's cry
Every black'ning Church appalls;
And the hapless Soldier's sigh
Runs in blood down Palace walls.

But most, thro' midnight streets I hear
How the youthful Harlot's curse
Blasts the new-born Infant's tear,
And blights with plagues the Marriage hearse.[40]

The concluding phrase repeats that of the second line of the *Ancient Proverb* and creates a crux on which I wish to focus. This dark city poem is about human "weakness" and "woe" as they may be observed in certain (uncertain) visual and auditory be-

39. Number XXXV of the Rossetti manuscript, in Joseph H. Wicksteed, *Blake's Innocence and Experience* (London, 1928), after p. 256, p. 261, and facing p. 285; cf. *Poetry and Prose of William Blake*, ed. Geoffrey Keynes (London, 1932), p. 96.
40. Keynes, p. 75; Wicksteed, after p. 244, and p. 252.

trayals ("marks" and "cries") and in certain (uncertain) imputed human causes (charters, bans, mind-forged manacles). The word "ban" as it is used in the second stanza of the poem no doubt includes many kinds of legal or official yells, proclamations, summonses, prohibitions, curses—no doubt even marriage bans. At this point let us consult one of the best informed and most soberly reliable of recent Blake critics.

> The one thing needful in achieving this transformation [of the human spirit] is the removal of the mind-forged manacles of the institutional tyrannies—marriage, the church, and the king.
> "Every ban" . . . is a multiple clank of the awful trinity of king, priest, and marriage.
> It is the marriage hearse that breeds youthful (and thus potentially innocent) harlots, by creating the necessity for prostitution. If there were no marriage, there would be no ungratified desires, and therefore no harlots. Thus it is ultimately the marriage hearse itself and not the youthful harlot which breeds the pestilence that blights the marriage hearse.[41]

Mr. E. D. Hirsch, as I have said, is well informed about Blake and reliable, and I believe he gives us an accurate reading of a sort of intention which Blake probably did entertain, a phase at least of Blake's habitual mind as it may be supposed to stand at some distance behind the poem. Mr. Hirsch gives us a good and learned instance of the new cryptography in Blake reading. "If there were no marriage, there would be no ungratified desires, and therefore no harlots." One thing, however, which perhaps he does not notice, or perhaps does not worry about, is that these ideas are silly. (Why wouldn't there be *many* ungratified desires, as many at least as there were losers in stag combats, or wooers rejected, or pursuers eluded, or matings frustrated? and *many* harlots? and *many* whoremasters?) An admirer of Blake the poet might well be content to leave these ideas, if he could, on a back shelf in the doctrinaire part of Blake's mind. What if we actually do find them or manage to put them in the poem? Won't this make the poem silly? And, since interpretation and evaluation are at the very least closely related, won't we be in danger of reading the poem as a pretty bad poem? And isn't this poem, in fact, supposed to be a masterpiece, "one of the best city poems ever written"?

41. E. D. Hirsch, Jr., *Innocence and Experience: An Introduction to Blake* (New Haven, 1964), pp. 263–65.

Isn't it, in fact, a masterpiece? It will be worthwhile to look closely at the difference between the last stanza of the engraved poem *London* and the crude second line of *An ancient Proverb*, which stayed in the sketchbook. Blake's struggle with *London* was in part a struggle to make the last line of the last stanza viable. The tough fact was that the word "marriage" in the history of English usage and culture was not the name of an evil. ("Let me not to the marriage of true minds admit impediments.") It was the name of a sacred institution and a first principle of stability for nearly every important value in a whole religiously and ethically oriented civilization and culture. The explosive force of the two violently juxtaposed terms at the end of the last line of *London* is a poetic fact. But this was not to be achieved by the easy way of simple supposition or assertion (though that may be a rationale which very well suits the aims of the biographical critic or cryptographer). Here the angry conscience of William Blake the doctrinaire prophet and activist clashed violently with the more tactful and skillful conscience of William Blake the poet, master and servant of the English language.[42] The latter conscience, apparently after a hard struggle, won and (perhaps without Blake's being fully aware of what happened—who knows?) saved him from engraving a poem with a lame, perhaps even silly and ruinous, last line. Let us imagine that some inquisitor of school curricula, reading Mr. Hirsch's gloss on *London*, were to file a protest against corrupting the minds of schoolchildren by the required study of this depraved poem. One sort of answer, from the defenders of the English curriculum, might be that it was good for children to hear all views and to be exposed to a liberal assault upon the mores in which home, church, and state were trying to educate them. But another answer that surely would not be long delayed would be to the effect that Blake's *London* in fact says no such thing. True, the English teacher or the school principal would say, the poem stresses charters and mind-forged manacles, but circumstances, real and symbolic (the cry of sweeps, the decay of churches, the blood of soldiers), are adduced to give specific topical color to the imputations. We are dealing with very concretely colored instances. And in the last stanza it is potently suggested that there is a very real and evil antecedent cause why

42. The evidence of the Rossetti manuscript supports the biographical dimension which I introduce for the sake of dialogue with the biographically minded. The distinction between the doctrinaire man and the subtle poem would remain even if the poetic achievement had cost Blake no trouble at all.

the marriage bed turns to a hearse. For an initiate reading of the last stanza, consult the career of an eighteenth-century Londoner like James Boswell or Charles Hanbury Williams.

In sum, a critic who says that the "poem" means that "if there were no marriage, there would be no ungratified desires," ought to show that this meaning actually operates in the poem or is generated by it—and is not merely a concealed or balked idea entertained by the author as revolutionary person. I myself think the poem is better than that meaning, and to judge from the contexts where the poem has often appeared and from earlier critiques, it would seem that most readers have also thought so.

Yet even these [blackened churches and blood-stained palace walls] are less terrible than the hideous perversion of the fairest joy on earth, voiced in the midnight cry of the young harlot. Love itself and the beauty of marriage and birth are stained by this most cruel misery of all.[43]

I have set up this discussion of the poem as a frame of reference within which a student may be able to see the direction in which his own mind moves in search of evidence for the meaning and value of a poem. When he can really see the difference between the directions and the results, then let him decide.

Mr. Hirsch's method of reading *London* is not an isolated instance, though his clarity in realizing what he is doing and his frankness in admitting it may be unusual. A new mode in historical studies, which I would describe as a kind of attempted Vista-Vision intentionalism, searches reasons for inferring an author's intention not only in the whole canon of his own works and life record, early and late, but in motifs selected from anywhere in the intellectual ambient of his era. Let me cite a remarkable instance of this new mode in Paul de Man's essay of 1956, "Keats and Hölderlin."[44] Here, with the pursuit of the poet as philosopher-hero in full cry and the method of theme and analogy rampant, we bring Keats's *Endymion* into line with his own later *Hyperion* and with Hölderlin's novel *Hyperion* by the simple if eloquently disguised method of arguing that throughout the poem Keats failed to say what he meant. His interest in another kind of meaning was just too much for him. Keats should have been writing, or he wished to be writing,

43. Wicksteed, p. 190. "I do not doubt that he continued to accept marriage at its face value even after his mind had learnt to entertain the revolutionary suggestions of the rationalistic and antinomian circles he came to mingle in" (p. 215).
44. *Comparative Literature* 8 (Winter 1956): 28–45, esp. 36–38.

about a very serious subject, the "eccentric road" of man's repetitive search for recovery of "unity of being." But he wrote actually about love (erotic love). "No wonder it becomes difficult to keep apart the passages in which love is an actual experience, among others, from those in which it is a symbol for something else. But only at the expense of this effort [i.e. violence] can *Endymion* be given a thematic coherence which Keats's *Hyperion* amply substantiates" (p. 36). We proceed to a reading of *Endymion* which makes its point only at the expense of finding the imagery "incongruous," "confusing," "bizarre," "stifled," "awkward" (pp. 37–38)—in short, utterly ineffectual (or inexpressive) and hence unpoetic. This is Keats's *Endymion.* "A thing of beauty is a joy for ever."

Some of our critics have argued that Mr. Beardsley and I have examined the term "intention" in too restricted and too simply mentalistic a sense (intention in the mind of the artist); at the same time they have adduced statements by us that show that we do not in fact object to certain broader invocations of "intention" (in effect, "intention" as present and verifiable "intent" in works of art themselves). And they have praised other writers, or themselves, for taking the term "intention" in a broader (or at least other) and more "generous" sense.[45] One writer has pointed out that we selected an example which showed what we meant and tended to support our argument, and thus he considers our example "tendentious."[46] It is difficult to see how such arguments are better than obscurantist devices of one-upmanship. We took "intention" in a specific or limited sense, because it was just the difference between this sense and the broader (or other) sense that we believed to be often obscured in critical argument, with consequent concealed dilution of, or escape from, objective criticism. At the same time, we tried to make the idea of "intention" a focal point (and I still believe it was a well-chosen focal point) for a cluster of genetically oriented ideas (inspiration, expression, authenticity, sincerity, purpose, and the like). What might seem at first glance a merely verbal and ambiguous cluster turns out on acquaintance to be a dynamic pattern that is well treated with as much unity of vision as possible. It is my opinion that as criteria for criticism these ideas stand or fall together. Both in our essay of 1945 and in our earlier dictionary article,

45. Margolis, pp. 103 and 189, citing Isabel Hungerland, "The Concept of Intention in Art Criticism," *Journal of Philosophy* 52 (24 November 1955): 733–42, and other sources.
46. Dr. Cioffi, p. 167.

Mr. Beardsley and I argued "that the design or intention of the author is neither available nor desirable as a standard for judging the success of a work of literary art." A recent writer on the same theme has accused Mr. Beardsley of having, in 1958, weakened this thesis by asserting merely that the "specific intention" of the artist outside the work is "practically never available"—thus, it would appear, making the question only empirical and forfeiting its "theoretical" and "philosophical" status.[47] What we meant in 1945, and what in effect I think we managed to say, was that the closest one could ever get to the artist's intending or meaning mind, outside his work, would be still short of his *effective* intention or *operative* mind as it appears in the work itself and can be read from the work. Such is the concrete and fully answerable character of words as aesthetic medium.[48] The intention outside the poem is always subject to the corroboration of the poem itself. No better evidence, in the nature of things, can be adduced than the poem itself. This observation seems to me less needed in meeting the directly evaluative form of the argument (see above, pp. 23–25) than in meeting the interpretive form which we have just been considering. The statement in our essay of 1945 should certainly have read: "The design or intention of the author is neither available nor desirable as a standard for judging either the meaning or the value of a work of literary art."

We have never said that the way of the objective critic could be smooth, easy, or perfect. Still we have tried to delineate one of the principles by which this critic will have to discipline his efforts unless he wishes to surrender to the flux, the gossip, the muddle and the "motley" for which philosophers like Dr. Cioffi, Professor Aldridge, and Mr. Cruttwell seem so earnestly to yearn.

It is true that verbal compositions do not subsist metaphysically, by or in themselves, as visual words on paper. The differ-

47. Margolis, p. 103, quoting Beardsley, p. 490.
48. One of our critics, Emilio Roma III, seems to grasp this principle firmly enough and to accept it ("The Scope of the Intentional Fallacy," *The Monist* 50 [April 1966] : 250–65, esp. 250–51, 256, 265). It is perhaps his main reason for recognizing a sort of "minimal" and "pitifully easy" meaning in our notion of the "intentional fallacy." But he believes that a distinction between what the speaker means and what the "sentence" means, urged very explicitly by Mr. Beardsley in 1958, is not to be found in our essay of 1945. Mr. Roma writes with the air (e.g. p. 254) of painfully spelling out what we said. "Style," he says, "is treated [by us] as though it had nothing whatsoever to do with content" (p. 265). To me at least, and I think to Mr. Beardsley, this can come only as a matter of surprise. How much of what we have written, in the essay of 1945 and elsewhere, is really understood by Mr. Roma?

ence between "inside" the poem and "outside" the poem (to which some of our critics object)[49] is not like the difference between the printed words and the margin of the page. But neither are verbal compositions merely passing acts or moments of the human spirit, sounds heard then or now but not again. The words have their peculiar existence in their meaning, and that derives from and is determined by their context or their history. The study of poems in their public contexts of language and culture sees them in a spread-out and universalized relation to those contexts. It is a study of pattern and ideal and is the only study which is capable of discriminating between the cogently organized artistic structure (both concrete and universal) and the mere particularities of personal moments, accidental and nonce meanings. What kind of unity or entity is the most valid object of literary study? Roughly, there are three possible answers: the Age, the Author, the Work. Various kinds of interest in race, milieu, and moment (so familiar to academic literary criticism for more than two centuries) come under the first head. Studies of literary genre come here when they get out of hand, and also the more extreme instances of deference to the historical audience.[50] One kind of ultimate metaphysician in favor of the author may be found in Benedetto Croce, who hardly believes in the literary work at all, certainly not in works of any length, but sees the whole duty of the critic as the pursuit of the "poetical motive," the "poetic personality" which he can find anthologically here and there in writers like Goethe, Corneille, and Dante. A newer sort of canonical historicist, as we have seen, makes the idolatrous assumption that a given author's mind or vision during his whole career is necessarily a coherent whole or a dialectic development, as good an entity as, or better than, any one of his works. For the objective critic of literary works, an author has as much unity as he can demonstrate in any given work or in a part of a work. The whole for which the critic looks is the coherently expressive structure, large or small. The poet's canon and life are "the most essential

---

49. Roma, pp. 251–52, 258, 262; Cioffi, pp. 167, 170 (on excluding "illicit sources" of interpretation). The word "motley" in our text just above is from Cioffi, pp. 176, 183, taken by him "probably" from Wittgenstein.

50. This may involve what Mr. E. D. Hirsch calls the "fallacy of the homogeneous past." "The homogeneous critic assumes that everybody in a given cultural milieu shares the same basic attitudes and beliefs. He is content to speak of the Greek Mind, the Medieval Mind, the Victorian Mind" ("Criticism versus Historicism," mimeograph of a paper read at the meeting of the Modern Language Association, December 1963).

part of the context of the poem"[51] only to the extent that the
poet is talking to himself. The words which the poet writes in a
given passage depend for their meaning in one sense on the per-
sonal context and the author's intention (his word as *parole*),
but they depend also, in a sense more important to the critic,
on the wider context of the language (his words as *langue*) and
culture.[52] Otherwise they would never, here and now, there and
then, make sense to anybody but the author himself. Authors
characteristically graduate from earlier, naïve stages and write
masterpieces. Characteristically also they write later weaker
works. To appreciate *Lear* and *Hamlet* it is not necessary to take
into account *A Comedy of Errors* or *Timon of Athens* (or such
parts of the latter as Shakespeare wrote) or even *The Tempest*.
The search for the author's generative intention as context of
the poem is a search for a temporal moment which must, as the
author and the poem live on, recede and ever recede into the
forgotten, as all moments do. Poems, on this theory of their
meaning, must always steadily grow less and less correctly known
and knowable; they must dwindle in meaning and being toward

51. Hyatt H. Waggoner, in *What to Say About a Poem*, *CEA Chapbook*,
by W. K. Wimsatt, Jr., and others, ed. Donald A. Sears (College English
Association, 1963), pp. 22, 32.
52. See Mr. Hirsch's exposition of Saussure's distinction ("Objective
Interpretation," pp. 473–75), where *langue*, the "system of linguistic
possibilities shared by a speech community," "contains words and
sentence-forming principles, but it contains no sentences." A poem or any
other verbal text containing sentences cannot then simply "represent a
segment of *langue*" (as modern literary theorists are said to hold) but must
be a *parole*, "a particular, selective actualization from *langue*," a deter-
minate individual expression. "Only individuals utter *paroles*," and "a
parole of the speech community is non-existent." "Meaning requires a
meaner." When we come to the difficulty of the "bungled text," the
"freshman essay," the malapropism (which, let me add, is the basic diffi-
culty of poem and purpose made large and unavoidable), we solve it by
saying that the author's text, failing to "represent the *parole* he desired to
convey," "represents no *parole* at all." But such an intuitionist and abso-
lute (or Crocean) conclusion does not sit well in the abstractive and scien-
tific premises (of *langue* and *parole*) with which we have begun. If we are
going to have "words" and "principles" conceived as prior to *parole*, we
must face the possibility of their being badly put together. A "house" put
together of ill-matched cardboard prefabrications would not be no-house-
at-all, or nothing, but simply a bad house.
Mr. Hirsch's *Validity in Interpretation* (New Haven, 1967), which urges
his views in greater detail and usefully reprints his essay of 1960, appeared
only some time after I had completed the present essay. Mr. Beardsley, in
an essay entitled "Textual Meaning and Authorial Meaning," has written
what I consider a shrewd critique of the book, scheduled to appear in a
symposium in *Genre* 1, no. 3 (July 1968), pp. 169–81.

a vanishing point. The best known and most valuable poem must be that written but a moment ago—and its best or only possible audience must be the author. But poems we know are not really like that. The most self-assured authors publish their works and hang upon public recognition. Shakespeare has more meaning and value now than he had in his own day. There is a sense in which even Homer, though we construe his language with pain and are not sure how many persons he was, has more meaning and is more valuable today than ever before.

1968

LAOKOÖN:
AN ORACLE RECONSULTED

Painting, Sir, can illustrate, but cannot inform.
—Samuel Johnson

And pray, sir, *Who is Bach?* Is he a piper?
—Samuel Johnson

Media

"One would have to be a young man again," wrote Goethe, "to realize the effect wrought upon us by Lessing's Laokoön." This book "transported us from the region of slavish observation into the free fields of speculative thought. The long misunderstood *ut pictura poesis* was at once set aside. The difference between picture and poetry made clear—the peaks of both appeared separate, however near might be their bases."[1] One would indeed have to be a young man again. The master distinction urged in Lessing's central chapters, XVI-XXII, between objects in motion, i.e. actions (the proper business of poetry) and objects at rest, i.e. bodies (the proper business of painting and sculpture), was both too little and too much. Lessing must have been aware of the notions about a color clavecin entertained by Father Castel at Paris;[2] but he had never heard of moving pictures—cinema. And only in a partly mock appreciation, a passage about some old pedantic grammarian's imagined commentary on Agamemnon's sceptre in Homer, does he seem to pay enough

This paper was delivered at the December 1967 Modern Language Association meeting. When I wrote it I was not aware of Murray Krieger's "The Ekphrastic Principle and the Still Movement of Poetry; Or Laokoön Revisited" in his *The Play and Place of Criticism* (Baltimore, 1967), which employs an idiom of metaphor and paradox that I will not attempt to relate to my own.
Concerning the epigraphs I have chosen, the remark on painting was made most likely in March 1772 (Boswell, *Journal*, London, 22 March 1772; *Life of Johnson*, June 1784); that on Bach was made on the occasion of Johnson's first visit to Dr. Charles Burney, on 20 March 1777 (Fanny Burney, *Early Diary*, 1889, II:153, 156; *Letters of Samuel Johnson*, 19 March 1777, no. 512; Roger Lonsdale, *Dr. Charles Burney*, 1965, p. 236).
1. *Dichtung und Wahrheit* VIII, trans. Minna S. Smith (London, 1908), II:282.
2. Lessing's friend Moses Mendelssohn had treated the topic and had objected to the confusion of sense modalities in his *Briefe über die Empfindungen*, 1755 and 1761. See Wilton Mason, "Father Castel and His Color Clavecin," *JAAC* 17 (September 1958): 103-16, esp. 107-08, 116.

attention to the inexplicit and symbolic power of image-working
—the subterranean area of the unified roots of all the arts to
which Goethe alludes. We no longer think of either poetry or
picture as simple representation (mimesis) of any externally, or
even any internally, identifiable thing. Even our mechanical
recorders and transmitters have nowadays assumed a more and
more well-recognized role in the enslavement of our imagination.
A young man with a Polaroid camera takes a snapshot of a wed-
ding party standing in bright sunlight. A few moments later, the
party is still standing, waiting for other cameras, when he pulls
out the fully developed color print (wonder of recent tech-
nology). A friend reaches for it, says, "Let me see it. Let me see
what they look like."

"A reader with any artistic sense," wrote Benedetto Croce for
the Fourteenth Edition of the *Encyclopaedia Britannica*, "finds
in a single line from a poet at once musical and picturesque
qualities, a sculpturesque strength and architectural structure;
and the same with a picture, which is never a mere thing of the
eyes but an affair of the whole soul . . . art is one and cannot be
divided into arts." At the level of truism, Croce argues that the
formal principle of all the arts is the same. At the level of fac-
tual discovery and historical information, the research scholar is
able to point out how some of the arts in fact supply materials
for, or are reflected in, some of the others. From a different
angle of study, looking at specific forms, techniques, and media,
I am concerned today to lay some stress on the truth that the
arts are in fact considerably different from one another.

Certain kinds of analysis seem to send us back to differences
which were more evident before we attempted the analysis. We
can tell the difference between cornflakes and snowflakes, a
hawk and a "handsaw," even without a microscope. We can
count the number of horses in a field more quickly than we can
count their legs and divide by four. Lessing's appeal to time and
movement, against space and repose, has become in the course
of time less convincing than the original unanalyzed difference
between a picture and a poem. On the one hand, pictures can
move; and on the other, the ongoing temporal literary experi-
ence has its moment of simultaneity. Both texts and moving
pictures are arrested in memory—more or less. Hence, in part,
all those excellent analogies representing the poem as urn, icon,
and the like. Hence, too, what is sometimes nowadays discerned
as "spatial form" in literature. Lessing's distinction was less in-
structive than another which was already better established in
his time, that between "natural" signs and "artificial" signs. As

42   Contraries

we might put it today, the difference between pictographic or ideographic writing and alphabetical or syllabic. In each kind, to be sure, there is a picture. But the picture of a zebra and that of the letter Z differ profoundly in that the zebra is visible at the zoo, whereas Z is not externally visible anywhere but in its picture. Perhaps we have not yet advanced very far, and never shall, beyond the simple formulation of La Fontaine: "Colors and words are not comparable things. The eyes are not the ears."[3] Or, more accurately, the mind using either eye or ear in a linguistic way is not the same as the mind using the eye in a pictorial way. The supposed power of the pictograph in Chinese poetry was an occasion for mysterious talk by Fenollosa and Pound. It is not taken very seriously by professors of Chinese literature.[4]

A good forger, as E. H. Gombrich in his marvelous book *Art and Illusion* observes, can perfectly reproduce a ten-dollar bank note.[5] Chatterton or Macpherson can forge, not very successfully, the imagined poetic idiom and language of a past era. But given a known particular sonnet by Keats and challenged to forge it, we have a choice between, on the one hand, reciting or transcribing it, and, on the other, writing a parody. If we are T. J. Wise, we forge, not the poem, but the printed paper.

Language succeeds in being more or less simply *iconic* of some auditory qualities and (far more important) in being variously *diagrammatic* of numerous logical relationships—parallels and oppositions, crescendos and diminuendos. This has been an important theme of linguistic analysis from Plato's *Cratylus* to C. S. Peirce and Roman Jakobson.[6] Artificial signs, as Lessing and his century would put it, strive in poetry to become natural signs. Still the artifice is always deeply pervasive. The boy in the comic strip blows up his balloon and it breaks. POP! Onomatopoeia, of course. But his father looks in from the other room and asks, "Did you call me, Henry?" In a parallel way Gombrich has cunningly and convincingly stressed the role of pre-existent visual formulas or schemas (and their modification or adjustment)[7] in the artist's production of a picture of something. We

3. *Conte du Tableau.*
4. Achilles Fang, "Fenollosa and Pound," *Harvard Journal of Asiatic Studies* 20 (1957): 213–38, esp. 215–20; James J. Y. Liu, *The Art of Chinese Poetry* (Chicago, 1962), pp. 3, 6, 14, 18–19; George Kennedy, "Fenollosa, Pound and the Chinese Character," *Yale Literary Magazine* 127 (December 1958): 24–36.
5. *Art and Illusion* (Pantheon Books, 2d ed., 1965), p. 90.
6. Roman Jakobson, "Quest for the Essence of Language," *Diogenes* 51 (1965): 21–37.
7. *Art and Illusion*, pp. 73–74, 356–57.

have a shape first and next we discover that, viewed in a certain way, it looks like something. On the other hand, it does look like something. A picture is at least a "relational model" of visual experience.[8] Recent studious simulacra in the order of Pop Art, whatever else they may be, are a sabotage protest against the too-long triumphant and cliché reign of expressionism and creationism. The notion of "nonrepresentational" visual art was always a mistake. Physical art objects (framed or pedestaled) inevitably resemble classes of physical natural objects or other art objects and therefore inevitably imitate them. Words, on the other hand, resemble mainly other words. Words work toward their apparent naturalness or directness, not in consort with the babbling brook, the howling wind, the whispering leaves, but through their own affinities and families. If we insist on the dramatic aspect, that words imitate human speech,[9] this will remove them even further from the pictorial. What I am driving at is that questions about illusion and about imagination are greatly different for the art of words and for the art of colored shapes.

Interpretation

"Literature and the Visual Arts: The Problem of Critical Terms." This rubric covers a considerable range of problems. One job of even a half-hour paper may be to sort some of them out. In the field of art history and art interpretation, a massive penetration by ideological and literary elements has long been an accomplished fact. The walls of the museum have been removed in large chunks.[10] Plenary and dazzling instances of research may be adduced from the books of such authors as Erwin Panofsky and Edgar Wind: Titian's *Sacred and Profane Love*, the naked Venus and the clothed, representing in fact the heavenly and the human kinds of "chastened" love;[11] the shepherds by the tombstone: *Et in Arcadia Ego*;[12] and a host of other Pagan

8. Ibid., p. 90.
9. Ibid., p. 363.
10. Cf. Geoffrey H. Hartman, "The Taming of History: A Comparison of Poetry with Painting Based on Malraux's *The Voices of Silence*," *Yale French Studies*, no. 18 (1957), pp. 114-15.
11. Edgar Wind, *Pagan Mysteries in the Renaissance* (New Haven, 1958), pp. 121-28; Erwin Panofsky, *Studies in Iconology: Humanistic Themes in the Art of the Renaissance* (Oxford, 1939), Harper Torchbook (New York, 1962), pp. 150-59, figure 108.
12. Erwin Panofsky, *Meaning in the Visual Arts* (Doubleday Anchor Book, 1955), pp. 307, 311, 313, 316, and plates 90-92.

Mysteries of the Renaissance. Still, there may be a kind of mind
or a taste which, inclining more both to the "pre-iconographical"
and to the "iconological" (the immediate sensory or "formal"
and the ultimate ideational or symbolic) than to the middle
ground of local convention and "iconography,"[13] will find in
many such learned instances a greater degree of cultural or ideo-
logical revelation than of the aesthetic. A seventeenth-century
Venetian painting[14] of a handsome young woman, with a sword
in her left hand and in her right a charger on which rests the
head of a man! Is this a picture of Salome? or of Judith? Lo!
while we cannot adduce a single Salome with a sword, we en-
counter in Germany and North Italy several sixteenth-century
paintings which show Judith (incorrectly) with a charger. There
was a type of "Judith with a charger."[15] Many symbols and
emblems in portraits by Lorenzo Lotto and others of that
allegorical and cryptographic school are now undecipherable, but
the artistic value of these paintings, some of them homely
enough pieces of family piety and encomium, might not be
greatly enhanced by the discovery of their secret. "Of their
nature," says John Pope-Hennessy in his fine chapter on such
puzzles, "emblems are intrusive." And he describes a "whole
series" of paintings by one Bartolomeo Veneto, "emblematic
portraits of ladies wreathed with symbolic flowers and bran-
dishing symbolic hammers, of which the meaning is invariably
arcane, and which have more interest as riddles than as works
of art."[16] There may well be a kind of lover of the pictorial
arts who turns from the study or even from the triumphant
solution of such problems, with relief, toward such a simple
celebration as Goethe's of the Laokoön group:—a "tragic
idyll. . . . A father sleeps next to his sons. They are encircled
by snakes, and waking, strive to tear themselves free from the
living mesh."[17]

Mélange

If pictures need to be interpreted by texts, the idea of juncture
between these forms and other forms is scarcely to be ques-

13. Panofsky, *Meaning in the Visual Arts*, pp. 40–41.
14. By Francesco Maffei.
15. Panofsky, *Meaning in the Visual Arts*, pp. 36–37.
16. *The Portrait in the Renaissance* (Pantheon Books, 1966),' pp. 231,
226.
17. *Ueber Laokoön*, 1797–1798; quoted by Margarete Bieber, *Laokoön*
(New York, 1942), pp. 12–13.

tioned. What Irving Babbitt was to chronicle as the romantic mélange of the aesthetic media, with a musical orientation, was never put in doubt by Lessing's argument. The *Gesamtkunstwerk* continued to expand with as much confidence as today the methods of art history. Despite a *New Laokoön* of 1910, many before-undreamed uses of the media have been witnessed in our century of technological advance. Today's critical "anti-interpreter" rejoices in the trampling of barriers and in a philosophy that understands the non-reality of all art entities and presumably of most natural ones. "A tree, a river, and a mountain are no more a single entity than are a ballet, the Leaves of Grass, or a Rembrandt painting."[18] We arrive at "multimedia," the barrage and "massage," the "supersaturated attack" on the senses, the "overload," the "blitz," contrived with elaborately inventive care in the "total environment" discothèque, at sales meetings of the Scott Paper Company, at electronic theater events, or in the halls of Expo and the Royal Ontario Museum: —batteries of pulsing and eye-searing strobe lights, wailing sirens and high-decibel modern rock, flashing and jumping screens, electronically tinted mists, incidental smells and touches, all these for the purpose of "turning on" the patron—in a total experience which approximates the effect of the psychedelic drug—a deepening and merging of sensory experience, a release of the mind from the "rational ordering" of perception.[19]

Still it may occur to a certain mind or taste to remark that so far as any past art happenings have had the chance to be recorded or embodied as entities of art history, the media have often enough shown a tendency to mingle like oil and water. Sometimes it is true that each is thin enough to be little or nothing without the other. The whirligig bundled clichés of a Robin Hood ballad and the runaway rasping syllables and lute of Wallace House achieve their aesthetic interest (as it may be distinguished from the simply antiquarian) mainly or only when joined in mutual aid. But a single medium is likely enough to be dominant, considerably superior, and even somewhat resistant to invasion. The text of a song in the Elizabethan John Dowland's *Songs or Ayres*, as Professor Bronson instructs us, may be a shoddy makeshift to provide syllables for singing the music. Or, Waller's exquisite poem *Goe Lovely Rose* is reported to be hardly singable. In another variation, the chastely modulated words of Dryden or Pope are stretched like rubber bands or

18. Susan Sontag, "On Art and the Total Art-Work," lecture at Yale University, quoted in the *New Haven Register*, 13 April 1967, p. 52.
19. Grace Glueck, *New York Times*, 16 September 1967, p. 29.

repetitiously treadmilled as occasions for the baroque embel-
lishments of a Handelian setting.[20] Dryden himself has recorded
the anguish of the poet in writing for an opera. This kind of
poetry must "please hearing rather than gratify understanding."
"The same reasons which depress thought in an opera have a
stronger effect upon the words." "I was then a slave to the
composition, which I will never be again."[21] We love the music
of Purcell and the electrifying voice of Flagstad, or the lovely
vocal lament of Kathleen Ferrier, but we do not set the text of
Nahum Tate or of the song *Willow, Willow* as exercises in critical
exegesis.[22]

Stage drama is a long-established and highly successful union
of auditory and visual art, a kind of primitive or unphotographed
moving picture, the bard present in person or in a collection of
persons, in costume—with scenery, incidental music, even
oranges and candy. Yet certain sensibilities have set little store
by this union of media—Aristotle, for instance, who said that
the *opsis* was a matter *not* of art *but* of scene shifting, and the
very non-Aristotelian Charles Lamb, who preferred not to see
the tragedies of Shakespeare acted. "What you see upon the stage
is body and bodily action; what we are conscious of in reading
is almost exclusively the mind, and its movements"— a "very
different sort of delight."[23]

Immobile pictures can scarcely speak texts. But they can
stand beside them. And thus we have the situation where it may
well be that "the pictures for the page atone, And Quarles is
saved by Beauties not his own." If it happens, however, that the
poet has illustrated or illuminated his own text, the literary
scholar, for reasons very deeply inherent in his mystery, will be
much more likely to look upon the adjacency as a matter of
great moment. Blake is the instance that today will most vividly

20. Bertrand H. Bronson, "Musical Tunes and Recited Verse," lecture
at the English Institute, Columbia University, 7 September 1967. And see
his "Literature and Music," in *Relations of Literary Study*, ed. James A.
Thorpe (New York: Modern Language Association of America, 1967), pp.
127-48, esp. pp. 128-30, 135, 137, 140, 142, 146.

21. Preface to *Albion and Albanius* (1685), near the end.

22. Cf. Evelyn K. Wells, *The Ballad Tree* (New York, 1950), pp. 101,
103, a British version of *Lord Randal* with music and an American version
of *Edward* with music, both collected by Cecil James Sharp.

23. *On the Tragedies of Shakespeare*, six paragraphs from the end. But
even so mixed an art as the theater can be defended as a pure conception.
"Theatre," says Eugene Ionesco, "can be nothing but theatre" (*Notes and
Counter Notes: Writings on the Theatre*, trans. Donald Watson, New York,
1964, pp. 33-34—"Experience of the Theatre," from the *Nouvelle Revue
Française*, February 1958).

spring to mind. "What Blake hath joined together," we are admonished by Professor Jean Hagstrum in his informative book on this theme, "let no man put asunder!"[24] And an eminent art scholar who reviews the book finds this thesis "undeniably correct," for the odd reason that picture and text "form an indissoluble whole, so that each can throw light on the other."[25] In such ticklish issues stylistic confusions are likely to betray deeper ones. It is my own pronounced view that we can subscribe to the thesis only if we have performed the preliminary rite of making Blake the god of our idolatry. Like all other human beings, which includes all other artists, Blake could do things both more and less deeply and accurately. Blake's poems are enmeshed visually in the design of his plates. It is possible for this to have no closer relation to the linguistic achievement of a poem than the egg or altar shapes of an earlier age or the experimentally scattered typography of our own. One of the best, because one of the most accomplished and self-contained of the *Songs of Experience*, is that entitled *London*, to which is joined a design where against a rude suggestion of London masonry appear a long-bearded old man (a decrepit Urizen figure) and a spritely boy, both attired in the flowing shrouds of Blake's allegory world.[26] The same design could be readily adapted later for plate 84 of *Jerusalem*. "Distinct General Form cannot exist," Blake wrote in his marginalia on Reynolds' *Discourses*. "To Generalize is to be an Idiot." We may wonder whether he was aware how far and how many times he himself had outgeneralized Reynolds. "In the most famous of all the Songs," says Hagstrum, "the magnificent verbal 'Tyger' is unworthily illustrated by a simpering animal."[27] The observation is a sound one, and Professor Hagstrum is the more to be congratulated in that it shows his independence of the reigning apocalypse. In the *Songs of Innocence*, a very little girl gets lost in the woods with lions, leopards, and tigers, but one of the pictures that goes with this episode seems to show a not so little girl who will get lost in a different way in the *Songs of Experience*.[28] Anticipation,

24. Jean H. Hagstrum, *William Blake, Poet and Painter* (Chicago, 1964), p. viii.
25. Anthony Blunt, "Blake and the Scholars: I," *New York Review of Books*, 28 October 1965, p. 22.
26. Hagstrum, *William Blake*, p. 84. " . . . a broken old man, who appears in the design but not the text of 'London,' heading for his grave, an image of his god, Urizen, whose victim he is."
27. Hagstrum, p. 86.
28. F. W. Bateson, *Selected Poems of William Blake* (New York, 1957), p. 100. Cf. Hagstrum, p. 79.

transfer, metaphor? Perhaps so. There is no doubt some truth in the contention that some of Blake's *Songs* receive in their pictures either a positive complement of thematic detail or a negative counterpoint. But it will be a nicer question how much this does in fact either to complete or to justify the texts. "The illustration of *The Blossom*," observes F. W. Bateson sanely, "has been used to give that poem an elaborate phallic interpretation . . . that would never occur to anyone who had only the words in front of him."[29] If it is true, and it may well be true, that the wispy text of *Infant Joy* reaches out its tendrils and *needs* the support of intimations about Holy Birth and Annunciation in the fine illumination, this is interesting. Yet we may feel a failure. The words standing alone, says Hagstrum, "seem gnomic and incomplete."[30] By such partial stencils, the deep craving of the poetic and critical taste for the achieved verbal presentment is not appeased. Just as the taste for good conversation, we may suppose, would have been frustrated for an Augustan man of the world meeting one of Swift's philosophers at the Grand Academy of Lagado, who instead of attempting the imperfect medium of speech, would exhibit various well-chosen physical objects which they produced from their pockets.

At this point in our account, if there were room for everything, might come a discussion of the landscape poetry of J. M. W. Turner,[31] or the Petrarchan *Rime* of Michelangelo,[32] or the portrait-painting of Alexander Pope. Here too insert the yearning of the painter Degas to write sonnets, and the advice of Mallarmé: "You don't make sonnets with ideas, Degas. You make them with words."[33] The celebrated parallel between the arts, whatever else it supposes, supposes different kinds of artistic competence, not often united in the same artist.[34]

29. Bateson, *Selected Poems of William Blake*, p. 101. Cf. Hagstrum, p. 82: "The flame-flower could be phallic; tiny cupids have taken the place of the textual sparrow, who appears nowhere in the design. . . . the merry sparrow who seeks his narrow cradle with the swiftness of an arrow is an exquisite rendition of sexual experience. . . ." Cf. Bateson, pp. 104–05, on *The Sick Rose*.

30. Hagstrum, p. 6.

31. *The Sunset Ship, The Poems of J. M. W. Turner*, ed. Jack Lindsay (Lowestoft, Suffolk, 1966).

32. Robert J. Clements, *The Poetry of Michelangelo* (New York, 1965), pp. 315–24. "The value of the *Rime* is not an autonomous one." "The *Rime* without Michelangelo are not the *Iliad* without Homer" (pp. xiii, 341).

33. Recorded by Valéry: Wallace Fowlie, "Paul Valéry," *Poetry* 76 (August 1950): 284.

34. W. B. Yeats was literally tone-deaf.

Parallels

Interpretation, mélange, parallel. At what point does one of these slide into another? If we suppose, for the sake of conversation, that there are at least five or six distinguishable fine arts, then so far as any one of these arts is a representational or mimetic art, the other four or five arts constitute an important part of the human life, the world both contemporary and historical, which the given mimetic art reflects or assimilates. The arts thus assimilated enjoy an aesthetic status no different from that of other human and divine affairs and institutions—religion, for instance, government, philosophy, science, games, clubs, wars, love, marriages, or feasting. Beyond question, there is a kind of widely obvious succession of reciprocal relations between pictorial and literary art which even a slight knowledge of history over the span of a few centuries enables us to recognize. Certain stanzas in Spenser will remind us of a painted panel by Lorenzo Lotto or of a springtime scene of Venus with the Graces and Flora by Botticelli; Thomson's *Seasons* (and perhaps Pope's Homer too)[35] have landscape vistas which remind us of Claude Lorrain. The four allegorical panoramas by William Kent for the collected *Seasons* of 1730 may well seem a more adequate image of the poem than the human-interest vignettes of skating, fishing, or nutting selected by illustrators about the turn of the century. (Picture as a form of commentary on the text revealing more about the commentator than about the text has recently made a legitimate claim for recognition.)[36] Grecian marbles, both genuine and concocted, arrived in England in considerable numbers during the later eighteenth century and the early nineteenth. They were mentioned in English poems, including that by Keats on those brought by Lord Elgin.[37] The humors of Charles Dickens were illustrated by George Cruikshank, and picture and text will easily remind us of each other. In all such parallels, it seems worth while to note and stress the role of one art as a *material* that is flattered in *assimilation* by another. No special problems of artistic terminology or artistic technique need arise. The spectrum of colors described by Isaac Newton in

35. David Ridgley Clark, "Landscape Painting Effects in Pope's Homer," *JAAC* 22 (Fall 1963): 25–28.

36. Ralph Cohen, *The Art of Discrimination: Thomson's "The Seasons" and the Language of Criticism* (Berkeley, 1964), chap. 5, "Literary Criticism and Illustrations of 'The Seasons'," pp. 248–307.

37. Stephen Larrabee, *English Bards and Grecian Marbles* (New York, 1943), pp. 94–97, 209–14; R. H. Wilenski, *The Meaning of Modern Sculpture* (London, c. 1933), pp. 41–64.

his *Opticks* of 1704 became a frequent metaphoric allusion in English poetry, but it did not make a new poetic technique—though that has been claimed by the devoted researcher. If Pope's Moral Essay *Of the Characters of Women* is organized in part by a recurrent motif of allusions to the art of portrait painting, pastoral countesses and Magdalens and the like, these materials work in the poem on the same formal literary principle as the recurrent images of disease and of lower animal life in the *Epistle to Arbuthnot*. It is not as if the art of painting had shown a way to the art of verse moralizing—despite frequent analogies drawn by Augustan essayists between the diction and the argument of poetry, the color and the design of painting. Equally, if Poussin's *Fall of Manna in the Desert* shows in successive postures of the figures and degrees of light on the scenery the beginning, middle, and end of an action, and even a *peripeteia*, these are features of narrative organization in history painting; they may be allusions to Aristotle's "rules." But it is the brush and pictorial imagination of Poussin, and not Aristotle's rules or the ingeniously evasive homage paid to them by Corneille, which validate the painting. A richly antique philosophy *ut pictura poesis* was widely cherished by academicians, poets, and painters of that long neo-classic era, without anybody's being worried by the fact that a piece of Roman house-wall decoration, the Aldobrandini *Marriage Scene*, discovered about 1605, was the sole available evidence of what painting in antiquity *looked* like.[38]

I have come close to suggesting that a really formal, stylistic, or aesthetic dependence of one art upon another is not possible. I will commit myself to the opinion at least that it is not likely to be demonstrated—that where the possibility of demonstration is conceivable, the application proves very difficult. The categories thin out. The pictures disappear. The application may become truistic. Perhaps a maximum opportunity has been constructed in the recently much enhanced and debated issue of the "Baroque."

Eleven years ago, at the MLA meeting in Washington, D.C., I had the privilege of delivering a comment on a paper and a book (Professor Wylie Sypher's *Four Stages of Renaissance Style*, 1955) which then represented the latest approach to these matters by a student of English literature. I meant it as a compliment when I said that Professor Sypher's analogical criticism (distinguishing Renaissance, Mannerist, Baroque, and Late

38. T. J. B. Spencer, "The Imperfect Parallel Betwixt Painting and Poetry," *Greece & Rome*, Second Series, 7 (October 1960): 173–86, esp. 183–84.

Baroque visual and literary styles) was itself couched in a very rich, a very suggestive, flexible, plastic, even fluid vocabulary— something like a Baroque style—or perhaps a Mannerist style—in the art of literary criticism. Professor Sypher, drawing his key concepts from Geoffrey Scott's *Architecture of Humanism* (1941) and Anton Ehrenzweig's *Psychoanalysis of Artistic Vision and Hearing*, was able to see Milton's *Paradise Lost*, for instance, as a gigantic Baroque organism, in which certain sub-liminal, eruptive Miltonic drives writhe and surge up through a canon of classical epic decorum, never being encrusted or de-feated by that decorum, informing it at every point with a vigorous new life. Or, to shift the emphasis slightly, one of the main ideas of *Paradise Lost* that I took away from the book was that of an overfleshly, too plump, Baroque resolution of insta-bilities which the earlier style of Mannerism in a more ascetic way would have been brave enough to confront as such. Milton's Puritan conscience, deflected into a Titanic binge by the influ-ence of irrational decisions made at the Council of Trent, in-dulges in a rosy, Rubens-like celebration of spirit enfleshed in matter, a triumph of the sensorium in volume and energy. A large element of the painterly Baroque, immense perspectives of clouds and climbing angels in big church ceilings and altar pieces, seems to get into that account. And that might leave us, so far as mode of parallelism is concerned, almost where we were with Claudian landscapes in Thomson's *Seasons*.

But we are reminded nowadays by the literary adventurer in Baroque, and I think properly, that the representational arts, painting and sculpture, were secondary and tertiary in the high Baroque Roman mode. The primary and immensely dominant art was architecture. Our own day, or our immediate past, sup-plies a context of art thinking which encourages the use of architecture as a special ground of aesthetic analogy. The once boastfully mimetic visual arts (painting and sculpture) have been passing through an era when they have become much less mimetic, or much more abstractly and shyly mimetic. (Consis-tent with this, a division of labor between designer and execu-tant can appear. The smaller visual fine arts move in the direction of architecture and engineering—invention by Picasso, construc-tion by the American Bridge Division of the United States Steel Corporation in Gary, Indiana.)[39] A plausible counterpart appears when the visual art which is most largely and most obviously ab-stract, structural, and utilitarian, even if inevitably also symbolic

39. *New York Times*, 16 August 1967, pp. 1, 38; Sunday, 27 August 1967, p. 23: Picasso's 163-ton, 50-foot-high steel sculpture for the Chicago Civic Center plaza.

LAKE TAHOE COMMUNITY COLLEGE

LEARNING RESOURCES CENTER

and culturally expressive, moves in a complementary direction
in the theorist's view and is seen in a more and more openly ex-
pressive light, a pronounced challenge to psychological and
moral interpretation. Architecture becomes available more and
more as a metaphor of the aspirations of a people or an age, a
mimesis of the inside of the architect's head. The account of this
by critics of a literary bent can take on a distinctly personal and
biographical accent—for example, in recurrent invocations of the
Baroque or the Mannerist builder's tortured genius, emotional
instability, apprehensiveness, and melancholy. His soul wrestles
with authoritarian *com*pressions to produce an *ex*pression of
personal anguish in an edifice which naively we might have
thought a library or a house of worship. Michelangelo "draws
his breath in pain to tell a complex and infinitely rewarding
story."[40]

Professor Roy Daniells, drawing on such weighty art author-
ities as Arnold Hauser, Nikolaus Pevsner, and Rudolf Wittkower,
describes the Mannerist style in plastic art, centered in Michel-
angelo's Chapel and Library at Florence, as an unorthodox,
tortured, and astonishing re-use of traditional themes and mate-
rials. Mannerism creates "an uneasy neutrality rife with potential
disturbance everywhere."[41]   Professor Daniells describes the
Baroque, centering in the High Roman period of Bernini and St.
Peter's, in terms of Wölfflin's fivefold change from the classical
Renaissance. The clarity and coordination of closed, stable lines
and planes are exploded into an open, yet fused and unified
chiaroscuro and spiral and mobile penetration of space toward
infinity.[42] Like Mannerism, Baroque "represents a perpetuation
of traditional forms accompanied by a reaction against them."
These generic definitions of Mannerism and Baroque, both
strongly stressing the novel employment of established motifs,
will indeed seem to the literary critic to have a great deal in
common. The literary critic will reflect: What artist, what poet
at least, without fresh vision, without some species of violence,
ever successfully took up his old materials? Or ever indeed
worked in any other way than by the adaptation of old mate-
rials?—as Professor Frye has nowadays taken the lead in so in-
sistently reminding us. All creative art and literature, we have

40. Roy Daniells, *Milton, Mannerism and Baroque* (Toronto, 1963),
pp. 8, 18, 55, Pontormo, Michelangelo, Borromini, Cortona.

41. Daniells, p. 7, quoting Pevsner, "The Architecture of Mannerism,"
The Mint, ed. G. Grigson (London, 1946), pp. 116–38.

42. Daniells, pp. 54, 56. Cf. Heinrich Wölfflin, *Principles of Art History*
(1915), trans. M. D. Hottinger (Dover Publications, 1932), pp. 15, 18–19,
73, 124, 161.

come closer and closer to thinking, is but Parson Yorick taking the cream off the drummer's love letter and whipping it up to his own purpose.

In his account of the Baroque in *Paradise Lost*, Professor Daniells drives hard on the informing theological concepts of unity, will, and power; he sees their analogues, symbols, and implications everywhere in the vast vertically axial space and time of Milton's cosmos, from the heights of Heaven to the depths of hell, and no less in the varied jets and bursts of energy, the campaigns, assaults, journeys, and explorations, demonic and angelic, which shoot meteor-like, diagonally, through the awful chiaroscuro.[43] And he reads the Baroque also in the several "archetypal" characters which people the huge canvas, in Milton's lavish verbal ingenuities, his wit and paradox (*Paradoxia Epidemica*), and even in such pleasantries as those exchanged during the long Sunday-school session of Adam with Raphael—that, for instance, about the sex life of angels—which we are asked to call Baroque humor.

But let us back off and away from that wealthy complex of Baroque colorations and analogies—for the half-hour paper, I fear, inevitably a Serbonian bog. In the book about representation and illusion in graphic art which I have already cited, E. H. Gombrich, invoking for a moment the advice of Roman Jakobson, offers some speculations about verbal mimesis and especially the role played by what he describes as the "register," "scale," or "matrix" of available expressions in assisting the apparently pure expressiveness or representative power which words sometimes seem to have. If we are required to give names to two animals, and if just two monosyllables constitute the vocabulary permitted us—*ping* and *pong*—we will say *ping* is the cat, *pong* is the elephant.[44] If that be correct, and I believe it is, then clearly the way to analogy in expression is open—endless.[45] Our historical knowledge, both promoting and limiting our choices,

43. In the chapter on "Space and Time," "the varied roles of Messiah throughout the long succession of events are like a row of columns forming a single colonnade upon which much structural weight can be sustained" (p. 99).

44. Gombrich, *Art and Illusion*, pp. 370–71, 381. "The individual meaning of Lorenzo Lotto's *Allegory* . . . may be hard to decipher, but the relationships, the ping pong of it all, are as clear to us as they were to Lotto's contemporaries." Gombrich (p. 362) believes "There is more in common between the language of words and visual representation than we are sometimes prone to allow."

45. As Oswald Spengler exulted to discover. In 1941 Professor René Wellek narrated for us the fantasies in the mode of Baroque, Classic, and Romantic *Geistesgeschichte* which had luxuriated in German books on

plays many curious roles in giving courage to our convictions
that this or that is like or parallel to some other thing. Make the
supposition that there *are* parallels between the arts—add the
almost necessary further supposition that chronology will have
something to do with these parallels. Dante's *Divina Commedia*
is more like St. Peter's at Rome or Notre Dame de Paris? Mil-
ton's *Paradise Lost* is more like Notre Dame or St. Peter's?
Milton's *Lycidas* is more like St. Peter's or the Medici Chapel at
Florence? *Paradise Lost* is more like which one? As we read to
the end of Professor Daniells' book, we discover that *Paradise
Regained* too has its specially appropriate architectural analogue,
in Longhena's church of S. Maria della Salute at Venice, and
Samson Agonistes too, in Bernini's church of S. Andrea al Quir-
inale.

What then are we to conclude? I reach the conclusion, at least
tentative, that writers like Professor Sypher twelve years ago in
his *Four Stages of Renaissance Style*, and Professor Daniells (in
1963) are employing a highly metaphoric, a highly imaginative
and inventive, idiom. I find this rewarding in its peculiar way,
and I enjoy it. As I believe that literary criticism should be imag-
inative, and metaphoric, I can only applaud this phase of the
development. At the same time, I feel impelled to remind us all
that the life of the imagination languishes in the atmosphere of
solemn debate, dialectic distinction, and real or supposed scien-
tific scrutiny. Such imaginative insights and judgments, calling
on cathedrals, churches, chapels, libraries, for the description of
poems, are valid only so far as explained, substantiated, or made
convincing by the critic in his own context and idiom. They are
not to be contended about syllogistically, statistically, scientif-
ically.

The Baroque, says Professor Daniells, is probably a cyclic or
universally recurrent cultural phenomenon. "The Athenian
Erechtheum and the Temple of Venus at Baalbec have features
which may reasonably be called Baroque."[46] Precisely!—or,
rather, imprecisely. We are supposed to be discussing a "Prob-
lem of Critical Terms." I must confess that my earnest hope is

---

English literature during the preceding two decades. See Wellek, "The
Parallelism between the Arts," *English Institute Annual, 1941* (New York,
1942), esp. 32–44; pp. 34–36, Spengler's *Decline of the West*, 1918. The
meaning and utility of "Baroque" and "Mannerism" as period terms in
literary history is, of course, not in question. See the excellent articles by
Lowry Nelson in Alex Preminger et al., eds., *Encyclopedia of Poetry and
Poetics* (Princeton, 1965), pp. 66–68, 473.

46. Daniells, p. 58.

that such terms as we have been discussing will never clarify or harden into any kind of determinate or literal validity for literary criticism. It is not true that there is such a thing as a Baroque Poem or a Mannerist Poem in the same sense that there is a Petrarchan Sonnet, a Senecan Tragedy, a Comedy of Humors, a Heroic Poem, a Horatian Satire, a Pindaric Ode, an Elegy, or a Pastoral. (It is not even true that there is such a thing as some of these venerable entities in the senses which sometimes seem to be supposed.) *Paradise Lost* IS a Baroque Poem in the same way that architecture is frozen music. Configurational analysis of the Baroque style, of the Mannerist style—*Strukturforschung* into these styles[47]—does more for the macrocosm than for the microcosm. The individual art works under scrutiny become something like highly abstractive *scrims* (or theatrical screens). Looking through St. Peter's, we can see a kind of removed or Platonic entity which we call the Baroque. Looking through *Paradise Lost*, we can perhaps see the same. But looking through St. Peter's, we cannot really see *Paradise Lost*, or *vice versa*.

Establish the Baroque Poem as a literal concept, a literal genre (something that is capable of being fed into a computer), and the scholar is waiting, he is just around the corner, who will step forth with a set of conventions for this genre—what is permitted by it and what is thus explained and must be all right. (Genre was once used as a norm for censures and prohibitions; it is used by the new genre men as a major premise for deductive tolerations.) We know that art history and criticism were not born yesterday. We are aware of Vitruvius and Pliny, Vasari and Bellori and Félibien. Still it seems safe to say that since the times of Aristotle and Longinus, literary scholarship and criticism have passed through more numerous and more varied phases both of orthodoxy and revolt. Literary criticism has had a long enough and polemic enough career to have known both a J. C. Scaliger and a Gottsched, an F. W. Schlegel and a Coleridge, and, above all, in the present context, a Benedetto Croce. Literary criticism has made some mistakes, of old, and has partly recovered from them. It should not be eager to repeat them. Let us not run out to welcome the High, Low, and Middle Baroque styles in poetry. (We have, in fact, Early, High, and Late Baroque well, and no

---

47. We are in the area of thinking where Homeric poetry is found parallel to eighth-century geometric vase painting. Cf. George Kubler, *The Shape of Time: Remarks on the History of Things* (New Haven, 1962-67), p. 27; Cedric H. Whitman, *Homer and the Heroic Tradition* (Cambridge, Mass., 1958), pp. 249–84, and fold-out chart at back.

doubt properly, established in the history of architecture.) A "kind of osmosis," says Professor Daniells, carries such terms from one art to the others. "Experience shows" it, he says.[48] Experience shows many things. Criticism has the responsibility of discriminating among those things.

1967

48.   Daniells, p. 60.

IN SEARCH OF VERBAL MIMESIS (SUPPLEMENT TO "LAOKOÖN: AN ORACLE RECONSULTED")

> 4.016 In order to understand the essential
> nature of a proposition, we should consider
> hieroglyphic script, which depicts the facts
> that it describes.
> And alphabetic script developed out of it
> without losing what was essential to depiction.
> —Ludwig Wittgenstein*

I. *Introductory.* In search of a truly verbal mimesis or iconicity, and especially a truly verbo-visual mimesis or iconicity. This essay attempts not to demonstrate anything novel and not even to push any theme to an ample illustration, but only to sort out certain more or less well known relations between words and what they refer to and in the process of sorting perhaps to arrive at some improved realizations. In an essay published a few years ago under the title "Laokoön: An Oracle Reconsulted," I alluded to four generic areas conspicuous in modern studies of visual art and literature: (1) interpretation of visual art, notably Renaissance paintings, in literary terms; (2) the parallel or analogy between visual and literary art (*ut pictura poesis, ut poesis pictura*) as it flourished notably in the late Renaissance and Baroque eras; (3) the mélange or harmonious union of more or less analogous arts in various assembled arts (*Gesamtkunstwerke*)—as song, drama, opera; (4) the question of medium—words compared to music and pictures—resemblances and differences. It is arbitrary that the present essay aims to move as strictly as possible within the limits of the last of those topics, No. 4, medium—but arbitrary only in the sense that it is always arbitrary to choose any topic, in preference to others. Topic No. 1, interpretation, is a modern aspect of attention to No. 2, analogy. Nos. 2 and 3, analogy and mélange, can logically be put to one side here, for the sake of our getting ahead with No. 4, medium, the topic of the essay. They will intrude briefly, however, at points where they seem to me to make the closest connection with what I am trying to distinguish from them.

I am taking "mimesis" in a narrow, intensified, or saturated, and I hope usefully precise sense. In the Aristotelian sense, tragedy is an "imitation" of a human action. But this is a very broad sense. The mimesis, or representation, so far as it is not scenic

Tractatus Logico-Philosophicus, trans. D. F. Pears and B. F. McGuinness (Humanities Press, 1961), p. 39.

or theatrical, inheres in or depends on very large measures of *expression* and of *reference*. About expression a few words later. Let me stress here briefly the difference between, on the one hand, mimesis (representation or iconicity) and, on the other hand, reference. We will say that the word "murmur" refers to the murmur of a human being, of running water, or hiving bees, or wind in leaves, but that also, in a qualified sense (see below, III.a) the word sounds like or represents these nonverbal sounds. We will say that the word "dog" refers to a dog but not, in any very convincing sense, that it sounds like, looks like, or feels like a dog. The unquestionable (if rather loosely defined) fact of parallels or analogues between poetry and other arts[1] and the fact of mélange or *Gesamtkunstwerk*, the "perennial syncretism" of the arts[2] (grossly evident in such phenomena as drama, opera, and song) relate to verbal mimesis mainly, perhaps only, in the very broad or Aristotelian sense.

Language as spoken, or speakable, may be, but need not be, for the purpose of my exposition, conceived as the primary medium of literature. In the modern era the language of literature is usually experienced with the visual intervention of graphemes. We may even suppose, if we wish, that the literary status does not arrive before that intervention—or fixation.[3] In any event, we are talking about a real distinction and a difference. A first major sorting of mimetic possibilities can plausibly divide them into (1) the graphemic and (2) the phonetic-lexical. (The reasons for the hyphenation of the latter two terms will appear as we proceed.) My sorting out pursues first some topics under heading 1, the graphemic (the simpler, and perhaps more speciously attractive if we have strong eidetic propensities), and then under 2, the more treacherously various phonetic-lexical. And thus:

II.a. The *alphabet* (an exercise in deconstructive realization). The human being, especially the human being as child, or as art-

1. James D. Merriam, "The Parallel of the Arts: Some Misgivings and a Faint Affirmation," Parts 1 and 2, *JAAC* 31 (Winter 1972): 153-64, and (Spring 1973): 309-22; Jean H. Hagstrum, "Verbal and Visual Caricature in the Age of Dryden, Swift, and Pope," *England in the Restoration and Early Eighteenth Century*, ed. H. T. Swedenberg, Jr. (Berkeley, 1972), pp. 173-95; Ronald Paulson, "The Pictorial Circuit and Related Structures in 18th-Century England," *The Varied Pattern: Studies in the 18th Century*, ed. Peter Hughes and David Williams (Toronto, 1971), pp. 165-87.
2. Edward Stankiewicz, "Structural Poetics and Linguistics," forthcoming in *Current Trends in Linguistics*, vol. 12, ed. Thomas Sebeok.
3. Plato, *Phaedrus* 274B-278B; E. D. Hirsch, *Validity in Interpretation* (New Haven, 1967), pp. 248-50, a review of Hans-Georg Gadamer, *Wahrheit und Methode*, 1960.

ist, often hovers on the verge of reversing the transitions of his technical history—the primitive inventions. Children hunt alley cats with ineffective bows and arrows, or with spears, pointed sticks hardened in flame. At summer camp they almost make fire with a bow drill, a cedar slab, and shavings. A few expert Texan hobbyists flake excellent flint blades, as narrated in an exciting little book, *Manual for Neanderthals*, by the Houston journalist H. Mewhinney.[4] One may well conceive that he and his friends could survive in the mountains after an atomic Armageddon. A very similar flirting, lingering, on an invisible threshold may be said, I believe, to occur in the presence of certain childish riddles.

> A B C D goldfish.
> L M N O goldfish.
> O S A R goldfish.

A gifted artist of the grotesque and comic, William Steig, throws off a byproduct of his savage primitive cartoonery, a little book of "small-fry" situations illustrating the depths of the English alphabet. C D B. A lesson in natural history. Do you see it? The bee—on the flower. I M A U-M B-N. U R N N-M-L. The brat looks down smugly upon his puzzled pooch.[5] A clipped, pinched, deformed dialect of American English (recognizable, no doubt, as an exaggeration of what can actually be heard in Brooklyn) is rendered by letters used not as actual letters but only as the *names* of letters. We confront the first stage in a more vivid realization that the graphemes of our alphabet carry names, which are sounds, lively, charged with a capacity for joking, puns. Certain letters in our alphabet can be used in a fictitious deconstruction that illustrates a fourfold, perhaps fivefold, value that is sunk in the structure of graphemic letters. Consider:

1. "I" (*ai*) is a visual or auditory word, meaning "ego."
2. "I" (*ai*), the word meaning "ego," is a homophone of a word "eye," meaning "organ of sight."
3. (*ai*) is the name of a grapheme—"I," and a homophone of both 1 and 2.
4. "I" (the grapheme) is a written letter, the cue to uttering a syllable—as in "i-o-nize," "i-o-dine."
5. "I" (the grapheme) is a written letter, the cue to uttering certain less than syllabic phonemes—as in "Ides," "in."

---

4. Austin, 1957.
5. William Steig, *C D B!* (New York, 1963), pp. [1], [11].

Or the slightly different instance of "B."

1. Lacking.
2. "Be" (*bi*) is a monosyllabic word meaning "esse."
3. "Bee" (*bi*) is a homophone of "be," and a word naming an insect.
4. (*bi*) is the name of a grapheme, "B," a homophone of "be" and "bee."
5. "Be-" (*bi*) is a syllable, as in "be-fore."
6. "B" (the grapheme) is a written letter, the cue to uttering a less than syllabic phoneme—as in "bid," "crib."

Our written language, the borrowed English alphabet, did not evolve in those ways—"eye" to "I" in "Ides," or "bee" to "b" in "bid." The slight difficulty one may experience in holding apart the four or five values just now listed, the modest explosion of surprise and fun in the inventions of William Steig (I F-N N-E N-R-G. M N X S L-T 4 U! —Be resolute in pronouncing the *names* of the letters, not the letters themselves)[6] may, however, help our realization of what happened when in the proto-Semitic to Phoenician sequence, something like Egyptian hieroglyphics (pictures with names) worked as puns or rebuses for words and syllables and then as names of letters—when for the only time in human history a sufficient alphabet was invented, in short when written language arrived at an adequately intimate and fitted relation with the prior spoken act. The alphabet—via the punning syllabic grapheme—becomes the first system of graphemes which are not pictures of anything visible.[7]

If we try next to imagine how the written language *began* as pictures, we will realize, I think, an even greater early step by which it depictorialized itself. This must have occurred as soon as any picture became in fact a pictogram—that is, when any

6. *C D B!*, pp. [36], [29].
7. David Diringer, *The Alphabet: A Key to the History of Mankind*, 3d ed., rev. with Reinhold Regensburger (New York, 1968), I: 160-69; Hans Jensen, *Sign, Symbol and Script, An Account of Man's Efforts to Write*, trans. George Unwin (London, 1970), pp. 50-53, 264, 270, 280-83. Some of the "alphabetologists" (including Diringer, I: 168) have argued that the *names* of the Semitic letters were not, like Egyptian rebus syllables, a punning part of the alphabetical or acrophonic evolution, but were added only *after* the letters were established. The older and more common view seems the easier to imagine.
All the consonant names of the English alphabet are—unlike those of the Hebrew or Greek—single-consonant monosyllables, and they are divided between eleven consonant-initials (*bi, di*) and eight consonant-terminals (*el, em*). These are circumstances which greatly favor Mr. Steig's agreeable game.

definite idea became attached to it. From then on, for prac-
tical purposes, much of the picture would be irrelevant and
might even be misleading. The supposed pictorial and poetic
value of modern Mandarin characters, dreamed of by Fenollosa
and Pound, commands scant respect from Chinese scholars.[8] In
the opposite scale, the name of a picture, "The Blue Boy,"
"The Age of Innocence," "Mrs. Siddons as the Tragic Muse,"
does not represent the whole meaning or the aesthetic value of
the picture. The cave bisons of Lascaux seem more concrete (if
only by clustering, or herding), less formalized, certainly less
conventionalized, than the characters of any known pictographic
language. (We can witness instances of ambiguous surplus today
in contexts where pictograms are still used—in highway signs,
for instance, where the arrow on the THRU TRUCK sign points
in one direction, , but the highway-department pic-
togram for truck points in the opposite,). Picto-
grams become progressively abstract, and the difference between
pictograms and sheer ideograms is difficult to define and not very
clearly important. On the one hand, the Chinese character for
tree , the Roman numbers I, II, III, and the Arabic num-
bers 1, 2, 3, 4. On the other hand, the barbed-wire cuneiform
character for ox, the sign ampersand & (and-per-se-and), and the
Arabic numbers 5, 6, 7, 8. When a picture can function as a
visual *word*, or insofar as it does function as a visual word, it has
lost most or all of its need to be a picture. The next stage in its
abstraction, from residual picture to formalized, even arbitrary,
ideogram, is far less radical than the transition from picture to
pictogram. The same kind of abstraction, convention, and fixa-
tion may be observed in the difference between sound mimicry
(bird or animal calls) and true verbal onomatopoeia (see below,
III.a). The depictorialization of graphemes at each stage ac-
corded with the deepest nature of verbal discourse and explains
the wide diffusion of the alphabet from a single invention and
its superiority to the manifold syllabaries of fossilized picto-
grams.

    II.b. *Mélange (Cum Pictura Poesis)*. There is a certain sense
in which the literature of the modern world, especially the po-
etry, has gone heavily visual. A prominent feature of the Guten-

---

    8. James J. Y. Liu, *The Art of Chinese Poetry* (Chicago, 1962), pp. 3,
6, 14, 18-19; Achilles Fang, "Fenollosa and Pound," *Harvard Journal of
Asiatic Studies* 20 (1957): 213-38, esp. 215-17.

berg era is the linear and paragraphic layout of the printed page
—with a special visual emphasis for lines and masses of verse.
Modern poetry, or poets collectively, seem to have been bent on
regaining the lost thickness of the pictorial word—but perhaps
often in mistaken ways. We most often consult our poetry in
graphemes and often enough in some sort of fancy or sophis-
ticated kind of graphemes. Much pictorial or quasi-pictorial
manipulation has been invited and has taken place. It remains,
however, an important question whether the visually aesthetic
properties of graphemes are always in fact very deeply tied in
with the phonological-semiotic structures which are the reason
for the occurrence of the graphemes: whether in fact we encoun-
ter illustrations of the supposed principle *ut pictura poesis*—or
not rather certain ingenious contrivances of a game that ought
to be called *cum pictura poesis*. This skeptical question, with its
implicitly severe answer, I conceive as embracing a wide spec-
trum of speciously varied but closely akin phenomena of visual
mélange, suggestions of a living alliance between very disparate
media: *viz.*, for one thing and mainly, all the "shaped" poems
both the more and less ancient and the modern, the *techno-
paignia*[9] of the *Greek Anthology* (stigmatized as a "Species of
false Wit" by Addison in *Spectator* 58), the formulations in the
Art of English Poesie by Puttenham in 1589, the fresh realiza-
tions by Herbert in typographical wings and altar, and in our
own time most notably the *Calligrammes* of Apollinaire—e.g.,
the poems shaped like a heart, a crown, a mirror reflecting the
name of the poet, and that which sprinkles the words in a show-
er of rain—and feeling (*Il pleut*).[10] All those are ways of dispos-
ing the graphemes of the poem itself into shapes that have some
kind of superficial or cold relation with the subject of the poem.
"The Poetry," says Addison, "was to contract or dilate itself
according to the Mould in which it was cast. In a Word, the
Verses were to be cramped or extended to the Dimensions of
the Frame that was prepared for them; and to undergo the Fate
of those Persons whom the Tyrant *Procrustes* used to lodge in

9. For the poems, see the *Greek Anthology*, Book XV, nos. 21-27: the
Axe, Wings of Love, and *Egg* of Simias, the *Altar* of Dosiadas, and that of
Besantinus, the *Pipe* of Theocritus (Loeb Library, V: 127-33). The term
technopaignion, as applied to a shaped poem, is apparently post-classical.
The *Technopaegnion* of Ausonius (Works, Bk. XII) is a collection of short
pieces illustrating the trick of ending each verse with a stopping mono-
syllable.
10. Guillaume Apollinaire, *Calligrammes, Poèmes de la paix et de la
guerre (1913-1916)*, Preface by Michel Butor (Editions Gallimard, 1966),
pp. 58, 64; a second shower, p. 159.

his Iron Bed." (Certain examples involve the arbitrary disjunc-
tion of letters—word shredding. The typographic dispersals of
E. E. Cummings run the gamut of such devices.)[11]

Another main type of mélange introduces more or less subtly,
and even beautifully, various additives, the illuminated capitals
and marginal and interlinear ornaments of medieval parchments,
the woodcuts in Renaissance emblem books ("pictures that for
the page atone"), the tendrils and bird, animal, human, and
fairy figures that creep gracefully in among the words etched at
the center of Blake's illuminated plates.[12] Somewhere alongside
such instances of the *cum pictura* and the fully shaped whole
poem, we may perhaps locate a department of wit termed "Word
Play," to be consulted nowadays appropriately in the magazine
Playboy—where, through an assortment of devices, words or
phrases are made into something like autonyms. Thus the word

touc⊢down, and the word b◯s◯m.[13] A German

poem (by Christian Morgenstern) about two funnels that drink
moonlight tapers in shorter and shorter lines; the concluding
phrase is *und so weiter—*

u.s.
w.

—the inverted V in the center of the W being admired as an image
of the opening of the spout.[14] "Concrete Poems," varied reduc-
tions of the linguistic structure in favor of visual order, like re-
peating wallpaper or carpet patterns, crossword puzzles, magic
squares, or computer print-outs, are a more modern experiment;
the real verbal element all but disappears.[15]

11. W (New York, 1931) shows the extremes of two opposite
devices, "calligram—or picture writing . . . word scramble . . . cryptogram"
(Malcolm Cowley, "Cummings: One Man Alone," *Yale Review* 62 [Spring
1973]: 343).

12. Roman Jakobson, "On the Verbal Art of William Blake and other
Poet-Painters," *Linguistic Enquiry* 1 (January 1970): 3–10, finds structural
analogies between Blake's "Infant Sorrow" and its illumination.

13. Robert Carola, "Word Play," *Playboy* 19 (February 1972): 161;
17 (April 1970): 163.

14. Quoted by John Lotz, "Elements of Versification," in *Versification*:
Major Language Types, ed. W. K. Wimsatt (New York, 1972), p. 18.

15. See the pot of FORSYTHIA that sends up sprays of its repeated
letters, the *F* spray, the *O* spray, etc., black ink against yellow, on the
cover of *Concrete Poetry: A World View*, ed. Mary Ellen Solt (poet of the
Forsythia) (Bloomington, 1970).

II.c.   But it would be unfair, and it is not my purpose, to end this section without indicating another kind of visual possibility in graphemes. There *are* features of language structure which can be accentuated by visual patterns, which perhaps fuse with these patterns, yet also lie deeper in the linguistic grain. The simple signals of a paragraph indentation and that of a capital letter are easy graphic instances. More complicated, but indubitable instances in English occur conspicuously in the kind of rhymed closed pentameter couplets written by Alexander Pope. The stair-like progressions of the Russian poet Mayakovsky, closely related to Slavic traditions of oral and musical emphasis, belong in an adjacent area.[16] We shall wish to distinguish degrees of visual imposition, degrees of dominance between the phonological-semiotic and the graphemic—and hence I believe degrees of depth and vitality in the union, and a gradation or shading of superficiality toward the arbitrariness of the "shaped" poem. But the matter may now conveniently remain hanging for a while, until we reach the end of some sorting in our second main series, the phonological-semiotic.

III.a.   *Onomatopoeia.*   C. S. Peirce, followed by Roman Jakobson, has divided iconic (or mimetic) expression into *image* and *diagram.* The latter inheres in relations, patterns of words (above, II.c., and below, V); the former, *image*, is atomic and simple.[17] Yet *image* embraces the greater number of subclasses more usually distinguished by linguists. If we argue that a simple verbal mimesis or icon can properly be only a mimesis of a sound, then we locate *onomatopoeia* as the most direct, most physically textured instance of verbal image. Such words as *murmur, whisper, hiss, pop* do seem indubitably to sound like what they say. We speculate that they have been developed into

16.   See them displayed in Russian and English in Vladimir Mayakovsky, *The Bedbug and Selected Poetry*, ed. Patricia Blake (New York, 1970), pp. 173-235, "Brooklyn Bridge" and other poems. These visual structures are a way (perhaps too easy) of separating and emphasizing phrases, parallels, contrasts. Mallarmé's *Un Coup de dés jamais n'abolira le hasard* (1897) combines stepping with simultaneous or shredded and interspersed messages in several kinds of type.

17.   *Collected Papers of Charles Sanders Peirce*, ed. Charles Hartshorne and Paul Weiss, vols. 1 and 2 in one (Cambridge, Mass., 1960); vol. 2, *Elements of Logic*, Book II, chap. 3, "The Icon, Index, and Symbol," ¶ 277-282, pp. 157-59 (Icons "which partake of simple qualities . . . are *images*; those which represent the relations, mainly dyadic, or so regarded, of the parts of one thing by analogous relations in their own parts, are *diagrams.* . . ." ¶ 277); Roman Jakobson, "Quest for the Essence of Language," *Diogenes* 51 (1965): 21-37.

words perhaps from simply mimetic noises. It may be necessary to remind ourselves now and then that, as true idea-bearing words, these all have, in addition to whatever degree of natural fitness, a distinct component of linguistic convention. We confront in onomatopoeic words a character analogous in the realm of sound to that in the realm of sight which we note in the picture partly surviving as pictogram. Dogs bark, we have often been told, cats meow, pigs grunt, guns bang, machines rattle, click, or chatter with different noises in different languages. One curious illustration of the principle occurs now and then in a certain self-betrayal technique of the comic-strip artist. A boy carries a balloon on a string; it breaks; the word "POP!" appears in the midst of the explosion. In the next frame the boy's father looks in from another room. "Did you call me, Henry?" At the same time, it seems probable that any name of a sound we can think of in our own language will strike us with a degree of onomatopoeic force. Consider, e.g.: *pop, fizz, bang, boom, murmur, whisper, groan, roar, tinkle, jingle, jangle, click, clatter, chatter, clank, clang, whistle, rumble, yell, yelp, scream, yip, screech, buzz, crack, growl.* Try to think of the name of a sound that does *not* have a degree of such suggestiveness. No doubt a number of principles are at work in various words of the above list. (Perhaps in the end we may conceive a very special category for sounds made by the human voice?)

III.b. *Root-forming Morphemes (Phonaesthemes)*. What used to be thought of as a sort of vaguely extended and mysterious onomatopoeia, a verbal magic, is better explained by modern linguistics as a paradigmatic echo, a property which words in a given language, especially the native words, the oldest (often the most physically or emotively expressive), exhibit in virtue of their kinship with other words. Intricate systems of such quasi-morphemic (or phonaesthemic)[18] affinities extend throughout the lexicon of the only language which this writer speaks fluently. It is a pleasant exercise to lie half-asleep and invite such sequences to filter into the mind. Run through the alphabet, for instance, forming monosyllables by adding initial consonants to the emergent or root-forming morpheme *-ash*. You can hardly miss: *bash, brash, clash, crash, dash, fash, gash,*

---

18. Leonard Bloomfield, *Language* (New York, 1933), p. 246; Dwight L. Bolinger, "On Defining the Morpheme," *Word* 4 (April 1948): 18–23, esp. 22; "Rime, Assonance, and Morpheme Analysis," *Word* 6 (August 1950): 117–36, esp. 130, "phonaestheme"; Rulon Wells and Jay Keyser, *The Common Feature Method* (Sociology Department, Yale University, 1961), on the initial phoneme sequence *fl*, esp. pp. 7–12.

gnash, *hash*, *lash*, *mash*, *pash*, (*quash*), *rash*, *slash*, *smash*, *splash*, (*squash*), *thrash*, *trash* (especially the recent American verb). A few polysyllables come to mind: *calabash*, *succotash*, *mishmash*, *balderdash*. It is difficult to know whether we have thought of them all. (In some of the most richly imitative poetic expressions we can think of—for instance, Tennyson's "Moan of doves in immemorial elms, And murmuring of innumerable bees"—we may see a union of true onomatopoeia and a kind of momentary morphemic echoing. We may call this "orchestration"[19] or a punning extension of onomatopoeia.) The well-known principle of the portmanteau readily joins the game. *Flash*, for instance, is a juncture between the *-ash* family and the small cluster that includes also *flame*, *flare*, *flicker*, *flimmer*. An *ambler* who ranges or roves is a *rambler*. And surely a *jilt* is a *Jill* who *jolts*.

The phonaesthemic or emergently morphemic meanings are lexical and conventional; they do not really depend on any resemblance between word and thing. Yet such families of words have a kind of "natural" or felt force that makes them at least *seem* mimetically expressive. Thus they demand a kind of *verbal* attention not demanded by the literal and explicit lexical controls so prominent in the verbal "paintings" of the tradition *ut pictura poesis*[20] and its progeny the numerous parallels and mélanges of the verbal and visual arts.

In an essay of 1953 David Masson has delicately subtilized and extended this theme of the lexically implicit. He argues that the English word *night* has a range of implicit or potentially expressive values that include brilliance (from *bright*, *white*, *light*, *sight*, *shine*), the numinous and the spacious (from *height*, *might*, *rite*, *right*, *flight*, *high*), alarms and excursions (from *smite*, *fright*, *bite*, *fight*, *excite*, *flight*). In contrast, the French *nuit* has values that include glimmer and glow (from *lueur*, *luir*, *lustre*, *lune*), scream or hoot (from *cri*, *aigu*, *heur*, *huée*), ruin and danger (from *nuis*, *nuire*, *puni*, *fui*, *fini*), intimacy (from *nid*, *uni*, *bénit*, *lui*). And German *Nacht* has splendor (from *Pracht*, *Strahl*), violence, power, fear, awe, cruelty (from *Schlacht*, *Macht*, *Acht*, *Rache*, *Gefahr*, *Gram*, *Ahnung*, *Ahndung*), temporality (from *Sucht*, *noch*, *nach*), negation (from *nicht*, *nichts*), damp (from *nass*, *feucht*).[21]

19.   René Wellek and Austin Warren, *Theory of Literature* (New York, 1949), pp. 163–64.

20.   See above, note 1, recent studies by Paulson and Hagstrum.

21.   David I. Masson, "Vowel and Consonant Patterns in Poetry," *JAAC* 12 (December 1953), reprinted in *Essays on the Language of Literature*, ed. Seymour Chatman and Samuel R. Levin (Boston, 1967), pp. 11–12.

III.c. *Kinaesthesis.* There is something that a few decades ago used to be called "sound symbolism," and something else that Samuel Johnson, in writing about Pope, called "representative verse." Either might be mistaken for, but neither is, I believe, the same as either onomatopoeia (III.a, above) or phonaesthemic echoing (III.b). Although one of these (sound symbolism) can be more or less located in the timbre even of single syllables or in simple accumulations of syllables, and the other inheres in, or at least needs the special aid of, *sequences* of syllables or accents (especially verse patterns), the two may be put correctly, I believe, together under the head of analogies generated kinaesthetically (or internally and physically)[22] in the articulation (even silent articulation) of verbal utterance. The analogies seem to include notably the heavy and the light, the dark and the light, the slow and the fast, the rough and the smooth, and perhaps the hard and the soft. The difference between E. A. Poe's celebrated refrain "Quoth the Raven, 'Nevermore,'" (recently re-celebrated so effectively by Roman Jakobson)[23] and Mallarmé's curious translation of it, "Le Corbeau dit: 'Jamais plus,'" may suffice to suggest the difference between the *syllabically* heavy (or dark) and the light. The verse *movement* asserting the heavy or light, the slow or fast, may be very conveniently, I believe, illustrated from Alexander Pope's *tour de force* of sound and sense in the second part of his *Essay on Critisism*. The neoclassic or baroque age of *ut pictura* was indeed specially concerned to make verses "representative"; the illustrations seem convenient, apt, and lively.

> A needless Alexandrine ends the song,
> That, like a wounded snake, drags its slow length along.

> When Ajax strives some rock's vast weight to throw,
> The line too labours, and the words move slow.
> Not so, when swift Camilla scours the plain,
> Flies o'er th'unbending corn, and skims along the main.

These resemblances of sound to sense, thought Samuel Johnson (in the *Rambler*), were "chimerical"—fancies dictated to our willing belief by the overt assertion of the sense. In his *Life of*

---

22. Masson, in Chatman and Levin, p. 12, uses the term "proprioceptive sensations." A category of "acoustic" associations is for Masson wider than the traditional "onomatopoeia" (III.a, above) and very close to the "kinaesthetic." His categories are in general oriented toward the emotive or "evocative" power of words rather than toward mimesis. His "kinaesthetic" associations generally lie dormant unless activated by proximity to appropriate lexical forces.

23. "Language in Operation," *Mélanges Alexandre Koyré* (Paris, 1964), II: 269-81.

Pope he performed the experiment of changing the sense of a line, keeping approximately the same sounds—and observed of course a quietus upon the sound effect. A like operation has been performed by Mr. J. C. Ransom upon a line of Edna St. Vincent Millay's, and he adds the analogy of the chameleon, that takes its color from the green of the tree.[24] (I myself have observed that the bluish-greenish eyes of a girl will assume a marvelously intensified deep blue if she is wearing a blue coat or even a large brooch of lapis lazuli.) But it seems doubtful if such arguments are really disabling to the fact, or the theory, of kin-aesthetic analogy. A delicate, perhaps tenuous, fitness is none the less real in that it disappears when it has nothing to fit—or perhaps changes, within limits, depending upon what it has the opportunity to fit. Dryden, doing better than Pope with St. Cecilia odes, blends a series of slow-fast movements, rough-smooth words, and perhaps onomatopoeias, persuasively, or at least suggestively, with overt assertions about musical instruments.

> The trumpet's loud clangor
>   Excites us to arms. . . .

> The double, double, double beat
>   Of the thund'ring drum
> Cries: "Hark! The foes come. . . ."

III.d. *Autonymy (Auto-iconicity?)*

> And ten low words oft creep in one dull line.

> Tho' oft the ear the open vowels tire.

Pope's verse passage is full of these autonymic grafts or blends—in virtue of the fact that its theme *is* (it talks about) such special verse arrangements. It not only illustrates but names and asserts them. The autonymy envelopes the mimesis.

> Wher'er you hear the cooling western breeze,
> In the next line it whispers through the trees.

> That, like a wounded snake, drags its slow length along.

> The line too labours, and the words move slow.

Can the notion of autonymy be expanded, so as to include a wider sort of something, a kind of auto-iconicity? Probably not. An auto*nym* is not an image of *itself*, but an *instance* of what it

    24. "The Poet as Woman," *The World's Body* (New York, 1938), pp. 94–97.

names, or refers to. Thus: *word, noun, polysyllable.*[25] Autonymy comes out of the peculiar abstractive, universalizing, and reflexive power of word-thought. We may speak loosely of the "auto-icon" of Jeremy Bentham kept in a cabinet at University College, London. But only the wax head is an icon. The rest is a clothed mummy or skeleton—a relic. Perhaps a typewriter on a pedestal in a certain kind of art show, and a tube of toothpaste in a picture frame, may be thought of as mounted, framed, or foregrounded in such a way that they become icons of themselves. Or perhaps not. Perhaps they are just what they are. I saw a movie once in which William Powell, who had lately returned from World War II duty in the Pacific, acted the part of a homecoming veteran. The effect was amusing for an admirer of Powell. There is a sense in which every famous actor becomes a partial auto-icon—only partial! Himself now mimes himself then. Mimesis involves difference. Long ago Plato disposed of the idea of the complete auto-icon. "We should have not an image of Cratylus, but two Cratyluses." This may help us to evaluate a celebrated thesis of Lessing. Lessing thought that the *poetic* aim of making words, "artificial" signs (working by convention), into "natural" signs (working by likeness) was best realized in the theater, where words, presumably, were direct and natural imitations of words. But direct mimicry, whether on the stage or in life, must be distinguished from drama and poetry. So far as Samuel Foote, on the stage, mimicked Faulkner a Dublin bookseller or Apreece a Welsh aristocrat, he did indeed mimic them or take them off. So far as Garrick, in company, mimicked his schoolmaster Samuel Johnson making love to his wife Tetty, he did indeed mimic him, in action and word. But so far as Garrick acted Hamlet afraid of his father's ghost, he created an instance of a fictive universal. The words indeed were not a mimesis. They *were* Hamlet's words. (So far as any actor's words and gestures refer to an inner state, they are not a mimesis but an expression[26]—either of something pretended, as in the

25. "Since the name of a given object may be chosen arbitrarily, it is quite possible to take as a name for the thing, the thing itself, or, as a name for a kind of thing, the things of this kind. We can, for instance, adopt the rule that, instead of the word 'match', a match shall always be placed on the paper. But it is more often a linguistic expression than an extra-linguistic object that is used as its own designation. We call an expression which is used this way *autonymous*" (Rudolph Carnap, *The Logical Syntax of Language*, trans. Annette Smeaton [London, 1967], Part IV, §42, pp. 156–157). Cf. pp. 211–12, Grelling's antinomy.

26. "Inner or psychic reality cannot be imitated, only expressed. . . . 'We know about [feelings] in others *only by way of signs.* . . . Drama and

view of Diderot or Charles Lamb, or of something real, as with the school of Stanislavsky and Boleslavsky.)

IV. *Metaphor.* Under the Saussurian head of "motivation," the *reasons* why an expression means what it means or means it aptly or vividly, linguists correctly include metaphor.[27] And metaphor is a near equivalent of poetry, an aspect of the *drama* of words as the response of human consciousness to context. (Drama does not depend on the physical presence of theater and acoustic utterance.) Metaphor is always more than convention and more than simple reference. Here let us remember that visual art too can be metaphoric, or symbolic, and perhaps always is when it is "art." This happens in ways that verge on convention but are not simply convention. Visual art, like verbal art, is imaginative. "The eye," as Leo Steinberg has put it, "is a part of the mind."[28] And here are deeper and richer materials for sorting and realization than this essay will attempt. A book that I once published, entitled *The Verbal Icon*, was about iconicity in the wider sense.

V. *Diagram.* Ludwig Wittgenstein's widely cited "proposition . . . a picture of reality . . . a model of reality" (*Tractatus* 4.01) refers to a kind of "projection" or diagram which may be difficult for the literary scholar to assimilate. Compare the epigraph to the present essay with, for example, *Tractatus* 4.0311: "One name stands for one thing, another for another thing, and they are combined with one another. In this way the whole group—like a *tableau vivant*—presents a state of affairs." Less esoteric notions, however, are available. Distinct from the color or timbre of "image," a certain logic of diagrammatic relations is the second main division of iconicity in the Peirce-Jakobson account. In his article of 1965 on the "Essence of Language," Jakobson is interested in the paradigmatic forms of diagram, those that lie in the structure of language itself, and outside the syn-

painting express . . . the activity of the soul only *indirectly.* . . . [They] imitate the natural signs of these inner realities'" (David J. Gordon, "Form and Feeling," quoting Elias Schwartz, *The Form of Feeling: Toward a Mimetic Theory of Literature*, in *Yale Review* 62 (Summer 1973): 592.

27. Stephen Ullmann, *Semantics: An Introduction to the Science of Meaning* (Oxford, 1964), pp. 91-92. Cf. Peirce, *Elements of Logic* (above, note 17), ¶ 277. "Those [icons] which represent the representative character of a representamen by representing a parallelism in something else, are *metaphors.*"

28. "The Eye Is a Part of the Mind," *Partisan Review* 20 (1953): 194-212. Or see Wallace Stevens, "The Relations between Poetry and Painting," *The Necessary Angel* (New York, 1951), pp. 159-76; E. H. Gombrich, *Symbolic Images* (London, 1972); Rudolf Arnheim, *Visual Thinking* (Berkeley, 1969).

tactic patterns of any one utterance. Thus, the fact that the
comparative degree of an adjective nearly always has more
phonemes than the positive, and the superlative more than the
comparative. But such diagrams can also appear as syntactic
diagrams within the single utterance: "The balloon grew big,
bigger, biggest—and burst." Or a diagram of lexical irreversi-
bility may be framed in a classic instance by repeating morphol-
ogy: "Veni, vidi, vici." Jakobson in his celebrated analyses of
short poems has bestowed much loving attention on very com-
plicated syntactic diagrams that have hitherto passed unnoticed,
perhaps even unfelt, by many readers. Simple forms will suffice
for the present argument. Simplest or commonest of all is the
mere parallel of elements in prose enumeration, pairing, or
antithesis. And this is often most keenly noticed by the gram-
marian stylist when he encounters its curious distortion and
obliteration in the work of student writers, the most common
example perhaps being the enumeration of three or four sub-
divisions of a topic: 1.___; 2.___; 3.___; 4.___, in such a way
that the syntax of *each* member varies (either painstakingly or
carelessly) from that of all the others. In the absence of an
example, it requires some pains, and is painful, for the gram-
marian to construct one. But I once improved (or deteriorated)
a student sentence to the following extreme: "Let us beware
the falsification involved in focusing one's attention on a nar-
row segment of experience, interpreted on the basis of a limited
set of shallow principles, which are not sufficiently inclusive."
My purpose was to illustrate a clear opposite to the prose style
of Samuel Johnson. "According to the inclinations of nature, or
the impressions of precept, the daring and the cautious may
move in different directions without touching upon rashness or
cowardice." "If you are pleased with prognosticks of good, you
will be terrified likewise with tokens of evil." That kind of ex-
treme prose diagram (sometimes diagram in excess of semantics)
verges on verse and calls out for it.

> 'Tis hard to say, if greater want of skill
> Appear in writing or in judging ill;
> But, of the two, less dangerous is th'offence
> To tire out patience, than mislead our sense.

And with this example we arrive at that juncture of (1) the visual
page with (2) the auditory logic which I alluded to at the end of
my first section. It is my notion that so far as alphabetized
graphemes can have any *close* union with the phonological-
semiotic stratum which they are employed to betoken, this is

the way in which they have it. Some complications occur. The union and support may be in a straight logical pattern, such as we have just seen. Or it may occur in various subtler ways, such as I have once called "counterlogical": the metrical equalities of syllable and accent marching along with the disparate phrasal patterns, the paradox of antithetic or disparate words bearing the similarity of rhyme, the special secondary emphasis of caesural pause, or the emphasis which falls upon line-terminal words in secondary syntactic positions through the artifice of enjambment.

> Of man's first disobedience and the *fruit*
> Of that forbidden tree. . . .

Such counterlogical diagramming in meter and rhyme, and also in the strongly marked vowel and consonant patterns so well known in poetry, doubtless picks up various elusive elements of onomatopoeic, morphemic, and kinaesthetic intimation (see above, III.a, b, c)—and thus the "music" or the "magic" of the poetic sound patterns.[29]   Yet further ranges are possible in languages enjoying a more intricate morphology.

> *Natura* fieret laudabile carmen an *arte*,
> quaesitum est.—
>
> [*Ad Pisones*, 408-09]
>
> non cessavere poetae
> nocturno certare mero, putere diurno.—
> [*Epistolae* I. xix, 10-11; cf. *Ad Pisones*, 268-69]

In all such patterns, as we experience them perhaps first, and superficially, through the visual medium, we can ask whether the visual does in fact join and accentuate a diagram present independently in the semiotic and prosodic structure (Pope's syntax and couplets, Milton's syntax and blank verse, or the concentric hexameter of Horace, can be recognized by the attentive mind-ear even if written as prose), or whether in fact the visual only imposes, or attempts to impose, a diagram which otherwise has no existence, so that we have in fact an instance of *poesis cum pictura*, where poetry merely attempts to become a visual art. This latter is what happens, I believe, in the *technopaignia* or shaped poems of the classical tradition, in the *Calligrammes*

29. See the subtly detected examples in Masson's essay of 1953, in Chatman and Levin, pp. 3-10. See John Hollander, "'Sense Variously Drawn Out': Some Observations on English Enjambment," in *Literary Theory and Structure*, ed. Frank Brady et al. (New Haven, 1973), pp. 201-26.

of Apollinaire, in certain other merely typographical measures of modern verse (the column-width lines of William Carlos Williams, for example, the approximate syllabics of Marianne Moore), and certainly in some, though not in all, of the typographic arrangements of E. E. Cummings. But it is not a duty of this essay to adjudicate such examples.

VI. *Conclusion*—in the sense of a terminal remark. In Plato's *Cratylus*, the chief inquiry into mimetic linguistics that survives from ancient times, Socrates the fugleman delivers a prolonged etymological discourse in which he attempts, in large part playfully, to convince the "conventionalist" Hermogenes that words really do embody reasons for meaning what they mean. Then he turns to his other friend, the "naturalist" Cratylus, and says in effect: "Yes, like paint in pictures, words do bear some kind of resemblance to the things they mean. But after all, the resemblance is not perfect. If it were, we should have not an image of something, but two identical things. The principle of verbal imitation is really rather weak. To firm it up, so that we have a usable language, we must call in generous assistance from the complementary linguistic principle of convention." It is my own notion that today we stand at almost the same juncture in linguistic-poetic studies—though coming to it from an opposite direction. After the sweepingly successful assertion of the primacy of convention in language by the father of modern linguistics, Ferdinand de Saussure, students of the present era, and most notably and perhaps initially Roman Jakobson, reach back to the earlier insight and authority of C. S. Peirce, to renew and improve an awareness of the "natural" powers of language, both imagistic and diagrammatic, on a wide front.

1976

NORTHROP FRYE: CRITICISM AS MYTH

> . . . poetry must wait on fact
> And we have seen that when the hero lifts
> The vizor of his helmet to the gaze
> Of the ecstatic myth-mad populace
> . . . it is nothing but a shell, a voice
> Without a face. . . .
>
> —Karl Shapiro

> Not all critical statements or procedures
> can be equally valid.
>
> —Northrop Frye

In accepting the mandate of our chairman to write and deliver this paper,[1] I have been told that this is a program set up in honor of our subject, and that, though I am expected to be critical, "searching," even skeptical, I must be so "respectfully," that is, I must bear in mind the honor of the occasion. As I always write respectfully of literary theorists, I do not find this stipulation irksome. I think I have written in its spirit. I would add the reflection that, as the devil's advocate is not called in until the prospect of canonization is imminent, and furthermore as it is extraordinary that such proceedings should take place at all during the lifetime of the candidate, I believe the honor of the occasion can be in little danger.

The rapidly expanding volume of Frye's writing in the vein of Gnostic mythopoeia, as well as his many but elusively varied repetitions and his paradoxes, create for the critic of Frye an expository problem at least as difficult as the argumentative.

According to Frye, primitive man (somewhat like any person we can imagine beginning life on a desert island) begins by wishing the world were a more comfortable place, that is, more "like" human nature. He enacts certain rituals to try to make it that way. And also he tells himself certain metaphoric and analogical stories embodying his assimilative wishes, and when these wishes project a shape of heroic divinity, investing the natural environment, we have in the proper sense "myth."[2] There is one basic and inclusive myth, which takes the shape of

---

1. This paper was read before the English Institute, meeting at Columbia University in September 1965.

2. "Myths are stories about divine beings which are abstract and stylized stories in the sense that they are unaffected by canons of realism or probability" ("Blake after Two Centuries" [1957], *Fables of Identity: Studies in Poetic Mythology* [New York, 1963], p. 141).

a divine quest, death, and rebirth, following the cycle of the four seasons. Out of myth evolve literature and its very important primitive "conventions," with differences from original myth that may not be fully clear. In literature metaphoric imagination replaces the magic of ritual.[3] Yet literature demands of us, if we are in tune, a "primitive response."[4] Myth and literature do not imitate nature. Having begun apparently with some uneasy glances at nature, they go their own way, madly, transcending, absorbing, enveloping. So that the singing school is not the world (from the world poets have nothing to learn), but literature itself. Literature is made out of earlier literature. It develops into one master, apocalyptic structure, a "universal human form," the heights of heaven and the depths of hell.[5] It includes all partial constructions of myth anybody might conceive, no matter how ambitious—the White Goddess, the Hero with a Thousand Faces.[6] (The phrase "Myth of the Eternal Return" would appear to be another name for the same central ideas—ritual, repetition, divine archetype.) Man, if he has enough imagination, lives not in the supposed "real" world of "nature" but in and by this dream structure of "pure un-inhibited" wish-fulfillment and of obsessive anxiety.[7] It is important for young people to be educated into this structure, and this is done by the reading of the greatest bodies of myth, the Bible (which is total but vague) and the Greek and Roman classics (which are clear but fragmentary).[8] In some broader way, all the efforts of our verbal wisdom—philosophy, history, science, religion, law—are myths, all myths, that is, imaginative constructs. The actual ruling myths of the past have all proved illusory. Literary study helps us to see through false myths, half-truths, mob speech, and gabble idioms. It helps us, above all, to conceive the permanent myth, that which is not illusory, not imaginary, but imaginative, the vision of the possible ideal "real" world, the "real form of human society"—the "free, classless, and urbane society"—"hidden behind the one we see."[9] "Nature" in this

3. *A Natural Perspective: The Development of Shakespearean Comedy and Romance* (New York, 1965), pp. 59–60, 116, 146.

4. *A Natural Perspective*, pp. 61, 64.

5. *The Educated Imagination* (Bloomington, 1964), p. 42; *The Well-Tempered Critic* (Bloomington, 1963), p. 155: "The universe in human form"; "The Realistic Oriole: A Study of Wallace Stevens" (1957), *Fables of Identity*, pp. 250–51.

6. *The Educated Imagination*, pp. 20–21.

7. *The Educated Imagination*, p. 43.

8. *The Educated Imagination*, pp. 46–47.

9. *Anatomy of Criticism* (Princeton, 1957), pp. 115, 349; *The Educated Imagination*, pp. 44, 60–67; "The Archetypes of Literature" (1951),

apocalypse gets itself "inside the mind of an infinite man who builds his cities out of the Milky Way."[10]

Let me introduce here a brief bibliographical note. In this account of Frye's system, rude, but I believe fundamentally faithful and correct, I have been reflecting the organon of 1957 (*Anatomy of Criticism*). But the dimensions and some of my phrases are taken from more recent works and especially from the series of six CBC lectures published in 1963 as *The Educated Imagination*. This is Frye's best attempt to write a small-scale account of his system. Another set of lectures, delivered at the University of Virginia, and published, also in 1963, as *The Well-Tempered Critic*, begins with capriccio variations on the ancient theme of high, low, and middle styles, and on verbal rhythms, but ends with some instructive repetitions of central ideas. Other pregnant statements are to be found among sixteen of Frye's shorter essays collected under the title *Fables of Identity* in the same year, 1963. In that year appeared too his Evergreen Pilot Book *T. S. Eliot*. And in that year he delivered at Columbia University the lectures published in 1965 as *A Natural Perspective*; these deal with primitive conventional patterns in Shakespearean comedy and romance.

Let me now continue my exposition and begin my argument with Frye by quoting two authors in whose classic thought Frye finds several of his own starting points—Plato and Aristotle. Plato, in the *Ion* (540 B-C), where the rhapsode is quizzed to the point of saying that a rhapsode (that is, a literary critic) will know the right things (*ha prepei*) for a man to say, the right things for a woman, for a slave, or for a freeman—but not what the slave, if he is a cowherd, ought to say to his cows, or what the woman, if she is a spinning-woman, ought to say about the working of wool. And Aristotle in chapter IX of the *Poetics*, where in general he says that poetry is more philosophic and of graver import than history, and in chapter XXV, where he says that, if a poet utters technical inaccuracies about the pace of a horse or about medicine or any other art, the error is not essential to the poetry; and if he does not know that a doe has no horns, this is less serious than if he portrays the doe "inartistically," "indistinctly," "unimitatively," or "unrecognizably"—*amimētos*. No translation of this adverb makes very good sense, because with this word Aristotle is touching a tender spot in the

---

Fables of Identity, p. 18: ". . . the central myth of art must be the vision of the end of social effort, the innocent world of fulfilled desires, the free human society"; and "The Imaginative and the Imaginary" (1962), *Fables*, p. 167.

10. *Anatomy*, p. 119.

mind of criticism. He is defining a circle of paradox (or contradiction) within which literary theory has ever since that time continued to move—and Frye no less than any other thinker who makes a serious effort to explain the difficulty. I mean the double difficulty, of poetry in relation to the world, and of criticism in relation to value—the so-far irreducible critical experiences: that literature is both more lively and less lifelike than the real world (this impossible pig of a world); that criticism cannot demonstrate value but is at the same time inescapably concerned with trying to do so. Frye is in no different situation from Aristotle, Coleridge, Croce, or Richards, in having to confront these experiences and in being unsuccessful in trying to simplify them. In his thinking on these problems Frye differs from other literary theorists mainly in the extreme assurance, the magisterial sweep and energy, with which he at moments attempts (or pretends) to detach literature from the world of reality, and criticism from evaluation, and in the aplomb with which he involves himself in the oddities, implausibilities, even patent contradictions, required for this detachment. Thus, literature, on the one hand, has no reference to life, it is autonomous, like mathematics, and sufficient to itself; it "takes over" life, envelops and absorbs it,[11] swallows it.[12] Literature is made out of other literature.[13] At the same time literature

---

11. *Anatomy*, pp. 122, 349, 350.

12. Cf. *The Well-Tempered Critic*, pp. 149, 154-55; *The Educated Imagination*, pp. 33, 35: "literature as unlike life as possible." In "Nature and Homer" (1938), *Fables of Identity*, p. 41, the view is attributed to Aristotle and Longinus. The same essay, pp. 46-47, contains Frye's most resolute attempt to argue that literature is altogether allusive and verbal. It is "not externally or incidentally allusive, but substantially and integrally so." Apparent returns from convention to experience are only shifts to a different convention. Cf. *The Educated Imagination*, p. 16; and "Literature as Context: Milton's *Lycidas*" (1959), *Fables of Identity*, p. 125, on Wordsworth and ballad conventions; *Anatomy*, p. 122: "literature existing in its own universe . . . containing life and reality in a system of verbal relationships." See also Frye's *Selected Poetry and Prose of William Blake* (Modern Library, 1953), p. xxvii: "Suppose we could think away the external or non-human world: what would the shape of things be like then? Clearly the whole universe would then have the shape of a single infinite human body. Everything that we call 'real' in nature would then be inside the body and mind of this human being, just as in a dream the world of suppressed desire is all inside the mind of the dreamer."

13. *The Educated Imagination*, pp. 28-29: ". . . there's nothing new in literature that isn't the old reshaped. . . . there is really no such thing as self-expression in literature. . . . We relate . . . poems and plays and novels . . . to each other"; and pp. 15-16: "A writer's desire to write can only have come from previous experience of literature. . . . literature can only draw its forms from itself"; and *The Well-Tempered Critic*, p. 147.

does refer to life, it must;[14] it began with real life in a primitive situation, and it is concerned with promoting values for real life, the vision of the ideal society (unless we mean that this is only a dream—as perhaps we do—but then why all the talk about the difference between the genuine and the phoney?).[15] *Lincoln Wasn't There* is the title of a recent well-conceived spoof on the ritual theory of mythic origins. If we were to judge by numerous passages in Frye, we'd have to conclude that the ocean wasn't there either, the wine-dark ocean that washed the shores of Greece, nor the rosy-fingered dawn, nor the pine-clad mountains. Nothing was there but the blind bard himself, the *words* of some earlier ballads, and an audience, which presumably did not include any ox-eyed or white-armed women, or any men who were crafty, sulky, proud, brave, or cowardly.

In his Polemical Introduction of 1957, Frye is intent on purging criticism of several wrong kinds of valuing, the biographical or genetic, the rhetorical, the moralistic, and the socially prejudiced. Like Arnold in 1880, he wishes to distinguish such exercises of mere locally public taste from judgments of "positive value,"[16] which he says are the proper business of criticism. He can and is willing to distinguish "ephemeral rubbish,"[17] mediocre works, random and peripheral experience,[18] from the greatest classics, the profound masterpieces, in which may be discerned the converging patterns of the primitive formulas. At other moments, however, he says that criticism has nothing whatever to do with either the experience or the judging of literature. The direct experience of literature is *central* to criticism, yet somehow this center is excluded from it.[19] Criticism moves toward an undiscriminating catholicity of "interest."[20] The patterns of the 1957 Introduction have approximately re-

14. See, e.g., *The Educated Imagination*, p. 25: "There's always some literary reason for using them, and that means something in human life that they [sheep, flowers] correspond to or represent or resemble." Cf. *The Well-Tempered Critic*, p. 148. And see Meyer Abrams, "The Correspondent Breeze," in M. H. Abrams, ed., *English Romantic Poets* (New York, 1960), p. 49, an excellent passage on "the inescapable conditions of the human endowment and of its physical milieu."

15. Cf. "The Imaginative and the Imaginary" (1962), *Fables of Identity*, pp. 152–53: "Sense . . . tells us what kind of reality the imagination must found itself on."

16. *Anatomy*, p. 27.

17. *Anatomy*, p. 116.

18. *Anatomy*, p. 17.

19. *Anatomy*, pp. 20, 27, 28. Let us make a collection of banknotes and then proceed to use them as stage money, or a collection of ten-dollar gold pieces and then treat them as subway tokens.

20. *Anatomy*, p. 24.

peated themselves in later pronouncements. On a single page of a statement in an MLA pamphlet of 1963 on *Aims and Methods of Scholarship*, "good taste" and "value-judgment" are said to be based on direct experience; at the same time "good taste" is a skill founded on a structure of knowledge, and this knowledge (or at least an important part of it) is academic criticism, and critics who go wrong usually do so, "*not* through the failure of taste and judgment, *but* through not knowing enough about literature."[21] On one page of *The Well-Tempered Critic* the "study" and "understanding" of literature are "different things" from the "admiration" of it and the "wonder," but on the next page we hear of the "fallacy of separating the understanding of literature from the appreciation of it."[22] In his MLA pamphlet statement of 1963 and also in a lecture published in *College English* for October, 1964, Frye thinks critics ought to avoid the risk of working from their own likes and dislikes and keep a business eye open to their reputations and their effectiveness. Critics who attack Milton only damage their own images. In the latter essay, "good" and "bad" become "not something inherent in literary works themselves," but qualities of activity or passivity in our own "use" of literature, so that evaluative criticism itself is no longer to be directed toward literature but toward earlier bad criticism.[23] Frye is a candidate for the votes of all shades of appreciators and scientists in criticism—except that of the unhappy analyst who finds himself under obligation to make comparisons. His key terminology and his most picturesque statements suggest some kind of neutral anatomizing, but we must remain unsure, as he no doubt is unsure, whether he wishes to discredit all critical valuing whatever, or only the wrong kinds of valuing.

21. *The Aims and Methods of Scholarship in Modern Languages and Literatures*, ed. James E. Thorpe (New York, 1963), p. 62. The italics are mine.

22. *The Well-Tempered Critic*, pp. 136-37. ". . . there clearly are such standards [i.e., of taste]" (p. 132). ". . . both intellect and emotion are fully and simultaneously involved in all our literary experience" (p. 144).

23. "Criticism, Visible and Invisible," *College English* 26 (October 1964): 10, 12. This lecture flourishes a number of Frye's reneges and contradictions. The title is a religious metaphor. Criticism can be either "militant" or "triumphant." In the phase of triumph, "glorified and invisible," criticism is just not comprehended by darkness and ignorance.

A critic who undertakes to chart Frye's vagaries on the theme of criticism and value will suffer from an embarrassment of riches—as at least one other writer, Philip P. Hallie, in the *Partisan Review* (Fall 1964), has illustrated with his own series of passages from the *Anatomy*. See also the review of the *Anatomy* by Meyer Abrams in the *University of Toronto Quarterly* (January 1959), p. 192.

What is it that enables Frye to get away with these violations
of logic and order? Unquestionably, the speed and energy of his
style. Let me insert here a general encomium on the liveliness,
the moments of vivid wit and charm which Frye brings to the
contemporary critical scene—the freedom and swash and slash
with which he employs what in his lectures *The Well-Tempered
Critic* he himself has so well described as the rhythm of associa-
tion, the discontinuous, the aphoristic, the oracular style.[24] In
The Educated Imagination, Frye quotes a teacher of his, Pelham
Edgar, who once told him "that if the rhythm of a sentence was
right, its sense could look after itself." It is true that in order to
write, we must have something to say. But having something to
say, adds Frye, means "having a certain potential of verbal en-
ergy."[25] Frye has learned the lesson of his teacher surpassingly
well. Two other papers than the one I have written might take
their departure from this point: one in praise of Frye's many
brilliant theoretical, but local, insights, one in complaint against
his frequently shuffling associational logic and syntax, which at
the worst I would describe as a kind of verbal shell game. I have
written neither of those papers, but a paper on Frye's system,
which, despite one or two disclaimers on his part regarding its
importance,[26] is after all the most prominent feature of his
writing. At the moment, I am saying that Frye has contributed
much to the gaiety, the fun, and hence in a certain sense to the
health of modern American criticism. He has enlivened our
proceedings. For this we should be grateful. Frye's vigorously
urbane recitals will start in our minds echoes of many voices
in the idealist and mythopoeic tradition, from Blake to Frazer,
Cornford, or Lord Raglan. But most often I find myself hearing
again the masterly jokes which I read first as a boy in those
dialogues of Oscar Wilde *The Decay of Lying* and *The Critic
as Artist*. "Hours ago, Ernest, you asked me the use of Criticism.
You might just as well have asked me the use of thought." "The
elect spirits of each age, the critical and cultured spirits, will
grow less and less interested in actual life, and will seek to *gain
their impressions almost entirely from what Art has touched.*"
"As a method, realism is a complete failure. . . . wherever we
have returned to Life and Nature, our work has become vulgar,
common and uninteresting." "One touch of Nature may make

24. *The Well-Tempered Critic*, pp. 85, 92, 104. "Such techniques have
for their object the attempt to break down or through the whole structure
of verbal articulation" (p. 92). Cf. *Anatomy*, pp. 329-37.

25. *The Educated Imagination*, p. 52.

26. See, e.g., *Anatomy*, p. 29: "Whenever schematization appears in the
following pages, no importance is attached to the schematic form itself."

the whole world kin, but two touches of Nature will destroy any work of Art."

Because, of course, as Frye could have explained to Wilde, the work of art is made of other works of art, and other works of art are made of the mythic archetypes.[27] We are now in a position to undertake a more direct account of this distinguishing feature of Frye's literary theory. A number of things are to be observed. And first, and most momentous, that the mythic archetypes provide a set of predicates ("a specific conceptual framework")[28] which Frye considers to be in some special and exclusive sense proper to literary study, something scientifically reliable and self-sealing. No dialectical leaks are possible. The mythic predicates give us *real categories*; they are a ground of *valid comparisons*. They are like the scientific middle terms of Aristotle's demonstrative syllogisms; only Aristotle would never have found these in literature. These and only these predicates come together progressively to build a totally coherent order of literary genres, of conventions, and of words (or of literary experience). Hence they provide a method of critical taxonomy.[29] Such predicates are "centripetal" in the study of literature. All others are "centrifugal,"[30] taking the student away from literature. In itself the system of mythic predicates is neutral—or maybe it is not neutral. It may be inspected, or *perhaps* it may be inspected, sometimes better in ephemeral popular works than in the classics.[31] It does not provide a test of value. Or maybe it does. At least somehow it does provide the education the critic needs in order to move with security on the floor of that unstable stock exchange of literary values which has given Frye so much amused concern.[32]

27. ". . . mythology merges insensibly into, and with, literature" ("Myth, Fiction, and Displacement" [1961], *Fables of Identity*, p. 33).
28. *Anatomy*, p. 6.
29. "Literature as Context: Milton's *Lycidas*" (1959), *Fables of Identity*, pp. 127–29: "For literature is not simply an aggregate of books and poems and plays: it is an order of words" (p. 127); ". . . a recurring structural principle. The short, simple, and accurate name for this principle is myth" (p. 128). "It is part of the critic's business to show how all literary genres are derived from the quest-myth. . . . the quest-myth will constitute the first chapter of whatever future handbooks of criticism may be written that will be based on enough organized critical knowledge to call themselves 'introductions' or 'outlines' and still be able to live up to their titles" ("The Archetypes of Literature" [1951], *Fables of Identity*, p. 17).
30. "The Archetypes of Literature" (1951), *Fables of Identity*, p. 7.
31. *Anatomy*, pp. 104, 116. But see the opposite view, pp. 17, 19, and "The Archetypes of Literature" (1951), *Fables of Identity*, pp. 12–13.
32. *Anatomy*, pp. 9, 17–18. See in his "Myth, Fiction, and Displacement" (1961), the account of Arthur Miller's play *The Crucible* as having

In his MLA pamphlet statement of 1963, Frye, repeating in capsule form his earlier accounts, wishes to put all remarks about the mere structure, themes, imagery, and language of poems in a class which he calls "commentary" or "allegorical" commentary. A second sort of remarks, all those that look in the direction of genre, convention, classical allusion, and myth, he distinguishes radically from the former, and he calls these latter not commentary but "identification," and this is the supreme act of criticism.[33] Similarly, in his *Nature and Homer*, of 1958, he argues that we cannot say good or bad of a literary work unless we can say *what* it is, what kind of literary work. As if one were to say, "This is a good comedy," and Frye were to answer, "Oh no, it isn't. It's a good satire in the third comic phase." In this line of thought, we are reminded forcefully of the relative proximity of Toronto to Chicago. In Frye's system, conventions and genres constantly play the role of premature ultimates. So far as I can see, Frye has never offered a shred of evidence for this kind of exclusiveness and essentialism[34] —but rather much that tells specifically against it: for instance, in his lectures on Shakespeare,[35] the primitive conventionalism which he insists is the structural basis of such unsuccessful plays as *Pericles* and *Cymbeline*. There would seem to be no reason whatever why a comic convention, a pastoral allusion, or a mythic stereotype should be considered a trace of the tough and ab-

the "content" of "social hysteria," but the "form" of "purgatorial or triumphant tragedy." The latter is the element of permanence, what tends to give the play "an immense reverberating dimension of significance" (*Fables of Identity*, p. 37). A few pages earlier (p. 34) the "conventional comic form" in *Pride and Prejudice* "does not account for any of the merits of the novel." See the accounts of *Macbeth* in *The Educated Imagination*, p. 24 (". . . what a man feels like after he has gained a kingdom and lost his soul") and in *A Natural Perspective*, pp. 62–63: "It is not a play about the moral crime of murder; it is a play about the dramatically conventional crime of killing the lawful and anointed king." Take away "this mythical and conventional element . . . and Thomas Rymer himself could hardly do justice to the chaos that remains." And see *The Educated Imagination*, p. 48: "To see these resemblances in structure . . . will not, by itself, give any . . . notion why Shakespeare is better than the television movie."

33. Cf. the model account of five stages in seeing the grave-digger scene in *Hamlet*, in "The Archetypes of Literature" (1951), *Fables of Identity*, p. 13, and the four "creative principles" of criticism (convention, genre, archetype, autonomous form) in "Literature as Context: Milton's *Lycidas*" (1959), *Fables*, p. 123.

34. Frye, of course, finds occasions for explicit disavowals of every form of exclusivism. See, e.g., *Anatomy*, p. 62; *College English* 26 (October 1964): 8.

35. Hinted also in *Anatomy*, p. 117. Shakespeare in his later period was at the "bedrock" of drama.

struse essence and identification of literature, while a centrally
structured image, a dramatized theme, or a persistent verbal
technique should not be, but should be only something marginal,
"easy" enough to notice, as Frye says, a mere topic of "com-
mentary." The mythic archetypes, centering in the slain king,
are Frye's King Charles's Head—"his allegorical way of expressing
it"—turning up if not at the beginning, middle, and end of most
of his essays, at least by the end in those instances where we be-
gin to hope that they may have been forgotten.

Frye has indeed a keen and witty sense of the difficulties and
insufficiencies of various other kinds of criticism (which he calls
"comparative," not "positive"), the biographical kinds, the af-
fective, impressionistic, "rhetorical," mimetic, realistic, moral,
and sociological kinds. In some of his negative arguments he
scores brilliant bull's-eyes. He has invented some of the most
entertaining jokes I know in assault upon the wrong ways of
criticizing which I myself would group under the head of the
biographical or "intentional" fallacy. "There are critics who can
find things in the Public Record office, and there are critics," he
boasts, "who, like myself, could not find the Public Record
Office."[36] It would distract us from the main issue to notice
here at any length that in his MLA pamphlet statement of 1963
he becomes a renegade to such insights in the course of a
headlong safety-first piety to the scholarly techniques and to
the great names. He has found any kind of technical ignorance a
"constant handicap." And let Milton offend his taste and judg-
ment. Milton must have his reasons.[37]

But to return to the archetypes: One way to describe what is
original in Frye is to say that it consists in an extreme and vio-
lent conjunction of schematism and concreteness; that is, on the
one hand, of abstraction, universalism, archetype, inclusive
system, and on the other hand, of high coloration, detailed
specificity, a wildly luxuriant growth of the flora and fauna, the
constellations, of Frye's world of the imagination. Let us say a
little more first about the schematism. This is something which
Frye is often willing to labor. The study of literature seems to
become, not knowing more and more precisely the character of

36. "Literature as Context: Milton's *Lycidas*" (1959), *Fables of Iden-
tity*, p. 128.
37. Cf. Spenser lapsing into "muddled arguments, tasteless imagery, and
cacophonous doggerel" ("The Structural Imagery in *The Faerie Queene*"
[1961], *Fables of Identity*, p. 69) and "Milton's one obvious failure . . .
The Passion" ("Literature as Context: Milton's *Lycidas*" [1959], *Fables*,
p. 126). *Anatomy*, p. 110, urges that "biography will always be a part of
criticism."

each literary utterance (though we find at least token assertions of the individual and ineffable, as in the essay on Milton's *Ly-cidas*),[38] but just the opposite, knowing each one under the most universal aspects possible. Never mind the trees. "Everything is potentially identical with everything else."[39] *Metamorphoses* becomes *Fables of Identity*. Frye has pushed this ruthless, categorizing, assimilative, subsuming drive of his theory in various places, but in none I think with more complete self-exposure than in this toward the end of the third essay in *Anatomy of Criticism*.

> In looking at a picture, we may stand close to it and analyze the details of brush work and palette knife. This corresponds roughly to the rhetorical analysis of the new critics in literature. At a little distance back, the design comes into clearer view, and we study rather the content represented: This is the best distance for realistic Dutch pictures, for example, where we are in a sense reading the picture. The further back we go, the more conscious we are of the organizing design. At a great distance from, say, a Madonna, we can see nothing but the archetype of the Madonna, a large centripetal blue mass, with a contrasting point of interest at its center. In the criticism of literature, too, we often have to "stand back" from the poem to see its archetypal organization. [p. 140]

Long ago, Horace told us that poems are like pictures, *ut pictura poesis*, in that some demand closer inspection, some, like murals presumably, look better at a distance. It has remained for mythopoeic criticism to tell us that we must back away from all of them, until they merge in a common formalism or "stylization" of archetypal colors and crude shapes.[40] Who really wants to see a painting that way? Perhaps a pure neo-Kantian "formalist" in art criticism—a Clive Bell or a Roger Fry. Scarcely a critic who has literary interests in the verbal art of literature.

As a matter of fact, no system of sheer abstractionism or universalism has ever commended itself for long to the world of lit-

---

38. *Fables of Identity*, p. 128.
39. *Anatomy*, pp. 124, 136.
40. *Anatomy*, p. 135. And see *The Educated Imagination*, p. 54, where literature in education has the same relation to other verbal studies (history, philosophy, social sciences, law, theology) as mathematics to physical sciences. See also "Myth, Fiction, and Displacement" (1961), *Fables of Identity*, pp. 28, 31; and "The Archetypes of Literature" (1951), *Fables*, p. 13: "This inductive movement towards the archetype is a process of backing up, as it were, from structural analysis, as we back up from a painting if we want to see the composition instead of brushwork."

terateurs and critics, any more than to the world of poets. Plato's
purity, such as it was, was conspicuously the frame of reference
of an antipoetics. How Aristotle, countering Plato, used the con-
crete and rich colors of actual Greek epic and drama to give
conviction and interest to *his* system of universals is a story for
another day. A system does need its colors, its precious realiza-
tions, its exhibits. And so we come to the more specific side of
Frye's mythopoeia, the detailed realization. We can readily
enough see the reason for this contrasting side of the system.
Still it is odd, and it is strained. The *idea* turns out to have not
only a Greek or Latin name but a phallus, a mask, a goatskin
jacket, a red wig, a sword, a staff, or what not. As one reviewer
has remarked, Frye's *Anatomy* is "about as stripped and quint-
essential as the Albert Memorial."[41] "To generalize is to be an
Idiot," said Blake, and he left his dictum joined in the record
with the rebellious and exuberant particularity of his own art,
where Adam is wrapped in the coils of the big green serpent and
God has wings of brass. In his Introduction of 1957 Frye notices
this opinion of Blake's and in the name of the archetypes he re-
jects it. His own articulations of the archetype are more true to
his master—both in degree of specificity and in degree of fantasy.
(Concepts can be highly colored and still in a sense seem un-
contaminated by the touch of experience. The immediate illu-
sion of external, fallen Albion can be avoided.) "Critical theory
of genres," complains Frye, "is stuck precisely where Aristotle
left it."[42] This, however, can be remedied, and will be—as, long
since, the service for botany was performed by Linnaeus. Frye
wants all the idealism, autonomy, and absoluteness of a subjec-
tive humanization but at the same time a highly concrete typol-
ogy, variegated specific categories, a brimful inhabited world of
Aristotelian genres, styles, and characters. Occam! thou shouldst
be living at this hour! Benedetto Croce! thou shouldst be living
at this hour! I am thinking of such arrangements as Frye's twenty-
four overlapping divisions of the seasonal cycle of myths, or his
permutations of high, middle, and low styles, complicated by
the ideas of hieratic and demotic, and of verse, prose, and assoc-
ciative (or speech) rhythms, at primary, secondary, and tertiary
levels, or the endless recital of parallel conventions, or hopeful
parallels, or qualifications or exceptions to parallels, among
Shakespeare's comedies and romances.There is surely something
of the archetype of Polonius and of the sock and buskin in that
passage of Samuel Beckett's *Watt* where the eccentric house-

41. Robert M. Adams, *Hudson Review* 10 (Winter 1957-58): 617.
42. *Anatomy*, p. 13.

holder Mr. Knott "mooches" about his rooms in varied footgear: "As for his feet, sometimes he wore on each a sock, or on the one a sock and on the other a stocking, or a boot, or a shoe, or a slipper, or a sock and boot, or sock and shoe, or a sock and slipper, or a stocking and boot, or a stocking and shoe, or a stocking and slipper, or nothing at all. . . . And sometimes he wore. . . ."[43]

In his moments of most nearly pure archetypal abstraction, Frye's types are in a sense true patterns. But in that sense they are also truistic, simplistic, and uninteresting. More or less universally valid patterns of imagery and shapes of stories can of course be discerned in the canon of the world's literature. Fictional stories, it is true, are all about what we wish to have or to be and what we wish not to have or not to be, what we like and what we don't like. Love and marriage and banquets and dances and springtime and wheat and fruit and wine are good. Hate and strife and downfall and death, disease, blight, and poison, are bad. A lamb is a good animal, a wolf or a tiger is a bad one, and frightening, especially in a pastoral society or tradition. "Any symbolism founded on food," says Frye, "is universal."[44] We can live in a city or a garden, not in a stony or weedy wilderness. If we rummage out all the ideas of the desirable and undesirable we can think of, they fall inevitably under the heads of the supernatural, the human, the animal, vegetable, and mineral, as Frye himself comes close to explaining in his allusion to the game of Twenty Questions. See the catalogues of apocalyptic and demonic imagery in the essay of 1951 and in the third essay of the *Anatomy*.[45]

But the general problem of a literary theorist who would be a revolutionary leader with truisms is how to make them seem pregnant and novel. "One essential principle of archetypal criticism," Frye instructs us, "is that the individual and the universal forms of an image are identical, the reasons being too complicated for us just now."[46] Like Blake, Frye would number the streaks of the mythic tulip. But for the theorist there are some special difficulties. Not in the abstractionist and truis-

43. *Watt* (New York, 1959), p. 200.
44. *Anatomy*, p. 118.
45. And see the images of upper and lower, journeys of ascent and descent in the classical "topocosm" described in "New Directions from Old" (1960), *Fables of Identity*, pp. 58–65.
46. "The Archetypes of Literature" (1951), *Fables of Identity*, p. 19. Cf. "Literature as Context: Milton's *Lycidas*" (1959), *Fables*, p. 120: "By archetype I mean a literary symbol, or cluster of symbols, which are used recurrently throughout literature, and thereby become conventional."

tic half of the system, but in its needed complement the specific and the colorful, we come to the issue of the cliché. The cliché, as Rémy de Gourmont said in passages that have been well understood by the American New Critics, is more than a matter of triteness and repetition. In that sense, all of our established vocabulary is cliché. The true idea of the cliché (the offensive cliché) involves the notion of irrelevance, the impertinent gloss of a misplaced special effort to be bright. ("Do you live in New York? I like to visit New York. I wouldn't live in the place if you gave it to me.") Frye himself has given us a happy exposition of how this applies. In *The Well-Tempered Critic* (pp. 125-26) he speaks of a certain "mytho-historical" type of stock response, probably the "most common" type. He had a student once who admired "Good King Wenceslas" because he thought it had been written in the thirteenth century. But this student lost all interest when Frye explained that it was in fact "a kind of Victorian singing commercial." This, adds Frye, was "only a very common form of misplaced concreteness." But the mythopoeic system of Frye himself is a wholesale indulgence in that very fallacy of misplaced concreteness.

A cliché, being not simply a repetition, may even be ingenious and original (or at least novel). When a biographer of John Barrymore tells us that Barrymore took on "the Danish assignment" or that he decided to "draw on the black tights of the classic Scandinavian," we may never have heard these expressions before, but we feel their affinity for, if not identity with, the dismal kind of cliché. Similarly, to describe Hamlet's stage-tradition jump into Ophelia's grave as if it were an instance of the classic descent into the underworld is a cliché application of the archetype,[47] ingenious perhaps, but still a cliché, a mythopoeist's cliché. It is the same thing to call Leontes in *The Winter's Tale* a *senex iratus* out of the New Comedy,[48] or to describe Tom Sawyer and Becky Thatcher's adventures in the cave as a displaced version of the dragon-killing myth (thus raising in our minds irrelevant images of Theseus, St. George, and Beowulf), or to see Lemuel Gulliver, bound by the Lilliputians, as a parody Promethean figure,[49] or to see Belinda in *The Rape of the Lock* as a figure out of the Rape of Proserpine, or, even worse, to see Wordsworth's Lucy, "rolled round . . . with rocks, and

47. *Anatomy*, p. 140; "The Archetypes of Literature" (1951), *Fables of Identity*, p. 13.
48. *A Natural Perspective*, p. 74.
49. *Anatomy*, pp. 190, 321.

stones, and trees," as an underground companion of the same
unlucky goddess.[50] The type assumes the solidity of the char-
acter or action it is called in to "identify." The *tritos anthropos*,
the third man used by Parmenides and Aristotle against the Pla-
tonic ideas, becomes in such a context once more a relevant
invocation.[51] A universal idea ascends into the rainbow strato-
sphere of the archetypes and redescends to settle a cloak of
exotic and unearned colors on the shoulders of some Shake-
spearean or Dickensian character. Warm gules indeed on Made-
line's fair breast. Myth, like a dome of many-colored glass,
stains the white radiance of anagogy. The Anima Mundi swarms
with sputniks, Telstars, chattering back their advice for stability
in the art market.

A lurid glow, a feeling of rituals enacted in the deepest recesses
of the racial past, of a remotely primitive authentication, is no
doubt generated by the appearance of Frye's Hallowe'en cast of
characters and the mazes of their cyclic action. A "primitive re-
sponse," we are told, is demanded of us.[52] "If we neutralize the
archetype," says Meyer Abrams, "by eliminating dark allusions
to 'primordial images' or 'the racial memory' or 'timeless depths,'
archetypal criticism is drained of the mystique or pathos which
is an important part of its present vogue."[53] And of course we
can neutralize it. We must. The Ur-Myth, the Quest Myth, with
all its complications, its cycles, acts, scenes, characters, and spe-
cial symbols is not a historical fact. And this is so not only in
the obvious sense that the stories are not true, but in another
sense, which I think we tend to forget and which mythopoeic
writing does much to obscure: that such a coherent, cyclic, and
encyclopedic system, such a monomyth, cannot be shown ever
to have evolved actually, either from or with ritual, anywhere in
the world, or ever anywhere to have been entertained in whole
or even in any considerable part. We are talking about the myth
of myth. As Frye himself, in his moments of cautionary vision,

50. *Anatomy*, p. 183; "Literature as Context: Milton's *Lycidas*"
(1959), *Fables of Identity*, p. 125. See also, e.g., Kingsley's Mary rowed
in across the "cruel, crawling foam"—with a "faint coloring of the myth of
Andromeda" (*Anatomy*, p. 36), Lord Jim as "a lineal descendant of the
miles gloriosus" (*Anatomy*, p. 40), the detective-story murderer as a
pharmakos pursued by a man-hunter (*Anatomy*, p. 46), and Rousseau's
desire for a revolutionary revival of primitivism as "informed by the myth
of the sleeping beauty" (*Anatomy*, p. 353).
51. "The present facts," says Frye of the extreme historical versions of
mythopoeia, "are being compared to their own shadows" (*Anatomy*, p.
108).
52. *A Natural Perspective*, pp. 6, 64.
53. "The Correspondent Breeze" (1957), in *English Romantic Poets*, ed.
M. H. Abrams, p. 49.

observes, the "derivation" of the literary genres from the quest myth is "logical," not historical.[54] That is, it is made up according to desire, by the imagination of the critic. That brave old world, that had such people in it, is a conglomerate of extrapolations out of actual Greek literature by Frazer and other Cambridge anthropologists, of reports and speculations about modern primitive or isolated peoples, and of assumptions taken, whether explicitly or implicitly, from the psychology of the collective unconscious. "Anthropology tells us," says Frye in 1947. "Psychology tells us."[55]

It is true that Frye, after an early appeal to both Frazer and Jung, has vigorously disclaimed any reliance on them or on any "chronological" derivation of myth at all.[56] He may well disclaim Frazer and Jung. They may be an embarrassment; they are not strictly needed. What *is* needed, however, is some constant implication or intimation of the primordial, the more mysterious the better. And such an implication is surely present. For "primitive" and other terms, nearly synonymous, in Frye's system, let him substitute throughout simply "universal"; for "myth," substitute "story" or "idea" or even "preternatural" story or idea; for "archetype," simply "type" or "model." And let him remove the Greek and Latin names of his archetypal figures, especially the proper names, and his broad appeals to both the Bible and Greek mythology.[57] The loss of blood, the destruction of the system, will be terrible to contemplate. Let him remove, for that matter, simply the historic cycle from myth to irony, the "Great Year," in the first essay of the *Anatomy*. And let him not, as he has recently done, bring out Livy and Donatus—or any of the several other rumors of late antiquity which are known to classical scholarship[58]—as if these could improve the insufficient argument which has all along

54. *Anatomy*, p. 108; "The Archetypes of Literature" (1951), *Fables of Identity*, p. 17: "It is only when we try to expound the derivation chronologically that we find ourselves writing pseudo-historical fictions. . . . " Pages 16–17 stress Frazer along with Jung's *Psychology of the Unconscious* (1912). Cf. "New Directions from Old" (1960), *Fables*, p. 66, and "Literature as Context: Milton's *Lycidas*" (1959), *Fables*, p. 119.

55. *Fearful Symmetry* (Princeton, 1947), p. 424.

56. *Anatomy*, pp. 108–12.

57. *The Educated Imagination*, pp. 46–47.

58. Frye, *A Natural Perspective*, pp. 54, 58, invokes Livy vii.2.6–7 and Donatus, the latter as reported by Thomas Lodge. Only the first sentence of the passage quoted from Lodge is in fact from Donatus-Euanthius. See Donatus, [*Euanthius de Fabula*], I.1–4: "Initium tragoediae et comoediae a rebus divinis est inchoatum, quibus pro fructibus vota solventes operabantur antiqui. . . . res tragicae longe ante comicas inventae." For other authorities of late antiquity, see A. W. Pickard-Cambridge, *Dithyramb, Comedy and Tragedy* (Oxford, 1927), pp. 97–107.

rested on the brief and obscure passages of extrapolated history in Aristotle's *Poetics*.

If we take Frye at his word and attempt to deduce his system "logically," we will reject it, for the structure which he shows us is, as I have been saying, divided between truism and *ad libitum* fantasy. What really happens is that we yield to these apparitions a kind of suspended judgment, because we fear, or hope, that behind them some kind of historical or quasi-historical validation is only waiting for the right moment to be wheeled into the arena. They extort the same kind of respect as men from Mars on radio programs in days long before Mariner IV had sent back photographs revealing the great improbability of higher life on that "sterile promontory."

A certain fictive coloring manifests itself throughout the mythopoeic exposition in a number of other ways. For instance, in a frequently original employment of terminology. Frye needs not only his own cast of characters and his special plots but his own language or vocabulary of displaced diction—derangement of epitaphs. It is a strange language. Consider, for instance, in the Polemical Introduction of 1957, the term "tropical," with its marginal or archaic meaning of "figurative," apparently introduced here mainly because of its oddity.[59] It gives the reader something to wonder about and thus may make him fail to realize the momentary bizarre focus by which study of figures can be equated with "the rhetoric of verbal ornament" and at the same time can be imputed to social and moral prejudice. Frye's vocabulary is not an accident but a necessary engine for the projection of some of his slanted visions. Despite frequent complaints about merely "rhetorical" kinds of literary criticism, Frye will also assert, in other contexts, that rhetoric necessarily intervenes between grammar and logic and hence that there can be no really logical argument in words.[60] This is in effect his defense of his own style, which we have already seen in different phrasing. Consider, for a second example, the term "literal," at the bottom level of symbol-reading in the second essay of the *Anatomy*, whereas "literal" in the well-known medieval system, as Frye himself labors to point out,[61] means something which corresponds to the second level in his essay, the realistic "descriptive." Frye divides the term "literal," in his own way, between a tautology—"a poem cannot be literally anything but a

59. *Anatomy*, p. 21. Perhaps Kenneth Burke is partly to blame, and no doubt Hamlet.
60. *Anatomy*, pp. 335–37, 350.
61. *Anatomy*, pp. 76, 116.

poem"—and the notion of some kind of sheer verbal (or "let-
ter") music and sheer verbal (or "letter") imagery, apparently
independent of any sign value the words may have.[62] Nobody
else would use "literal" as Frye uses it here. The very thin slice
of symbolism which he is talking about ought to be called, if
anything, the "alphabetical" or perhaps the "phonemic," but
such a name would advertise the fact that no such kind of crit-
icism ever really occurs. To take a simpler and more sweeping
example, let us not forget the term "displacement," a key term
in Frye's system, itself a strange displacement,[63] by which re-
ality becomes anomalous, and "pure un-inhibited" fantasy the
norm. And notice the curiously willful use of the term "imag-
ination" and several related terms in the essay of 1961 "Myth,
Fiction, and Displacement," by which he manages to put Cole-
ridge "in the tradition of critical naturalism,"[64] because forsooth
Coleridge conceived a "secondary imagination" and thus avoided
the frenzy of the total identifying "vision."[65]

Frye says in the first essay of the *Anatomy* (on the status of
protagonists) that his alignments of "high" and "low" are not
evaluative but only "diagrammatic."[66] This, as I may already
have suggested, must be questioned. Evaluations, and diagram-
matic evaluations, do obtrude all through these essays. Consider,
for instance, the verbal critics, the New Critics, groveling in the

62. *Anatomy*, pp. 77-78.
63. *Anatomy*, pp. 136-37. The innocent-looking term "genre" is an-
other curiosity, functioning in the second essay to refer only to the
"mythical" or "archetypal" phase of reading, but turning up at the head
of the fourth essay ("Theory of Genres") to describe a rhythmic layout of
literature according to transactions between author and audience (epic,
dramatic, prose fictional, lyric).
64. *Fables of Identity*, pp. 29-30.
65. "Towards Defining an Age of Sensibility" (1956), *Fables of Iden-
tity*, pp. 134, 136. Or notice how myths are carefully, even insistently,
differentiated from folk tales (the latter lacking the element of divinity) in
Frye's essay of 1961 "Myth, Fiction, and Displacement" (*Fables*, pp. 31-
32), but in his Shakespeare lectures of 1963, *Cymbeline* is a "pure folk
tale," which three pages later adds to Shakespeare's problem comedies a
"primitive mythical dimension" (*A Natural Perspective*, pp. 67, 70).
66. *Anatomy*, p. 34. Cf. pp. 335, 350; and "How True A Twain" (1962),
Fables of Identity, p. 93, on "high" and "low" themes in Shakespeare's
Sonnets. In an early essay on Yeats, Frye quotes a warning from Blake
against "mathematical form" or the "Euclidean paraphernalia of diagrams,
figures, tables of symbols and the like, which inevitably appear when sym-
bolism is treated as a dead language." The examples of Elizabethan hand-
books and commentaries and that of Yeats's commentary on Blake which
Frye adduces in the same essay do not seem to have warned him that he
himself was in any danger ("Yeats and the Language of Symbolism" [1947],
Fables, pp. 218-19, 231-32).

wintry cellar of verbal irony,[67] and at the other end of things the heroes on the high sunlit plains of myth and romance lifting their gaze to the apocalyptic windows of the morning, But, to put value aside, diagrammatic descriptions ought at least to be capable of diagram. If they are not, there would seem to be a grave question as to what they are saying. Frye is really, in'the long run, not very careful with his diagramming. In the very complicated third essay of the *Anatomy*, on the mythic cycle, spring is comedy, and summer is romance. And much turns on that analogy. But in the essay on "The Archetypes" of 1951,[68] spring had been romance, and summer had been comedy. And in the collected *Fables* of 1963 Frye does not scruple to reproduce that essay without adjustment and without warning to his audience. Presumably we are not expected to notice such misalignments or to boggle at them.

The fact is that Frye moves from the descending *sequence* of his first essay—romance, high mimesis (most tragedy, central tragedy), low mimesis (most comedy), irony—to the embarrassment of a very different *sequence* of "broader categories" in the third essay: spring (comedy), summer (romance), autumn (tragedy), winter (irony-satire).[69] This no doubt has something to do with the complexities that emerge in the asserted correspondence of the first and second three of the six phases of each season with its adjacent seasons.[70] The key pages are: page 177, second three of comedy (spring) with the second three of romance (summer); page 219, first three of romance with the first three of tragedy (autumn); page 236, second three of tragedy with the second three of satire (winter); page 225, first three of satire with the first three of comedy. "There are thus four main types of mythical movement: within romance, within experience, down, and up."[71] "With Centric and Eccentric scribbl'd o'er, Cycle and Epicycle, Orb in Orb." Superimposed Fourth-of-July pinwheels, with a reversing sequence of rocket engines, may give a dim idea of the pyrotechnics involved here. By a proper attention to the *terminally* climactic structure of the spring and autumn seasons and the *medially* climactic structure of the winter

67. *Anatomy*, pp. 65–66.
68. *Kenyon Review* 13 (Winter 1951): 103–05.
69. *Anatomy*, pp. 34, 37, 154, 157, 163, 206. Cf. p. 75, "the sense of reality . . . far higher in tragedy than in comedy." The "parallel" between the five descending modes of the first essay and the ascending phases of symbolism in the second is explicitly asserted (p. 116).
70. "The four seasons of the year being the type" (*Anatomy*, p. 160).
71. *Anatomy*, p. 162. Romance and satire are complete cycles within the larger cycle of tragedy and comedy (pp. 198, 239).

and summer seasons, Frye might have worked out his diagram and might have succeeded in whirling his twenty-four literary subcategories at least *consistently* around the seasonal cycle. But even that would not have paralleled the pattern of his first essay, and furthermore it would not have helped the supposedly primordial and archetypal notion of the Spenglerian[72] four-season cycle. For the truth is that man's consciousness of seasonal change has varied much in various ages and climates. The ancient Greeks, as Sigmund Freud reminds us, generally distinguished only three seasons (spring, summer, and winter), the three Horai or daughters of Zeus and Themis.[73] The variations of lunar, solar, and pluvial calendars in Buddhist, Hindu, and Muslim cultures (three, six, and two being apparently favorite numbers) are too complicated for the present moment.[74] *Winter* and *summer* are the continuous, ancient, and Germanic names of seasons in English, and these two seasons prevail in Old English heroic poetry. The astronomical and Roman sophistication of the four-seasonal system finds its way only later into the English popular and poetic consciousness.[75]

The four seasons, as they function in Frye's system, are just about as primitive as the four strokes of a piston in a Rolls Royce engine.

I find it difficult at this point not to be reminded of genealogy. Frye, as we know from his *Fearful Symmetry*, 1947, and from a recent lecture, "The Road of Excess," found the interpretation of Blake the beginning of a revolution in his own reading of all poetry.[76] He gives perhaps a further, if less deliberate, clue in his essay of 1956 "Towards Defining an Age of Sensibility," where he achieves a definition which embraces Blake himself in the same madly visionary perspective with Ossian and

72. "Yeats and the Language of Symbolism" (1947), *Fables of Identity*, p. 224; "Quest and Cycle in *Finnegans Wake*" (1957), *Fables*, p. 258.

73. "The Theme of the Three Caskets," *Collected Papers* (New York, 1959), IV: 244–56.

74. "Festivals and Fasts," in James Hastings, ed., *Encyclopedia of Religion and Ethics* (Edinburgh, 1937), V: 837, 868; Rhadagovinda Basak, "The Hindu Conception of the Natural World," in Kenneth W. Morgan, ed., *The Religion of the Hindus* (New York, 1953), p. 96; Maurice Gaudefroy-Demombynes, *Muslim Institutions*, trans. John P. MacGregor (London, 1954), p. 182. I owe a special debt to Richard L. Greene, close student of the seasons.

75. Nils Erik Enkvist, *The Seasons of the Year: Chapters on a Motif from Beowulf to the Shepherd's Calendar* (Helsingfors, 1957), pp. 1–5, 196–210.

76. *Fearful Symmetry*, pp. 10–11, 418, 424; "The Road of Excess," in Bernice Slote, ed., *Myth and Symbol* (Lincoln, 1963), pp. 3–20.

Rowley.[77] "I Believe," wrote Blake, in a rebuke to the naturalism of Wordsworth's *Essay* of 1815, "I Believe both Macpherson & Chatterton, that what they say is Ancient Is so." "Precious memorandums," growled Wordsworth, "from the pocketbook of the blind Ossian." Only "the boy, Chatterton," already a forger, had ventured to imitate them. Wordsworth's taste and judgment were accurate. Still he was not far enough removed to have much perspective on the phase of primitivism he was examining. Macpherson's plush-covered Gaelic Homer was Macpherson's own literary idiom and, such as it was, a genuine literary creation. At the moment of its publication, however, it needed the excuse of a feigned antiquity. Chatterton too invented a scenery and a cast of characters—Rowley, Cannynge, John a Iscam, Aella, Sir Simon de Burton, and all the rest—and above all he created a language—as truly a poetic idiom, an expressive forgery out of the morphemic and phonemic elements of his native English—as Spenser's archaic "no language" had been or as Burns's partly synthetic Ayrshire Scots would soon be. Yet for Chatterton it was equally important for getting his idiom launched that he claim the warrant of an antique authenticity. With Macpherson and Chatterton we have a kind of expressiveness balanced so nicely with a sham antiquity that it is difficult to say which gives more support to the other.[78] Blake as a boy tried out both idioms briefly, before entering as a man upon his own construction of myth, in purest English, line, and color, though in wildest apocalyptic fantasy. Blake solved the problem of belief in credentials by a simple fusion. No doubt there was little difference between the sense in which he said, "I Believe both Macpherson & Chatterton," and the

77. ". . . where the metaphor is conceived as part of an oracular and half-ecstatic process, there is a direct identification in which the poet himself is involved. . . . it is in this psychological self-identification that the central 'primitive' quality of this age really emerges" (*Fables of Identity*, p. 136).

78. "The Ossian and Rowley poems," says Frye correctly, "are not simple hoaxes; they are pseudepigrapha . . . they take what is psychologically primitive, the oracular process of composition, and project it as something historically primitive" ("Towards Defining an Age of Sensibility" [1956], *Fables of Identity*, p. 136). See the savage, the lunatic, the lover, and the poet treated repeatedly in *Fables*—e.g., "Towards Defining an Age of Sensibility" (1956), p. 136; "Blake after Two Centuries" (1957), p. 141; "Literature as Context: Milton's *Lycidas*" (1959), p. 128; "The Imaginative and the Imaginary" (1962), pp. 152, 154. The "fraudulent miracles," the "charlatanism" of Madame Blavatsky, says Frye, are "less a reflection on her than on an age that compelled her to express herself in such devious ways" ("Yeats and the Language of Symbolism" [1947], *Fables*, p. 221).

sense in which he believed in his own Urizen, Orc, Los, and all the rest of his varicose *dramatis personae.*

The eighteenth-century age of sensibility and much of the nineteenth century tended to validate literature by an appeal to the authentic heart and mind of the primitive folk and of the closely related childish and naïve. We recognize today, at least when we are wide awake and thinking about any identifiable time or place, that that heart and mind are no more authentic than any other. So far as that simple and sincere mind exists— outside of modern myths—it can be mistaken, uncouth, outlandish, stupid, and brutal, at least as much as any other. Yet such loyalties die hard. It is possible that we in our own way (we scholars, especially, saturated in our devotion to the past) have been turning to another deep part of the eighteenth-century preromantic mind—the inclination to authenticate certain visions by the method of forgery. Poetry itself is nowadays conceived, at least by some of our most progressive thinkers, as a kind of forgery, that is, a bold visionary mistake. "Literature, like mythology," writes our chief authority and the subject of this paper, "is largely an art of misleading analogies and mistaken identities."[79] Extend this idea to criticism, as seventy-five years ago Oscar Wilde showed the way. The idea of poetry as myth will readily extrapolate to the idea of criticism as myth, and thus, by the shortest of leaps, to that of criticism as forgery. Facts, apparently, are not needed. The deduction of our whole argument is logical, not historical. Still the envisioned facts of a literary ur-history and a prehistory serve the very useful purpose of suggesting a kind of antique authority and terminus for veneration. A "primitive response" is "demanded." It is no doubt as futile to try to bring mythopoeic criticism to the measure of observation and reason as it was for W. W. Skeat to normalize the language of Chatterton's Rowley—by which he succeeded only in purging Chatterton of his main poetic value. Visionary criticism enjoys, I think, not quite the immunities of visionary poetry. Yet this kind of criticism may be in a sense, in its own moment and for its own creator, indefeasible. For the rest of us, what if the cast of critical characters should all turn out to be phantoms? The priest of the Sacred Grove at Nemi "too," wrote Frazer near the end of his great work, he "too, for all the quaint garb he wears and the gravity with which he stalks across the stage, is merely a puppet, and it is time to unmask him be-

79. "Myth, Fiction, and Displacement" (1961), *Fables of Identity*, p. 35.

fore laying him up in the box."[80] "These our actors, As I fore-
told you, were all spirits and Are melted into air, into thin air."

1965

80. *The Golden Bough*, 3d ed., X (1913), vi. Cf. Stanley Edgar Hyman,
The Tangled Bank (New York, 1962), p. 266.

II

EIGHTEENTH-CENTURY ESSAYS

BELINDA LUDENS

I

The two stones of the Roman Neoplatonist Plotinus (*Enneads* V.viii and I.vi), one beautiful in virtue of a special form carved upon it by an artist, the other endowed with being, and hence in Plotinian terms with beauty, in virtue simply of its being one thing, may be considered archetypal for a sort of metaphysical explanation which explains too much—that is to say, which expands its focus upon a special idea until that idea coincides with the whole horizon of the knowable universe. The Plotinian system has had its modern inverted counterparts in forms of expressionist idealism, notably the Crocean. I think it has another sort of parallel in the view of art, or of the whole of cultivated life, as a form of play, which develops, from the aesthetic of Kant, 1790, to a kind of climax in the masterpiece of Johann Huizinga, 1938. *Homo Ludens* asserts that "play can be very serious indeed." "Ritual," for example, "is seriousness at its highest and holiest. Can it nevertheless be play?"[1] The trend of the argument is to say that play is the generator and the formula of all culture. It was not carrying things much further when Jacques Ehrmann, the editor of a volume in *Yale French Studies* entitled *Game, Play, Literature*, 1968, protested that Huizinga and some others were in fact taking reality too seriously. "Play is not played against a background of a fixed, stable, reality. . . . All reality is caught up in the play of the concepts which designate it."[2] This Berkeleyan moment in the philosophy of play idealism had been in part prepared by the work of a cosmic visionary, Kostas Axelos, whose preliminaries to "planetary thinking" (*Vers la Pensée planetaire*) of 1964 led to the simple announcement of his title page in 1969 *Le Jeu du monde*. Man as player and as toy; the universe as a game played and as itself an agent playing.

But the universe, of course, as Emerson once pointed out, is anything we wish to make it: "The world is a Dancer; it is a Rosary; it is a Torrent; it is a Boat; a Mist, a Spider's Snare; it is what you will. . . ."[3] I myself must confess to a double inclination: to take the concept of play very broadly, yet to stop short of making it a transcendental. It seems a more useful and a more interesting concept if it has some kind of bounds and

---

1. *Homo Ludens* (Boston, 1955), pp. 5, 18.
2. *"Homo Ludens* Revisited," in *Game, Play, Literature, Yale French Studies* 41 (1968): 56.
3. *Journals* (Boston, 1909–14), VI: 18.

makes some kind of antithesis to something else. Surely we can think of some things, some moments of action or experience, that are not play—jumping out of the path of an ondriving truck just in time to save your life, for instance, or making out an income tax return. The more spontaneous the action, I suppose, the more certainly we can distinguish play from what is not play. Thus a sudden skip and gambol on the green is not like the leap amid the traffic. But a person filling out a tax form may conceivably, either to relieve tension or to express resentment, evolve some half-conscious overlay of irony or ritual. Allow us a moment to feel safe, and the same is true on the street. I have witnessed a very distinguished academic person—a university president—confront the rush of automobile fenders at a busy corner in New Haven by turning sidewise, like a toreador, and flaunting the skirt of his topcoat.

We have the double sense that play is both clearly different from certain other things, and that it is a chameleon—or, as Wittgenstein would put it, only a collection of family resemblances.[4] We know that in our everyday usage *play* has not a single opposite, but a medley—what is real, serious, or necessary, what is work, war, or woe.

Perhaps we can usefully conceive the area approximately circumscribed by the term "play" as a polyhedron, in which our divisions according to genus and species will be determined by which side we think of the figure as resting on. Immanuel Kant initiated the modern discussion with a slant toward fine art when he conceived the pleasure of art as a "feeling" of freedom in the play of our cognitive faculties."[5] Such a *play* of faculties may be analogized very widely—to the play of water in a fountain, the play of firelight on a shadowy wall, the play of muscles in an athlete's body, the play of Aristotle's taws "upon the bottom of a king of kings." The English term "play" has that loose sort of connotation. And so have the German *Spiel* and *spielen*. But the Kantian tradition of art as free play of faculties need not be frittered away in such directions. As developed by Schiller and later by Groos and Lange, it gives us a notion of manifold and ordered freedom that makes an appropriate fit for the established fine arts and at the same time may extend to such plausible analogies as childish or savage forms of mimesis, game, and ritual, and to numerous forms of civilized gratification which

4. *Philosophical Investigations*, trans. G. E. M. Anscombe (New York, 1970), p. 32e, §67.
   5. *Critique of Judgment*, trans. J. C. Meredith (Oxford, 1911), §45.

Kant himself snubbed as merely sensate and pleasurable or amusing.[6]

The aesthetic or artistic emphasis on the concept of play invites us to conceive different kinds of play as realizing, with different degrees of prominence, three insistent aesthetic features: that is, expression, mimesis, and design (or pattern)— corresponding broadly to the three Kantian divisions (and features) of art: the speaking, the shaping, and the art of the beautiful play of sensation. The Kantian general aesthetic requirements of disinterest and of purposiveness without purpose reappear today in clauses concerning convention, unreality, isolation, autotelism, and freedom which make the definitions of play according to Huizinga and his successors.

"Play," however, is only one of two terms which commonly appear side by side, as if all but synonymous in recent literature of play theory. The other term is "game." The two terms are used almost interchangeably—as the French *jeu* is translated either *play* or *game*. It is my notion that the terms are not in fact synonymous, and that "play" does not always entail "game" —that "game" in fact is only one very special kind of play. Sometimes we play games; at other times, as when we gambol, or romp, or swim, or walk in the woods, or yodel, or doodle, we are just playing. At this juncture another of the inheritors of Kant and Huizinga, Roger Caillois, editor of the journal *Diogène*, comes to our aid with his articles on "play" and "games" published in 1955 and 1957.[7] Whatever else we may say in general about play and game, however many classes or qualities of either we distinguish, two common principles seem to Caillois certain: one a childlike, spontaneous principle of improvisation and insouciant self-expression (*paidia*), the other a sort of perverse complementary principle of self-imposed obstacle or deliberate convention of hindrance (*ludus*). It is never enough, for very long, to skip and gambol. We play leapfrog or hopscotch. "The unfettered leap of joy," says Schiller, "becomes a dance; the aimless gesture, a graceful and articulate miming speech."[8]

With convention, and only with convention, can the element of game enter into play. The idea of convention might carry us also very quickly in the direction of language, and into language games (that is to say, into the logical problem of shift-

6. Ibid., §45, §46.
7. Expanded into a book, *Les Jeux et les hommes* (1958, 1967) [*Man, Play, and Games*, trans. Meyer Barash (New York, 1961)].
8. *On the Aesthetic Education of Man*, Letter 27.

ing frames of reference). But a different idea from that is more relevant to my present purpose. And that is the idea of game as competition. Convention in games is the opportunity for and invitation to an orderly and limited competition.

The game of pure competitive skill (or *agōn*) and the game of chance (*alea*) are two forms of play which Caillois is specially interested in, which he would insistently distinguish, but which nevertheless he sees as very closely related. It is my own notion, though I think I need not argue it here at length, that chance has such a close affinity for competition that it is just as often an element intrinsic to some kind of competitive game (dice, poker, bridge) as it is a pure form (lottery, Russian roulette), where, as Caillois instructs us, it may be conceived as inviting only the passive surrender of the player to the decree of fate.

The relation of competitive game-play to forms of conspicuously aesthetic play may be very interesting and very difficult to state. The concept of mimesis[9] may be the hinge on which a comparison most instructively turns. A tragic drama is a mimesis of a combat (involving often murder and war), but no combat actually occurs in this drama, at least none corresponding to that which is mimed. A game of chess or a game of bridge may be conceived as a mimic warfare (*Ludimus effigiem belli*). But that is to say that such a game proceeds according to a set of conventions which are the conditions for a very strictly limited but nevertheless *actual* combat—one which bears a relation of *analogy* to larger combats and is in that sense a *mimesis* of them. (Let nobody be in any doubt about the actuality of the combat in chess or bridge or poker.)

At least two special sorts of connection can obtain between these two sorts of play, the aesthetic and the competitive. (1) The element of combat in the sheer game can be stylized and arrested in the shape of puzzle or problem, and in this case it is altered in the direction of aesthetic design. This happens notably in the kind of compositions known as chess "problems." (2) A second kind of rapprochement is of more direct literary significance: it happens that the competitive game can appear internally to the art play, as part of the story. And here the game may be treated with either more or less precise regard for its technical details, and in either case it may manifest either more or less formal and aesthetic interest as it seems to function either more or less as

9. Caillois's alignment of *agōn*, *alea*, *mimicry*, and yet another thing, *ilinx* (the vertigo of the roller coaster or ferris wheel), as four ways of escape from reality, and hence as four species of play, is a tidy unification which stands a little to one side of my own purpose.

an interior duplication or symbol of the gamesome or ludic nature which, in some sense, we may discover as a character of the work as a whole.[10]

II

Before I plunge more directly into the proposed topic of this paper—the game of cards in Pope's *The Rape of the Lock*—let me attempt one further classical perspective, this time invoking not Plotinus but Plato himself, in an analytic mood which is pretty much the opposite of anything Neoplatonic. I have in mind that dialogue in which a rhapsode, that is, a professional declaimer of Homeric poetry and a professor of poetry, is given a destructive Socratic quizzing. The question insistently, if engagingly, pursued is this: whether a professor of poetry, or for that matter his model and inspiration the poet, knows anything at all, or has anything to teach, in his own right. It appears that he does not. If he knows anything about medicine, for instance, or about steering a ship, or spinning wool, it will be in virtue of exactly the same kind of knowledge as the practitioner of those arts would have. The mind of a poet—Homer, for instance—who talks about nearly everything, is just a grab bag of various kinds of knowledge which are the proper business of various other kinds of experts. The application is made even to the knowledge of epic games:

"... does not Homer speak a good deal about arts, in a good many places? For instance, about chariot-driving. . . . Tell me what Nestor says to his son Antilochus. . . ." " 'Bend thyself in the polished car slightly to the left of them; and call to the right-hand horse and goad him on, while your hand slackens his reins' " [*Iliad* XXIII. 355 ff.]. . . . "Now, Ion, will a doctor or a charioteer be the better judge whether Homer speaks correctly or not in these lines?" "A charioteer, of course." "Because he has this art, or for some other reason?" "No, because it is his art" [*Ion*, 537-A].

Almost any modern reader, I suppose, is likely to believe that this question raised by Socrates is unimportant for the study of poetry. Forgetting perhaps that the Greeks of Plato's time did

10. In another essay in *Yale French Studies* 41 (1968), a member of the French Department at the University of Chicago, Bruce Morrissette, examines games as the centers of structures in the game-like fictions of Robbe-Grillet.

actually look on Homer as a chief authority about chariot rac-
ing, warfare, generalship, and related topics, and that in a sense
he was such an authority, the modern reader will think of poetry
about games, either outdoor or indoor games, most likely in the
light of some such passage as the following near the end of the
first book of Wordsworth's *Prelude*, where he recalls some of his
childhood pastimes:

> Eager and never weary we pursued
> Our home amusements by the warm peat-fire
> At evening . . .
>   round the naked table, snow-white deal,
> Cherry or maple, sate in close array,
> And to the combat, Lu or Whist, led on
> A thick-ribbed Army; not as in the world
> Neglected and ungratefully thrown by
> Even for the very service they had wrought,
> But husbanded through many a long campaign.
> Uncouth assemblage was it, where no few
> Had changed their functions, some, plebeian cards,
> Which Fate beyond the promise of their birth
> Had glorified, and call'd to represent
> The persons of departed Potentates.
> Oh! with what echoes on the Board they fell!
> Ironic Diamonds, Clubs, Hearts, Diamonds, Spades,
> A congregation piteously akin.
> Cheap matter did they give to boyish wit,
> Those sooty knaves, precipitated down
> With scoffs and taunts, like Vulcan out of Heaven,
> The paramount Ace, a moon in her eclipse,
> Queens, gleaming through their splendor's last decay,
> And Monarchs, surly at the wrongs sustain'd
> By royal visages.

[I. 534–36, 541–62]

The main thing we learn about that card game is that the cards
were dog-eared, very badly beaten up—a medley of survivals
from several different packs, some of them having been doctored
or altered to raise their value. A poet, we will of course say,
looks on a given technical routine, like playing cards, in just the
light needed for whatever he is trying to say in his poem; and
we will most likely imply that the precise rules and play of the
game—certainly its niceties and finesses—are not likely to be a
part of the poet's concern. Maybe a writer of stories about base-
ball—a Ring Lardner, a Bernard Malamud—will have to know
what he is talking about in order to convey the appearance and

feel of the thing. A very good story about chess, Vladimir Nabo-
kov's *The Defence*, manages to create a vivid impression of a
boy's experience of learning to play and of becoming a master.
In Stefan Zweig's celebrated *Schachnovelle* (*The Royal Game*),
the psychology of obsessive, schizoid game play seems to me
less finely informed with any authentic chess experience.[11] A
story involving a card game or a chess game is likely enough to
tell us something very indistinct about the game itself, or else
something utterly absurd. In one story about chess that I re-
member, an old man is able to cheat another old man, his in-
veterate rival, by allowing his beard to curl about a rook at one
corner of the board, thus lulling his opponent into a sense that
the rook is not there. Short stories have been written indeed
around the actual score of chess games—but these are just that,
chess stories, and they appear for the most part in chess maga-
zines. In one of Samuel Beckett's zero-degree novels, *Murphy*,
there is the actual score of a chess game, played in a kind of
madhouse, but the point of the game is its utter absurdity.
Neither player (neither male nurse nor mental patient) is able
to *find* the other—they play simultaneous games of solitaire.
Faulkner's short story "Was" (*Go Down, Moses* [1942]) manages
two hands of poker, one "Draw" and one "Stud," with an ar-
tistic economy made possible in part by the concealment and
bluffing which are intrinsic to this game that gives a name to the
studiously inexpressive countenance.

Wordsworth, we are told by his friend Coleridge, was a spe-
cialist in "spreading the tone." Generalization, even vagueness,
in imagery, idea, and mood, was his forte. It is difficult to imag-
ine a poem by Wordsworth in which a precise and technically
correct narration of a hand at cards would have been relevant to
his purpose. Is the same true for Alexander Pope? I have an idea
that most of us, if only from our general habit of reading poetry,
would read into Pope for the first time with no more expectation
of finding an exactly described card game than in Wordsworth. I
remember that when about twenty-five years ago I first studied
The Rape of the Lock closely enough to realize fully the pres-
ence of the card game, I was very much surprised. I had a special
sort of delight in the discovery—because I myself have always
been moderately addicted to table games, and so it gave me plea-
sure to work the puzzle out—but also because the precision of
the details seemed to me in a special way an achievement appro-

11. George Steiner, *Extraterritorial: Papers on Literature and the Lan-
guage Revolution* (New York, 1971), produces some ringing evocations
from Nabokov, Zweig, and other chess sources (pp. 47-57).

priate to Pope's art as a couplet poet and also a specially precise and exquisite miniature of this whole poem. For the modern eye or ear, this game may often pass in a somewhat sunken or muted way beneath the very colorful and rhythmic surface symbols in which the action is carried. It seems difficult to say to what degree it was hidden for Pope's readers, many of whom presumably were better up on the game of ombre than we are. For us, I think, part of the pleasure can come from the fact that the game is not awkwardly obtrusive or obviously technical, but is woven so subtly into the poetic fabric. It seems to me a merit of the passage that one may well read it without full awareness of what is going on.

III

There is now no way for me to avoid a degree of technicality in my exposition. The game of ombre as Pope narrates it is an impressive blend of visual technique and gamesmanship or technique according to Hoyle—the Hoyle of that day, a French book on ombre and piquet, translated into English in a volume entitled *The Court Gamester*, published at London only a few years after Pope's poem, 1719.[12] Beginning with a writer in *MacMillan's Magazine* in 1874 and a certain Lord Aldenham, who somewhat frivolously devoted a large book to *The Game of Ombre* (3rd ed., 1902), a succession of modern writers have commented on Pope's game. Geoffrey Tillotson's exposition in an appendix to his Twickenham edition of *The Rape of the Lock* in 1940 triggered a contentious correspondence in the columns of the *TLS*.[13] A short essay of my own, published in 1950, was an effort to tidy up the tradition and improve on it. Take a deck of cards and remove the 8s, 9s, and 10s of each suit (12 cards in all), leaving forty. Seat three players at a table, Belinda and two male courtiers. The man to Belinda's left, probably her chief antagonist, the Baron, deals nine cards to each player (27 in all); he puts the remaining 13 cards down in a stock or kitty. Belinda bids first, gets the bid, and declares spades trumps. The players then discard weak cards and draw an equal number of replacements from the kitty. The order of strength in the cards is not as in modern contract bridge. It differs from hand to hand, de-

12. *Le Royal Jeu de l'Hombre et du Piquet* (Paris, 1685). The English version includes a substantial quotation from Pope.
13. See especially F. W. Bateson, 1 March 1941, p. 108.

pending on which suit is trumps. For the present hand, the top
card is the Ace of spades, Spadillio; next the 2 of spades, Manillio;
next the Ace of clubs, Basto; then the spades in order, King
down to three. The red Aces are lower than the face cards in
their suits. In order to win the hand Belinda has to take more
tricks than her stronger opponent—5 against 4, or 4 against 3
and 2.

Four tricks unroll smoothly for Belinda as she leads in succes-
sion Spadillio, Manillio, Basto, and the King of spades—pulling
smaller spades from her opponents—except that on the third
and fourth tricks the third player, the anonymous one, fails to
come through. So the Baron may well have the last trump, the
Queen. Belinda has two winning cards left in her hand, the King
of hearts and the King of clubs. As the hand turns out, we can
see that it doesn't matter which King she plays. She gets her fifth
trick sooner or later. But what of the possibilities at that appar-
ently crucial moment as she leads on the fifth trick? Which
King shall she play?—if she is to live up to the epithet "skilful"
bestowed on her by the poet at the commencement of the
scene. ("The skilful Nymph reviews her Force with Care.")

We are not told every card in each player's hand. The xs in my
chart indicate the degree of indeterminacy in Pope's specifica-
tions. But the probabilities may be considered. In the event, for
instance, that the Baron has the Queen of spades and four dia-
monds, then no matter how the diamond tricks are divided be-
tween the Baron and the third player, producing either a win
with five tricks for the Baron, or a 4-3-2 win for Belinda, or a
4-4-1 Remise or drawn game, the outcome will not *depend* upon
Belinda's lead. Certain more complicated suppositions about the
Baron's holding one or two low hearts or one or two low clubs
(but *not* both hearts and clubs) can be made, and I have made
them, I believe exhaustively.[14] I will not recite them here. The
upshot of my analysis is that only if the third player captured a
diamond lead on the sixth trick and then went on to produce
the 4-4-1 Remise by taking three more diamond tricks himself

14. On the supposition that the Baron had the Queen of spades, two or
three diamonds, and one or two low hearts or one or two low clubs (but
not both hearts and clubs), and that his diamonds would take one or two
tricks and then lead into the third player's hand, so that the Baron would
throw his low heart or hearts or low club or clubs on a last trick or tricks
won by the third player with a diamond or diamonds—on this supposition,
the score would be 4-3-2, again a win for Belinda—different only in a non-
essential way from her 5-4 win if she led her King of hearts (or King of
clubs) on the fifth trick.

	BELINDA		THE BARON		SIR ANONYM
I. BELINDA ⟶	Spadillio Ace ♠		♠		♠
II. BELINDA ⟶	Manillio Two ♠		♠		♠
III. BELINDA ⟶	Basto Ace ♣		♠		Plebeian Card ✕
IV. BELINDA ⟶	King ♠		Knave ♠		Pam Knave ♣
V. BARON ⟶	King ♣		Queen ♠		✕
VI. BARON ⟶	✕		King ◇		✕
VII. BARON ⟶	✕		Queen ◇		✕
VIII. BARON ⟶	Queen ♡		Knave ◇		✕
IX. BELINDA ⟶	King ♡		Ace ♡		✕

(the Baron throwing down low hearts or clubs— but *not* both), could Belinda suffer an *unfavorable* outcome which *depended* on her leading the wrong suit at the fifth trick. But on this supposition, that the third player held four diamonds, or perhaps on any supposition at all, Belinda at the fifth trick could suppose very little about the number of either hearts or clubs in the Baron's hand and hence would have little reason to prefer either a club or a heart lead. A test by the calculus of foreseeable possibilities would be the correct test of Belinda's skill (of whether her play of the hand is, in the terms of Roger Caillois, a true *agōn* or is largely an instance of *alea*), but such a test will not quite pan out. We fall back on a more superficial, human, and plausible test by appearances. The discard of the Knave of clubs (Pam, who "mow'd down Armies in the Fights of Lu") by the third player on the fourth trick does look like a discard from weakness. Possibly his only club? In that case, the Baron may be thought somewhat more likely to have clubs than hearts. Dramatically, if not technically and mathematically, the Knave of clubs, so conspicuously heralded as a discard, advertises a certain plausibility in her next lead of the King of clubs. Belinda is a society belle and not a Charles H. Goren. It is by the standards of the polite card table (not necessarily profound) that we shall measure her skill. She is no doubt skillful in her own esteem. She leads her King of clubs, loses it to the Queen of spades. The Baron pours his diamonds apace for three tricks, his Knave on the eighth trick drawing even her Queen of hearts. Then the Baron's Ace of hearts (lower than the face cards) is forced out on the last trick, to fall a victim to the King lurking in her hand. "The Nymph exulting fills with Shouts the Sky,/The Walls, the Woods, and long Canals reply."

The pictorial features of a deck of cards, the royal faces, the plain plebeian spots, are well calculated for the symbolism of an epic battle (the "routed Army . . ./Of *Asia's* Troops, and *Africk's* Sable Sons"); for that of palace revolutions ("The hoary Majesty of *Spades*. . . . The Rebel-*Knave*"); and for that of the most important business of court life, the battle of the sexes (the warlike Amazonian Queen of spades, the wily Knave of diamonds, the "captive" Queen of hearts). Belinda's hubristic first sweep of four tricks, the sudden blow from fate, or the peripeteia, of the fifth trick, her narrow escape from the jaws of ruin and codille, her last-trick triumph and exultation—all these develop her portrait as the mock-heroine of a melodramatized tragic-epic action.

IV
.

An episode of epic games was one of the dozen or so ingre-
dients prescribed for the epic poem by René le Bossu in his
Treatise of 1675. But what is the significance of such contests
in the epic structure? The answer, broadly, must be that epic
games are a miniature emblem of the contest which is the heroic
panorama of the whole poem. Heroic fighters and leaders relax
and indulge themselves, not in games of tiddlywinks, or even
ombre, but in huge, manly, spectacular, circus-like feats: chariot
races, footraces, boxing, discus-throwing, spear-throwing, ar-
chery. The games have a kind of ready-made or prefabricated
relevance in the epic context—as in post-Homeric Greece the
epic spirit is annually recapitulated in the festival games.

That general kind of significance, however, is not all. The epic
poets in the Western succession each seems to have treated the
episode of the heroic games in his poem in such a way as to con-
fer on it some much more special slant. Happily for my purpose,
I am not the first to have thought of this. My colleague Professor
George Lord, for instance, has written an excellent essay[15]
pointing out how the funeral games in honor of Patroclus in
Iliad XXIII (which, we have seen, the rhapsode Ion knew so well
by heart) are not simply a résumé of the anger, division, and dis-
courtesy among the Greek leaders with which the poem opens,
but a kind of image in reverse, where courtesy and reconcilia-
tion—i.e., good sportsmanship—have their day as a countertheme
to the "wrath" of which the poet has been singing from the
opening word of the first book. Paris had long ago *stolen* Helen
from Menelaus, thus starting the war. In the first book of the
poem, Agamemnon at first angrily refuses to give up a captive
girl ("Her I will not let go"), then does so with bad grace and
snatches another, the property of Achilles. (Hence all that gi-
gantic sulking; hence the reverses of the Greeks on the plains be-
fore Troy and the death of Patroclus.) In the chariot race of the
funeral games, where the second prize is a fine mare, Antilochus
at first beats out Menelaus for that prize by some dirty driving,
but then he turns around, concedes the point, and gives the
mare to Menelaus, who in turn gives her back to Antilochus.
Sports, after all, are the appropriate arena for good sportsman-
ship—which is a ludic image of such virtues as courtesy, chivalry,
and gallantry. *Iliad* XXIII, says Professor Lord, is a comic reca-
pitulation or self-mockery of the tragic heroism of the whole.

The games which are narrated, by perhaps an elderly Homer

15. "Epic Mockery," *Touchstone* 2 (1965): 23-28.

or by perhaps a second Homer, in Book VIII of the *Odyssey* at the court of King Alcinoüs in the charmed kingdom of the Phaeacians, have about them both something of the healthy athletic mood of a college track meet, and the reveries which today characterize the secret life of Walter Mitty. In the *Iliad*, battle-scarred warriors lay aside armament for a moment of major league game-playing. In the *Odyssey*, the shipwrecked stranger, handsome and tall, but eldering, worn, and sorrowful, watches as the younger men among the oar-loving Phaeacians compete in footracing, wrestling, jumping, discus-throwing, and boxing. After a while somebody throws a few taunts at the stranger: "You old scrubby-looking sea captain, you wouldn't be so good at games of skill and strength like these, would you?" And then the transformation—the sudden heartwarming assertion. "I don't know about that," says the unrecognized hero of the Trojan-horse exploit. And he picks up a big stone discus, bigger than any the others have been handling; he gives it a skillful whirl, and it flies out a long way beyond what anybody else has done. Then this old stranger utters a boast, telling them what he can do if they wish to challenge him in boxing, wrestling, or footracing. Or, for that matter, in archery. He says he is very good at handling the polished bow, sending an arrow into a throng of foes. We all know, of course, what that bodes for certain insolent suitors who are at that very moment living high in the halls of a house at Ithaca.

It was a commonplace of Renaissance criticism, from the Italians of the sixteenth century, to Samuel Johnson, that Homer was the more profoundly original epic poet, but that Virgil achieved a greater degree of polished perfection. Virgil had no doubt a problem in how to give some original twist to the funeral games held in Book V of the *Aeneid*. The ideas of age and youth, paternity, filial piety, reverence, and a corresponding bright hope for the future are the keys to what he did. The whole poem is a prophecy and a preview of the history of Rome; and the more poetically successful first six books are prognostic of the more propagandistic second six. So in Book V, the boatrace, footrace, boxing, riding exhibition, and shooting matches, are a genealogical celebration, and both a rehearsal for war (like rugby at Eton) and a prefiguration of events to occur in the second half of the poem on the plains of Latium. Virgil, it has been said, was probably the first great writer to turn play into work.[16]

This survey of epic games might go on for a long time. But I compress it now by coming down to Pope's immediate pred-

16. George Lord, in a letter.

ecessor and a major model and sounding board for allusions in *The Rape of the Lock*—Milton, of course, in the games resorted to by the devils in the second book of *Paradise Lost*. *Paradise Lost* is remarkable for the spiritualization and subtle internalization which are pervasive throughout the grand murky and spiraling baroque cosmological structure. We read the war in Heaven or the allegory of Satan, Sin, and Death at the gates to chaos in our own hearts if we read them vividly at all. "Which way I fly is Hell; myself am Hell" (IV. 75). So it is only just, and the description is full of genius, when Satan's legions, left to their own amusement, express the consuming restlessness of their new state by setting out on long exploring expeditions through the dismal semichaotic realm of fire and ice which they have recently colonized. Even more acutely and poetically, Milton has some of them, more philosophic souls, sit down to animated disputes on the theological issues of freedom and necessity which touch them so closely. At these infernal games, there are wing, foot, and chariot races too, there is demonic harping and song. There is no card game. Cards, gambling, and drinking are possible demonic associations in some anti-saloon-league context, but such would be too low for the heroic damned of Milton's scene. The parlor game which *we* have in view would be obviously too dainty.

V

The contrasting wider context of the big epic tradition does much of Pope's work for him. The work is invited in a very special way by the other main part of the context, the immediate social one. It is perhaps easiest to invest literature with the colors of a game when the life represented is courtly, artificial, ritualistic, playful. Such a life, lived with a high degree of intensity and burnish, *is* a game—or a jest, as Pope and his closest friends might have said. It can also be a special sort of warfare. Pope's letter to Mrs. Arabella Fermor, prefixed to his second edition, in which the game of ombre first appears, may be read as a language game of teasing and flattery. It is not my idea that the poem itself can be said, in any useful sense, to be a game played by Pope either with himself or with his reader. The poem, however, is in a very notable way a poem about a gamesome way of life. The background life of the poem, the powders, patches, furbelows, flounces, and brocades, the smiles and curls, the china, the silver, the billet-doux, the lapdogs, and the fopperies and flirtations, are built-in elements of the higher social gamesmanship. The poem absorbs and represents this situation in a very immediate and vivid image, and thus in a very thorough sense it is a game poem.

Here we may as well recall some relevant insights of the late Dr. Eric Berne, whose best-selling book entitled *Games People Play* (1964) was developed from his less racy *Transactional Analysis in Psychotherapy* (1961). "Games" in the somewhat extrapolated but persuasive sense of certain slantwise and fictive stratagems employed in a variety of neurotic types of aggression. Instead of facing each other on the level, as adults, the role-players of Dr. Berne's analyses suffered either from assumptions of parental hauteur and inquisition or from childlike poses, sulks, and tantrums. They played, among many others, certain "Party" and "Sexual" games, to which he gave such names as "Kiss Off," "Ain't It Awful," "Rapo," "Indignation," "Let's You and Him Fight," and "Uproar." "Favors to none, to all she smiles extends."—"At every word a reputation dies."—"The Peer now spread the glittering Forfex wide."—"Then flashed the living lightning from her eyes."—"To arms, to arms! the fierce Virago cries."—"And bass and treble voices strike the skies." Let us think here also of the stubbornly contested betrothal gambits played between Congreve's Millamant and Mirabell. Think of the somberly mythologized combat between mentor and pupil, the dark luster, of Swift's *Cadenus and Vanessa*. In *The Rape of the Lock*, we witness the gladiatorial aspect of sex and courtship. Belinda "Burns to encounter two adventrous Knights,/At *Ombre* singly to decide their Doom."

The other epic games we have noticed are all highly episodic, off-center developments in the vast poems where they occur. The game of ombre occurs in a central or focal position which could be appropriate only in a poem of rococo dimensions. The game of ombre is the least deadly and most conventionalized combat in Pope's poem, and yet it is a real combat (game combats I have said and will repeat are real) and it is the most precisely delineated and most complete combat of the whole poem, appearing in the center as a kind of reducing or concentrating mirror of the larger, more important, but less decisive, kinds of strife and hints of strife that both precede and follow it.

Here perhaps we can invoke, with only a slight and forgivable degree of exaggeration, a pattern developed by Professor Cedric Whitman for ordering the complicated and lavishly repetitious procession of quarrels, councils, speeches, feasts, libations, sacrifices, battles, triumphs, defeats, and burials which make up the *Iliad* of Homer. There is a kind of center for the *Iliad* in two

anomalously conjunct nighttime episodes, the embassy to
Achilles of Book IX and the (perhaps genetically intrusive)
reconnaissance by the scout Dolan and his violent end in Book
X. Coming up to these and moving away from them are two
sequences of events and of days that unfold in mirror (or butter-
fly) patterns of partly antithetic, partly similar images, "ring
patterns." And this is in the manner of those Grecian pottery
vases or urns that have friezes of figures on them converging on
some central figure in a reflecting pattern (the huge vases of
Dipylon ware, for instance, manufactured at about the time
when Homer most likely was writing, 750 to 700 B.C.). (Or
think of that "leaf-fringed legend" or "brede of marble men and
maidens," priest and sacrificial heifer, that move, no doubt sym-
metrically from two sides, toward the "green altar" in Keats's
"Ode on a Grecian Urn.")

The card game at the center of Pope's poem is not only the
most precise and least earnest combat of the poem. It is at the
same time, though animated, the least animate, the most com-
pletely a work of art, in that the actors described so lovingly,
with such detail and color, are neither supernatural nor human
agents. They are in fact only cardboard—though the ambitious
animus of Belinda and the Baron are just behind them, and even
the sylphs "Descend, and sit on each important Card." Move
back from this artful center toward the beginning of the poem,
into the second canto, and we find the human epic element of a
journey or expedition (as prescribed by Bossu), Belinda's boat
ride on the Thames, which is convoyed by swarms of supernatural
agents, the sylphs, in attitudes of keen vigilance and readiness
for combat. Look then next in the opposite direction. The game
of ombre *ends* in Belinda's moment of greatest triumph. And
this is followed almost immediately by the Baron's counterattack
and victory as he snips off the lock. This is *his* moment of
greatest triumph. (If he loses the hand at ombre, he wins the
canto.) Immediately thereafter, in the fourth canto, we return
to the motif of a journey, this time a descent into a grotesque
allegorical region of the underworld (much as at the end of the
first canto of *The Faerie Queene* of Spenser). The element of
the supernatural, or preternatural, is prominent again now, both
in the destination and in the traveler, who is an agent of earth, a
gnome, descending to the Cave of Spleen on no benevolent mis-
sion.

Now move back to the very beginning of the poem, the first
canto. After the opening epic invocation, we first get our bear-
ings in a scene of the human and comic everyday, with Belinda
and her dog, rousing at noon to an afternoon of adventure. In

the first canto, too, appear the epic elements of extended discourse and encyclopedic knowledge, and of supernatural agency, as the doctrine concerning the elemental spirits is expounded by the guardian sylph, with premonitions of impending disaster. At the end of the canto, Belinda with the assistance of Betty arms herself like an epic hero for battle and at the same time practices her ritual of self-worship at the toilet table. At the level of such motifs, perhaps we must admit that a degree of sinuosity complicates our pursuit of an overall symmetry. The chief later moments of ritual, for instance, occur in the second canto with the Baron's piled up French romances, the gloves and garters sacrificed to the power of Love, and in the ombre canto with the ceremony of the coffee mill and "altars of Japan." We have what may perhaps be called only a complementary pattern of different emphasis, when we observe that the extended anaphoristic sequences of hyperbole and bathos ("While Fish in Streams, or Birds delight in Air,/Or in a Coach and Six the *British* Fair."), both in the author's own voice and in the voices of Belinda, the Baron, Thalestris, and Clarissa, are a conspicuous feature of the second half of the poem, beginning at the end of the third canto and recurring through the fourth and at the start of the fifth. But with these sustained speeches, especially with the inflammatory speech of Thalestris to Belinda near the end of the fourth canto and the ensuing episode of the vacuous Sir Plume's confrontation with the Baron, we are on lowly human and comic ground again, in a position roughly the counterpart of the opening of the poem in our geometric scheme. (The speeches as such may be set against the long initial discourse of the sylph.) The comic vein is conspicuously continued in the fifth and last canto with the lecture on good humour delivered by Clarissa and rejected by Belinda, and in the closing furious pitched battle between the belles and beaus.

The fury of this combat has no counterpart in the first half of the poem. We may say that the airy hints of danger and the vigilance in the first two cantos have been stepped up by the gamesome duel of the third canto, to a degree of violence where the Baron's rude aggression and the ensuing turmoil are poetically plausible. And now Pope finds himself in a special dilemma, and with also a special opportunity for brilliance, in this noisy combat. The more physically it is realized, the less it can be satisfactorily resolved. And so, as shouts "To Arms," clapping fans, rustling silks, and cracking whalebones shade into death at the eyes of fair ones, a show of Homeric gods in epic simile, and an allusion to Jove's "golden Scales in Air," weighing the "Men's Wits against the Lady's Hair," the strife shifts into the mode of metaphor and symbol, or of myth—like so many irresolvable combats we have known in story and on stage. Belinda resorts to throwing a physical pinch of snuff at the Baron and even threatens him with a deadly bodkin. But the only injury inflicted is a huge sneeze, which reechoes to the high dome. Apparently on the waves of sound or air generated by this sneeze, or by Belinda's cry of *"Restore the Lock,"* which too rebounds from the vaulted roofs, the Lock itself mounts and disappears. "But trust the Muse—she saw it upward rise,/Tho' mark'd by none but quick Poetic Eyes." Like a "sudden Star," or a comet, it "shot thro' liquid Air,/And drew behind a radiant *Trail of Hair.*" Vanished, it assumes the mythic proportions of the founder of Rome, Romulus, who withdrew to the heavens during a thunderstorm, or the constellated locks of the Egyptian queen Berenice (virtuously sacrificed for the safety of her husband), or the planet Venus worshiped by lovers at the Lake in St. James's Park.

Variation in kinds of combat is one of the main structural modes, or principles of progression, in this poem. The minutely delineated cardboard combat of the central canto is the concave mirror in which, as Samuel Johnson might have put it, the ultimately sidereal reaches of the rest of the poem (the sun of the first three cantos, the stars of the last) are focused—and clarified. Or, to shift my metaphor, and to bring in the concluding words of the short essay which I wrote on the poem twenty years ago: "The game of Ombre expands and reverberates delicately in the whole poem. The episode is a microcosm of the whole poem, a brilliant epitome of the combat between the sexes which is the theme of the whole."

1970

IMITATION AS FREEDOM—1717-1798

I have to begin with an embarrassing confession:—namely, that I suffer from a wrong theoretical orientation for this series of papers.[1] That is, I am more than a little inclined to question the critical accuracy or usefulness of the antithesis "necessity and freedom" (tradition and innovation, or, as we used to say when I was young, convention and revolt). This looks to me like a quasi-genetic sort of distinction—one which, for most or all critical or descriptive purposes, I should wish to translate into a corresponding distinction between the idiom (or language) which a poet inherits and what he manages to say by the use of or in virtue of that idiom. A poem is not a revolt, but an expression. At a meeting of savants which took place last winter in this city, I heard it said that such modern phenomena as the city riots of the past few summers (Watts, Detroit, Newark) were "happenings" and in that sense works of art, community expressions and hence community art works. This was said before the university sit-ins of last spring had occurred. These too, I feel sure, would have qualified. Academic, no doubt. But still art works. *Literature and Revolution* is the title of a recent volume in the series *Yale French Studies* (No. 39, 1967). A lovingly detailed diagram of a Molotov cocktail, we know, appeared during August 1967 as the cover ornament of a *Review of Books* published in this city. But I do not subscribe to that orientation. I do not accept a view of literature as essentially a rebellion. I think rather of an order of expressions, and of a departure from these which is a new expression but not a destruction. I think of the classic linguistic terms *langue* and *parole*, where *parole* is a particular utterance which has significance only as it is heard against the ground of a *language*. The little bronze figurines which in the Crocean analogy are thrown into a crucible and along with mere pieces of scrap metal lose their shape in contributing to the mass of the great statue are not in fact a good analogy to the words and ideas, the proverbs, the old metaphors, the jokes, the meters, rhymes, and rhetorical patterns which enter into a new work of literature. The old literary materials—even if strangely twisted—have to retain some sort of shape, or they do not function.

Freedom in poetic art?—it may be a sense of boldness, inventiveness, or independence, which the poet enjoys as he works

---

1. This paper was one of a series, under the general title "Necessity and Freedom in Lyric Form," read at the English Institute, Columbia University, New York, September 3-6, 1968. A select bibliography of secondary works was added to the printed version; see below, following note 17.

and which he thus imputes to his work. It may be some observable or even measurable kind of departure from what prevails or what has been done before—in short it may be novelty—though what relation to deeper literary values this has may be hard to decide. Or a Kantian sort of "freedom in the play of our cognitive faculties" may be indeed coterminous with, all but identical with, poetic achievement! Freedom *is* poetry—and poetry is meaning—or excellence of meaning. I think this in fact is a very frequently implied equation, which supports and seems to give deep significance to our use of the term "freedom" in literary criticism. What I undertake today is to conduct a sort of mixed discourse, flourishing perhaps a few dramatic and biographical aspects of poetic freedom in eighteenth-century England, but moving so far as I am able, in each instance, toward a description of what the poet in fact accomplished, or managed to say, by the exercise of, or in virtue of, his liberty—and, no less, in virtue of the enabling restraints of his bondage.

One shorter confession too: I am unable to distinguish with any confidence between poetic "form" and poetic "substance." True, there are ways of describing the whole achieved expression of a poem which bring out the notion of structure or "form" of meaning, rather than meaning as personal experience or as doctrine or teachable content. We can attempt to work always toward that formal emphasis. We can take pains also to say something, as often as possible, about such technical aspects of poetry as meter and rhyme, or syntax and vocabulary. But I do not think the term "form" in our rubric is meant to restrict us to any kind of structural, or technical, or stylistic features of poems. Despite the bad analogy of the Crocean figurines, I think we must consider ourselves invited to take "form" in a more nearly general Crocean sense—form as achieved expression—as, in fact, poetry—or, as we have just seen, freedom.

The period 1717 to 1798 in England (I have chosen the dates only somewhat arbitrarily) produces poems by Pope, by Swift, by Blake, by Wordsworth and Coleridge. But many of these, and among them the most exceptional poems of the century, occur near the beginning and near the end. The critical imagination in quest of the poetical essence of this period very readily, I believe, contracts, at least momentarily, to some shorter inside period—for the sake of neatness and convenience, say, from 1744 the death of Pope to 1784 the death of Johnson. Here in fact are found most of the characteristic lyrics of the century. This was a relatively weak or dim inner period, a poetic valley of a shadow. It is shot through, nevertheless, with many interesting flashes; it is a time full of somewhat fatigued and straining traditions, transitions, retrospective creations, hard-won, even unconscious, freedoms. One motif intrinsic to the poetry of the whole century may be observed with special concentration here—the method, the bondage, and the main freedom of all English neo-classic and preromantic poetry—the principle of imitation or free-running parallel. Imitation not only of the full, ancient, and classical models, Homer or Pindar, Horace or Juvenal, but also, increasingly, as the classical models became, or may have seemed to become, used up, imitation of the whole British tradition and especially of the English poets who had already best imitated or paralleled the ancients—Spenser and Milton especially and, though he was still very near, Pope. Such names remind us immediately that imitation was enacted for the most part on a very large scale. Translated epics, georgics, or pastorals were one conspicuous, if relatively unoriginal, sort. There was more obvious originality and fun in either high or low burlesque, the various shades of mock-heroic and parody, and in the kind of free translation most specially and no doubt most properly called "imitation," the satiric London parallel to Horace or Juvenal. These large-scale poems, dominantly narrative or discursive, do not of themselves tell us very much about lyric form. They do, however, mark out perspectives. The idea that burlesque and imitation were Augustan avenues of departure from the solemn models and constricting genre norms of the tradition, and thus of escape into a large, free realm of poetic creation, was expounded about twenty years ago by Austin Warren. I assume it as a demonstrated or at least as a persuasively argued and now more or less commonly received principle, which we can invoke to advantage—if only we keep reiterating the compensating principle that the escape from models *was* freedom, *was* expression, *was* fun, only so long as the models were preserved and were present as fields of reference for the realization of the new meanings. An imitation of a classic model is always a reference *to* and only thus a departure *from* the model. When does this mesothesis of likeness and difference succeed in being a free, original, interesting, genuine, and poetic expression? I have already alluded to the difficulty of treating freedom as a critically inspectable value. The ironies of Pope's *Epistle* to a blockhead *Augustus* give us one example of true freedom, and hence of brilliance, in the imitative mode. Some of the pieces in Dryden's collection of Juvenal translations might be adduced to illustrate the average drabness of a more literal kind of transfer.

II

The title of my paper will perhaps already have suggested the
fact that I have chosen, not the method of intensive local poetic
analysis, but rather that of a wider survey, with somewhat cur-
sory allusion to select, perhaps arbitrarily select, examples.
1717 (June 3rd) is the date of Pope's first collected edition of
poems—the handsome volume (in both quarto and folio) with
the foldout frontispiece engraving of Pope as the straight and
slender young cavalier, which along with *Eloisa to Abelard* and
the *Verses to the Memory of an Unfortunate Lady* made R. K.
Root say that had Pope died then, he would be remembered to-
day as a prematurely cut-off Shelley of the Augustan age. 1717
(July 13th) is the date of another publication by Pope, the anon-
ymously edited miscellany *Poems on Several Occasions*, con-
taining a number of his own minor pieces. One of these, a poem
which he was ultimately to polish into one of the few finest
lyrics of the age, is a short classical imitation, the *Ode on Soli-
tude.* Later he claimed to have drafted this when he was twelve
years old. "Happy the man whose wish and care / A few paternal
acres bound." The imitative virtues of this poem are not of the
parodistic sort, but consist rather in its plenary, if synoptic, re-
alization of a theme classically enshrined in Virgilian Georgic,
Horatian Ode and Epode, and Senecan chorus, in epigrams of
Martial, and in Claudian's portrait of an aged farmer. The well-
established medley of "retirement" images, the rural felicity
and innocence, the hardihood and piety, had been rendered too
by Ben Jonson, by Marvell, by Dryden, and especially by Cowley
in the garland of translations with which he adorned his essays
on such topics as *Obscurity*, *Agriculture*, and *The Dangers of an
Honest Man in Much Company.* Cowley's verses were favorite
reading and quoting for Pope, and in the grotto and garden of
his later years Pope, as we have recently been instructed in sev-
eral opulent essays by Maynard Mack, was bringing off an elab-
orate re-enactment of the ancient ideal of georgic wisdom. In
what way did the stanzas of Pope, matured from his boyhood
until he was nearly fifty, succeed in being free, different from,
or more genuine and successful than, the English translations of
his predecessors? One may say of course that he did not translate,
but made his own poem, a distillate of a whole tradition and
spirit. There would be no way of refuting the assertion that al-
most any feature of this poem, especially any that we find subtle,
novel, or pleasing, is a part of its freedom and its secret. It is

with a sense of some arbitrariness, then, but perhaps not too
much, that I select for comment the extraordinary freedom and
éclat with which Pope has managed with the aid of meter and
rhyme and phrasal parallels to tame English syntax and word
order into something very much like the effects of juncture,
momentary contrast, pivoting, sorting, suspension, closure, and
completeness which are characteristic of Augustan Latin poetry.
Such management was a tact and power of the Augustan Latin
literary language. Other English poets, notably Milton through-
out *Paradise Lost*, give us varied anthologies in the torment of
the English language into curiously Latinate patterns. The essen-
tial refractoriness of English word order in submitting to this
discipline may be illustrated in these lines from Cowley's second
chorus in Seneca's *Thyestes*:

> *Me*, O ye Gods, on Earth, or else so near
> That I no Fall to Earth may fear,
> And, O Ye Gods, at a good Distance *seat*
> From the long Ruins of the Great.

Pope does something different. Taking advantage of the strong
points of his tiny stanza and the metrical parallels, he proceeds
more smoothly, calmly, and coolly, more efficiently, in his
Latinate accomplishment. A few *hints* of the Latin syntactic
models are all that we need and all that is possible in oral
delivery.

> *Beatus ille qui* procul negotiis,
>   ut prisca gens mortalium,
>   paterna rura bobus exercet suis
>   *solutus* omni faenore
> neque excitatur classico *miles* truci . . .
>   [Horace, *Epode* II, 1-5]

> Felix, qui propriis aevum transegit in arvis,
>   *ipsa* domus *puerum* quem vidit, *ipsa senem*.
>   [Claudian, *De Sene Veronensi*, 1-2]

Or, to strengthen the syntactic illustration a little, the following
from a different context in Horace, but one also very well known
to Pope and actually translated by him in another poem.

>   vos exemplaria Graeca
>   nocturna versate manu, versate diurna.
>   [*Epistle to the Pisos*, 268]

And thus (on the overleaf):

Happy the man whose wish and care
A few paternal acres bound,
Content to breathe his native air,
In his own ground.

Whose herds with milk, whose fields with bread,
Whose flocks supply him with attire,
Whose trees in summer yield him shade,
In winter fire.

III

1736, the date of Pope's final revision of "Happy the Man,"
brings this poem within a few years of the time when Gray prob-
ably wrote a first version of his *Elegy in a Country Churchyard*,
and when Collins was meditating or writing his *Odes*. Gray's
Elegy is a poem which shares very much in imagery and tone
with a poem of Pope's 1717 works, the *Verses* (later *Elegy*) *to
the Memory of an Unfortunate Lady*. Not only did Gray con-
tinue the Augustan line of wit, as F. R. Leavis I believe was the
first to insist, but he was so close in time to Pope that we ought
not to be surprised. The generation of Gray and Collins, the
Wartons, Shenstone, Lyttelton, Akenside, Mason—in short, of
the gentlemen whose poems made up Dodsley's *Collection of
Poems* (1748-1758)—was a generation deeply sunk in a nos-
talgia for the age and presence of the Augustans, and above all
for Pope. Collins indeed is more patently an early romantic
than Gray. Nowadays the trend is to stress his allegiance to the
Popular Superstitions, and hence to the kind of imagination
represented by fairies, witches, and hobgoblins, and to discover
in his *Ode on the Poetical Character* a sort of pan-sexual Narcis-
sism or mythopoeic movement of identically Divine and human
creation. But he was recognizably a classicist too, psycho-
logically Aeschylean and Aristotelian in his allegorical odes on
the passions, and metrically both Pindaric and Horatian.

The three tetrameters and the closing dimeter of Pope's little
Ode on Solitude were an imitation of a Horatian lyric stanza.
("Ode. Sapphick," he entitled it in 1726). Collins too, in the
quietest and best and best-known of his poems, the *Ode to Eve-
ning*, was thinking of an ode in the Horatian sense. He chose a
different, perhaps a bolder, way of approximating a Latin stanza,
the Fourth Asclepiadean. Take three iambic pentameter lines,
add two syllables (one foot) to the third line, and make sure
that the sixth syllable (the end of the third foot) is always ac-
cented and is always the end of a word. Five, five, three, three—

without rhyme. As with Horace, the stanzaic effect inheres in
the varied numbers and the phrasing against the numbers. True,
this kind of thing had been done in English before. It had been
done first by Milton in a youthful translation, straight from
Horace: "The Fifth Ode of Horace, Lib. 1. *Quis multa gracilis
te puer in Rosa,* Rendered almost word for word without Rhyme
according to the Latin Measure, as near as the Language will per-
mit."

> What slender Youth bedew'd with liquid odours
> Courts thee on Roses in some pleasant Cave,
> Pyrrha? for whom bind'st thou
> In wreaths thy golden Hair . . . ?

After Milton the stanza was used not only by Collins but some-
what stiffly by all three of the Wartons, who wore it, as Oliver
Elton says, almost like the badge of a group. "Only Collins," he
says, "brought out its music." The greater freedom, the finer
tone, of Collins's stanzas to the "nymph reserved," "chaste Eve"
("Now teach me, maid composed, To breathe some softened
strain"), comes in part through his novel extension of a classic
form to enclose or shape the stuff of a newly intensified land-
scape melancholy—a mood, as Yvor Winters argues, that subsists
purely in its symbols, with no real motives. (Perhaps not so new
at that, but a subtly modulated old, Miltonic stuff.) This poem
is a deepening version of the retirement theme. One free formal
feature to be noted about it is surely that, whereas the dim land-
scape images and pensive mood are minor Miltonic, the movement
of the phrases through the tiny stanzas is not cut or segmented,
as in *Penseroso* couplets, but is like the actual movement of
Horatian odes and at the same time like Milton's *Paradise Lost*
style and his sonnet style too, continuous from line to line, and
even from stanza to stanza.

> . . . . some soften'd Strain,
> Whose Numbers stealing thro' thy darkning Vale,
> May not unseemly with its Stillness suit,
> As musing slow, I hail
> Thy genial lov'd Return!

We can see an instructive sort of contrast to Collins's well-
known verses in another *Ode to Evening,* included in the twin
small volume of odes published simultaneously in December
1746 by his Winchester and Oxford friend Joseph Warton.

> Hail, meek-eyed maiden, clad in sober gray,
> Whose soft approach the weary woodman loves

> As, homeward bent to kiss his prattling babes,
> He jocund whistles through the twilight groves.

Content without the rhyme of the first and third lines, this
pentameter quatrain insists, nevertheless, on a square enough
parallel, balanced halving of lines, and stanzaic closure to illus-
trate a minor poetic strain that was tuning quietly during the
decade toward its sudden and plenary fulfillment in Gray's
Elegy. The Colin Clout or *Nosce Teipsum* quatrain of alternating
rhymes had been employed by D'Avenant and Dryden at the
middle of the preceding century as a counterpart of classical
heroic hexameters, somewhat ampler than the English couplet.
It was a relatively obscure and very weak poet, James Ham-
mond, who about 1732, in a sequence of expurgated Tibullan
adaptations, seems first to have conceived this quatrain as a
counterpart of the Latin hexameter and pentameter, or elegiac
couplet—fit metrical emblem for the pensive melancholy of frus-
trate love. William Shenstone, who alluded to the stanza as
"Hammond's meter," wrote more of the same sort of watery
elegies, twenty-six in number, and an introductory theoretical
essay upon the genre. How did Gray succeed at one leap in car-
rying this slender tradition so far beyond the "necessities" or
timidities which had hitherto seemed to constrain it? Geoffrey
Tillotson suggests that one of Gray's inventions is the landscape
picture laid down in separate strips, line by line.

> The lowing herd winds slowly o'er the lea,
> The plowman homeward plods his weary way.

True, we have noted the same thing in Warton's relatively tame
Ode to Evening. Still, it may be that these landscape strips, as
Gray manages them, are a notable part of his unique quality.
Gray's *Elegy* shares with Pope's a preservative technique in
blending the softness of elegiac feeling with the tartness of satiric
commentary. Cleanth Brooks has observed the ironic reciproca-
tion between country churchyard and the funerary emblems of
the great abbey church. Perhaps we will be tempted to say that
Gray transcends and outdoes Hammond and Shenstone simply
because he writes a more poetic line, richer, fuller, more reso-
nant and memorable in all the ways in which we are accustomed
to analyze the poetic quality. There may be no other way of
describing his poetic freedom. I would not debate long against
that. Let me, however, add one more observation, one of my
own favorite notions about this poem (which I note too in
Brooks's essay, on re-reading it, and in a more recent essay by
Bertrand Bronson), that its resonance and fullness in the memory

come in good part from the concluding personal complement to, and affirmation of, the marmoreally impersonal main statement. The universalized meditation comes home, as Johnson said, to the reader's business and bosom through the final focus and intensification in the heart of the speaker himself, who sees (and, as Brooks argues, *chooses*) his own grave and epitaph. ("For thee, who mindful of th' unhonour'd Dead / Dost in these lines their artless tale relate . . ."—not Gray in any special personal sense, of course, not West, and not a village stonecutter—but the melancholy, sensitive unknown poet meditator and speaker —and hence you, I, we, anybody who happens to be reading the poem.) One reason why I come to rest on this idea is that it affords, I believe, a very instructive moment of comparison with one of Gray's two Pindaric Odes, *The Progress of Poesy*.

The Pindaric ode in English was one of the straightest or most serious ways of imitating the classic model. The sublimity of the models almost precluded the kind of freedom and significant parodic fun that was invited by satire and epic. Or if parody was attempted, as by Bonnell Thornton in his burlesque Saint Cecilia's Day ode set to music by Dr. Arne for Ranelagh in 1763, and by Lloyd and Colman in *Two Odes* (1760) ridiculing Gray and Mason, it almost necessarily fell to an extreme of contrast; it was low travesty. Dryden, improving on the neo-classic "free verse" of Cowley, had demonstrated a kind of bravura of musical mimesis, a wildly recitative ring, in two irregular St. Cecilia's Odes. Pope, despite his admiration for Dryden's feat in the *Essay on Criticism*, had done less than his best in an attempt at the same genre, published in 1713. Edward Young contrived weak adaptations of Dryden's style, in sublime celebration of the British navy (1728–1734).[2] Congreve had earlier (1706) come in to assert briefly that the Pindaric ode ought in fact to be a very regular three-phase construct—strophe, antistrophe, and epode (turn, counterturn, and stand, as Ben Jonson had put it), precisely repeated in successive triads. The lesson had been not much noticed for another thirty years. But with the *Odes* of Collins and the even more recent translation of Pindar by Gilbert West (1749), Gray was in a position to go all out in a highly intricate (countable and testable though probably never readily audible) triadic pattern, precisely repeated, and to add to this formidably classic quality, a range and depth of allusiveness which in the collected *Poems* of 1768 he permitted himself to

2. The episode is described by E. E. Reimer in his unpublished Yale doctoral dissertation of 1968, *The Paradoxical Sublime: Edward Young's Early Works*, chap. 5.

cover with a panoply of footnotes such as American students of
the present age are likely to associate mainly with the *Waste
Land* of Eliot. There *was* a kind of freedom in all this, a bold
originality—to which we find the most thunderous testimony in
the outrage vented by Samuel Johnson: ". . . glittering accumu-
lations of ungraceful ornaments; they strike, rather than please;
. . . the language is laboured into harshness . . . 'Double, double,
toil and trouble'. He has a kind of strutting dignity, and is tall
by walking on tiptoe."

But to return to the connection with the *Elegy* which I began
by hinting: the boldest, by far the most striking and shocking
thing about the *Progress of Poesy* seems to me to be the closing
stanza, the epode of the third triad, bringing to a conclusion, or
up to the latest date, the progress of poesy from Greece through
Italy to England, Shakespeare, Milton, Dryden. Thus far have
the "paths of glory" led. At the end of the *Elegy*, the humble
poet speaker, the melancholy "youth to fortune and to fame
unknown," was lying flat, in his grave, his "head upon the lap
of earth," his "frailties" sunk in "the bosom of his Father and
his God." (So far as obscurity is a choice, it is a choice which
Nature cooperates all too readily in helping us to make.) But
the "youth pined away with desire," as a later vision will instruct
us, does "arise from [his] grave and aspire, Where [the] sun-
flower wishes to go." The end of the *Progress of Poesy* is another
ending of one poet's recital, but the end of a far bigger story
also. No "mute inglorious" Miltons have appeared in the cast of
characters, but "he" himself "that rode sublime/Upon the
seraph-wings of Extasy." And now, today, in 1754?

> Oh! Lyre divine, what daring Spirit
> Wakes thee now? Tho' he inherit
> Nor the pride, nor ample pinion,
> That the Theban Eagle bear . . .
> Yet oft before his infant eyes would run
> Such forms, as glitter in the Muse's ray
> With orient hues, unborrow'd of the Sun:
> Yet shall he mount, and keep his distant way
> Beyond the limits of a vulgar fate,
> Beneath the Good how far—but far above the Great.

The epitaph which concludes that churchyard *Elegy*, I have ar-
gued, transcends or envelops the merely individual. It is the
individual focus of the universal. Can the same be said for the
galvanic resurrection which concludes the daring third epode of
the *Progress of Poesy*? I think not. For, after all, it is our com-

mon fate to be dead and to lie flat in the ground. It is a very special and eminent experience to mount and soar (even though a little lower than the Theban eagle) yet "beyond the limits of a vulgar fate." Gray, one might plead, is not thinking of himself, but just of the sublime English poet of the moment, whoever he may be. But who else could he be at this moment,[3] as this triumphant epode is penned? The stanza to my mind is rampant with the individuality, and the vanity, of the Cambridge scholar. In this it displays a very unusual degree of correctly wild Pindaric energy.[4] Nevertheless, it may seem, and be, like the rest of the ode, cold enough for us, even repellent. Freedom, we may wonder, but as in many a political issue, freedom to do what?

Gray's second Pindaric ode, *The Bard*, equally intricate and regular, is another celebration of the power and progress of poesy, urged with an even more intense degree of rhapsodic energy. The frenzied Welsh bard, joined in dreadful harmony by a chorus of ghostly colleagues, pronounces a doom upon the royal line of Edward I but adds a prophecy of long poetic glories for England under the Tudors. "Robed in a sable garb of woe,/ With haggard eyes the Poet stood;/Loose his beard, and hoary hair . . ." Every schoolboy knows, or once knew, that he punctuates his tirade by a leap from the side of Snowdon into the Conway's foaming flood. The visionary bardic afflatus, a form of wit to madness near allied, was appropriate matter for the throb of the wild Pindaric strophe. If one way to freedom was the irresponsibility of parody and burlesque, another way, known or hinted at since classic times, was madness. It was good, at any rate, as a literary device. Perhaps it was even better in actuality. The date of Horace Walpole's inauguration of the printing press at Strawberry Hill with Gray's two odes, 1757, was also the approximate date when another Cambridge scholar, a prolific London hack writer, went really mad, or at any rate entered a period of confinement in several madhouses. Christopher Smart's antiphonal logbook, *Jubilate Agno, Rejoice in the Lamb*, written during this time, recovered and published long after, bears the marks of a genuinely mad mind. It bears also the unmistakable marks of poetic genius.

3. His friend "Mr. Mason" is complimented but disposed of in the footnote attached to the earlier line: "But ah! 'tis heard no more."

4. Like the passage in Pindar's Second *Olympian* which Gray quotes in a footnote, or like Horace, *Exegi monumentum aere perennius*. But these too are satisfactory less as poetic expressions than as boasts that time proves to have been justified—curious moments of prophetic vanity. Perhaps my account of Gray's poem is overly biographical. A similar case might be urged, I believe, simply against the "speaker" of the poem.

For I will consider my Cat Jeoffry.

For he is a servant of the Living God duly and daily serving
him.

For at the first glance of the glory of God in the East he
worships in his way.

. . . .

For when his day's work is done his business more properly
begins.

For he keeps the Lord's watch in the night against the
adversary.

For he counteracts the powers of darkness by his electrical
skin & glaring eyes.

For he has the subtlety and hissing of a serpent, which in
goodness he suppresses.

For he will not do destruction, if he is well-fed, neither
will he spit without provocation.

For he purrs in thankfulness, when God tells him he's a
good Cat.

To my mind there is more poetic life in these disjunct antiphons
than in either of Gray's intricately labored *Odes*. What makes
the poetic freedom and success of this passage? To speak roughly:
loving and amused observation of a household animal is coupled
with the sacramental view of the universe and the prayerful form
of Scripture and liturgy. The freedom arises in a reverently ir-
reverent parody of Scripture and the Prayer Book. Madness was
the interior dynamic that issued the license for this kind of par-
ody.

IV

With Gray's Pindaric Odes and Samuel Johnson's imitation of
the Tenth Satire of Juvenal a few years earlier we arrive at an
approximate climax and end to the direct and straight imitation
of the classics in the English neo-classical movement. To carry
our narration of freedom through imitation any further, we need
now a new rubric, a new term or two—none the less valid be-
cause they may be our own favorite terms, rather than those the
age would most readily have applied to itself. I am thinking of
some such terms as *antiquarianism*[5] and *primitivism*.

Percy's *Reliques of Ancient English Poetry*, 1765, will imme-

_____

5. "A mere Antiquarian is a rugged being" (Samuel Johnson in Boswell's
Life, sub anno 1778).

diately come to mind, and in connection with this it is worth
our while to notice in passing one kind of native or folk free-
dom which flourished in that enlightened age but which an age
of modern scholars seems hardly to have suspected until Bertrand
Bronson brought it to light about twenty-three years ago in his
account of Mrs. Brown of Falkland, who was a ballad informant
of Sir Walter Scott's informants William Tytler and Alexander
Fraser Tytler, Lord Woodhouselee. Daughter of a professor at
Aberdeen and wife of a clergyman, this lady carried in her head,
from singing heard in childhood, no fixed or bookish text of a
ballad, but just the ballad itself, a narrative line or story poem
(a "fluid entity") which she felt free to cast and recast in nu-
merous rhetorical and prosodic variations.[6] In this instance, the
freedom seems to have produced no important creative results.
But it may help us to appreciate the fact that we are indebted
to free sources of the same kind for those sharply trimmed es-
sential versions of *Edward* and *Sir Patrick Spens* which an earlier
Scottish collector, Boswell's friend Lord Hailes, had given to
Percy. There is no reason to think these were any more ancient
or more genuine than any of the numerous inferior versions of
the same ballads which may be found in Child and Sharp. They
were the work of living eighteenth-century Scottish reciters.
The vital energy of the age in traditional song, as Bronson says,
put forth natural "flowers—proper to the season, not excavated
fossils." The eighteenth century no less than the fifteenth was
"a golden age" of Scottish balladry.

But for our purpose today, I have in mind in naming Percy
mainly another kind of freedom—one very effective mode of
escape from the rigors of the prevailing civilized norms of ele-
gance and good sense. This escape was somewhat like that of
imitation and burlesque. I mean the escape which Percy enjoyed
by the simple, half-apologetic, act of electing to put before the
public the rude rhymes of an earlier uncouth age. He and his
readers could thus innocently disport themselves in all this
raciness and vigor. The harshness and uncouthness was not their
responsibility. True, some of the pieces had to be touched up a
little by Percy and made more presentable. But this too was a
form of connivance and participation, of fiction, and hence of
freedom.

Percy's first edition of the *Reliques*, let us recall, was closely
contemporary with the Gaelic pseudo-documents of another
Scottish antiquary, James Macpherson, and the rhythmic Eng-

6. "Mrs. Brown and the Ballad," *California Folklore Quarterly* 4 (April
1945): 129-40.

lish prose translations which he produced in three volumes as
the poems of the ancient Fenian poet Ossian.[7] "We gave the
song to the kings. A hundred harps mixed their sound with our
voice." The plushy green headlands, the blue bays, the wind
groaning in the pines and oaks, the ships, halls, caves, tombs,
and campfires, the running deer and boars, the thrusting and the
bleeding warriors, the spears, swords, harps, armor and gems—
the whole bardic idiom of Homeric and Miltonic imitation—con-
stituted a distinct poetic invention on the part of Macpherson,
if no very subtle one. He gained the freedom to indulge in this
invention through the removal and protection of his fictive
plunge of fifteen centuries.

A very similar element of freedom in forgery appears in the
more sympathetic fraud committed not much later by Thomas
Chatterton, the sad and marvelous Bristol boy. The three post-
humous editions of his *Rowley Poems*, by the eminent Chau-
cerian Thomas Tyrwhitt, the third containing the solid philolog-
ical exposure, appeared in 1777 and 1778. Chatterton's Rowley
poems were an orphan's pathological flight from present reality
into an archaic world of fine fabling and of plangent filial yearn-
ing.

> Sprytes of the bleste, on goulden trones astedde
> Poure oute yer pleasaunce own mie fadres hedde.

More important for the formal side of our inquiry, Chatterton
used the sanction of a mock antique vocabulary and grammar to
create a new kind of free poetic idiom. Like the Spenser of Ben
Jonson's phrase, Chatterton-Rowley "writ no language." And
yet, like Spenser, he did write a language, and marvellously well.
He wrote his own expressionistic fusion of contemporary English
and certain freely mingled echoes of the past. The elements, the
phonemes and the morphemes, as we might say today, were all
pure English. The way they were run together was the oddity
and the achievement, something legitimized by the supposed
antiquity, but in large part determined by a rhythmic and ex-
pressive tact which, if it has to be explained in brief, we may
attempt to explain by an appeal to a principle expounded, in
humorous fantasy a hundred years later, as *Jabberwocky*. The
effects are only in part orthographic and ocular.

> Whanne Englonde, smeethynge from her lethal wounde,
> From her gall'd necke dyd twytte the chayne awaie,

7. 1760 is the date of the sixteen *Fragments*, 1762 that of the epic
poem in six books *Fingal*, 1763 that of *Temora*, in eight books.

Kennynge her legeful sonnes fall all arounde,
(Myghtie theie fell, 'Twas Honoure ledde the fraie,)
Thanne inne a dale, bie eve's dark surcote graie,
Twayne lonelie shepsterres dyd abrodden flie,
(The rostlyng liff doth theyr whytte hartes affraie,)
And wythe the owlette trembled and dyd crie . . . .

[*Eclogue* I]

The featherd songster chaunticleer
Han wounde hys bugle horne,
And told the earlie villager
The commynge of the morne.

[*Bristowe Tragedie*: *Or the Dethe
of Syr Charles Bawdin*, Stanza I]

A great nineteenth-century scholar, the Reverend W. W. Skeat,
tried to get at the essence of Chatterton's Rowley poems—"the
exact amount of merit" to which Chatterton had "attained"—
by translating them into correct modern English. "Han" is a
plural verb in Chaucerian English, not singular. And thus we get:

The feathered songster chanticleer
Has wound his bugle horn.

And thus in the interests of grammar is obliterated whatever
charm the tiny alliterative clarion of the line may have had.

It may seem too big a leap (in poetic idiom even if not in
chronology) from Chatterton to the publication in 1786 at
Kilmarnock in Ayrshire of Robert Burns's *Poems, Chiefly in the
Scottish Dialect.* But I believe there are good reasons for men-
tioning Burns immediately after Chatterton. Whatever we may
wish to say about the racy and earthy peasant freedom of Burns's
poems and his free lyric lilt and gusto, the language in which he
wrote (when he was not writing like James Thomson, in the
Spenserian stanzas of *The Cotter's Saturday Night*), the Lowland
Scots dialect, whatever precisely that is, is of great importance
for understanding the free expressive power which Burns en-
joyed. The eighteenth century, we know, was full of humble and
uneducated poets—in Pope's time Stephen Duck the "Poetical
Thresher"; later Henry Jones the "Poetical Bricklayer"; Mrs. Ann
Yearsley, of Bristol, the poetical Milk-Woman, Lactilla; James
Woodhouse, the Poetical Shoemaker. And others too. The mar-
velous thing about all these poets was that, although of lowly
origin and meager opportunity, they wrote the standard style of
high varnish and poetic diction, like all the other bad and medio-
cre poets of the era. That was their achievement. The marvelous

thing about Burns, on the contrary, was that, being a peasant,
he managed to write in what was apparently the language of a
peasant. But just how precisely or literally he wrote in such a
language, or, so far as he did, what were its peculiar capacities
for poetic expression, is a difficult question. Is such a language
an initial opaque obstacle to understanding, which the English
reader, by historical linguistic research, penetrates, in order to
get at a hidden rich meaning? Or is it not possible that in some
way such a language is in fact a specially and immediately ex-
pressive medium, a contrivance for a much more direct, if inex-
plicit, presentation, than the civilized literary language permits?
Let me suggest the nature of this problem by quoting first a few
lines from an early Scottish contemporary of Burns, Robert
Fergusson, who died young in 1774, a university and city man
and a satirical poet of the city, Edinburgh. Still he wrote also of
the country, as in the following lines from his poem entitled
The Farmer's Ingle.

> Niest the gude wife her hireling damsels bids
>   Glowr thro' the byre, and see the hawkies bound,
> Take tent case Crummy tak her wonted tids,
>   And ca' the leglen's treasure on the ground,
>   Whilk spills a kebbuck nice, or yellow pound.

Your students will have trouble understanding those lines, writ-
ten in a very genuine, unquestionable eighteenth-century Scots.
Hawkies, *Crummy*, *tids*, *leglen*, *kebbuck*? The passage is about a
farm wife, her milkmaids, and her cows. And now, by contrast, a
few lines from Burns. From *Tam O'Shanter* (1791):

> O Tam had'st thou but been sae wise,
> As taen thy ain wife Kate's advice!
> She tauld thee well thou wast a skellum
> A blethering, blustering, drunken blellum.

From a poetical epistle to a friend, in the 1786 volume:

> O, sweet are Coila's haughs an' woods,
> When lintwhites chant amang the buds,
> And jinkin hares, in amorous whids,
>   Their loves enjoy;
> While thro' the braes the cushat croods
>   With wailfu' cry!

Here again the words may be strange to us, but I dare say they
will scarcely seem an obstacle to our getting a strong impression
of what the passages are saying. The country Scots chosen by

Burns and mixed with literary Scots and with straight English is
for the most part not an opaque language to you, nor was it to
Wordsworth or Keats, who in 1803 and 1818 wrote poems at
Burns's grave. Nor do I think it could have been to Burns's Eng-
lish contemporaries, nor to the Edinburgh literati (despite a ges-
ture of glossing in Mackenzie's review). The glossary prefixed to
the Kilmarnock volume by Burns himself may be taken as part
of the act. Burns's dialect in his best-known poems—his vocab-
ulary of the wee, the sleekit, timorous, cowrin, and generally
comic and sympathetic diminutive, or at an opposite pole, of
the braw, fou, blethering, blustering, blellum and skellum—is
very largely transparent to an educated English reader. (Some of
the pleasure which we get from it is very similar to that which
we get on recognizing slapstick and indecent jokes in Shake-
speare.) Let us remember again the principle of Jabberwocky.
"How high browse thou, brown cow?"[8]

V

   Imitation or burlesque of the Greek and Roman classic mod-
els. Imitation or forgery of the British archaic past or the prim-
itive present. A third strain of imitation, as we have said at the
start, was imitation of the English classics, from Chaucer to
Pope, or in a broader sense, imitation of the classic tradition.
Sometimes free and expressive, sometimes a mere nostalgic ex-
ercise! The landscape gardener and elegist William Shenstone's
three versions (1737, 1742, 1748) of his Spenserian *School-
mistress*, showing an evolution from rudely comic archaism in
the manner of Pope's *Alley* to idyllic reminiscence and senti-
mental village portraiture, may be set in contrast to the Cam-
bridge litterateur William Mason's *Musaeus: A Monody to the
Memory of Mr. Pope, In Imitation of Milton's Lycidas*, 1747.
Here not only Milton but also Spenser and Chaucer (in both
poem and engraved vignette) convene at Pope's death in his
grotto, and each speaks some verses in parody of his own style—
curious and moving for the antiquarian in any of us, I dare say,
but cold and merely negative emblems of what the power of
Augustan imitation might ideally be. Alexander Pope's four
glossy Virgilian eclogues and his friend Gay's burlesque Theoc-
ritan and Spenserian *Shepherd's Week* (which Samuel Johnson

   8. The matters on which I touch briefly here are in the course of being
treated at length by Mr. James McArdle in a dissertation on the poetic lan-
guage of Burns.

said was a comic way of reaching serious truth) were followed
during the mid-century by Collins's four *Persian Eclogues*, in
which the freedom of the Oriental decor joined the antithesis of
two idyllic against two tormented recitals; by the satirical coup-
let writer Charles Churchill's anti-Scot pastoral dialogue *The
Prophecy of Famine*, one of the cruelest and ugliest poems ever
written; by Goldsmith's couplet celebration of the "loveliest
village of the plain," where pastoral nostalgia is fortified by allu-
sion to a partly invented contemporary economics of depopula-
tion; and by Chatterton's three stanzaic medieval eclogues, from
which I have already quoted. Such are the immediate anteced-
ents of the wry and bitter anti-pastoral couplet poem *The Village*,
published by the Rev. George Crabbe in 1783. It is a poem which
has the distinction of containing a theory of realistic imagination
in a couplet revised by Samuel Johnson, so as to say better what
Crabbe wrote—or perhaps the reverse of what Crabbe wrote—as
our theoretical intelligence happens to grasp it.

> From Truth and Nature, shall we widely stray
> [Where Fancy leads, or Virgil led the way?] [9]
> Where Virgil, not where Fancy, leads the way?

But Crabbe could make himself unmistakably clear;

> . . . cast by Fortune on a frowning coast,
> Which neither groves nor happy valleys boast;
> Where other cares than those the Muse relates,
> And other shepherds dwell with other mates;
> By such examples taught, I paint the Cot,
> As truth will paint it, and as Bards will not.

I am now aiming at a convergence of themes and a focus upon
a period of four years, 1782–1785, toward the end of which oc-
curred the death of Samuel Johnson. During the early 1760's in
London the satirist Charles Churchill had been a member of a
set of gay young fellows which included a student of law and
resident of the Inner Temple named William Cowper. Cowper
went terribly mad in 1763, tried to commit suicide, and after
that fled into a life of rural and domestic retirement—alternating
for the rest of a fairly long life between further attacks of a
severe religious melancholy and periods of troubled sanity. Un-
like Christopher Smart, he wrote his best poems in his periods
of sanity, during one of which he produced a volume of wiry
and restrained couplet satires (*Poems*, 1782). The best of these,

9. Crabbe's original line, preserved by Boswell, *Life of Johnson*, March
1783.

entitled *Table Talk*, a dialogue, interweaves political themes in
the vein of Pope's *Epistle to Augustus* with literary and personal
parallels to both *Augustus* and Pope's *Epistle to Arbuthnot*.
One of the remarkable things about these poems is that Cowper
was apparently unaware of the extent to which his rhetoric and
rhymes were echoes of Pope. Pope, he tells us,

> (his musical finesse was such,
> So nice his ear, so delicate his touch)
> Made poetry a mere mechanic art;
> And every warbler has his tune by heart.

In a letter to a friend he once wrote: "I have not read an Eng-
lish poet these thirteen years. Imitation, even of the best mod-
els, is my aversion; it is servile and mechanical."[10] He could not
have been more thoroughly deceived. It was difficult for the
poets of that age to be conscious how closely they were envel-
oped by the idiom of Pope and by that of Milton. Cowper was a
subtle poet, not in spite of his derivations, but in large part just
because of his virtuoso capacity to play variations on the tunes
of Pope and Milton. If we pick up and follow the line of Miltonic
influence, seen at its best during the early century probably in
the parodies of John Philips and in the freely upholstered blank
verse and medley of *Paradise Lost* images and themes that dis-
tinguish Thomson's *Seasons*, we arrive again at our focal period
with the publication in 1785 of Cowper's long blank-verse dem-
onstration *The Task*. In many parts this is a light Miltonic parody.
It is a poem which as a whole occupies a place in the Georgic, or
farm-and-garden, inheritance from the classical world similar to
that which Goldsmith's *Deserted Village* occupies in the pastoral.

   That concludes a brief detour away from the lyric which I have
undertaken for the sake of sketching the wide context of imita-
tive and parodistic assumptions which enveloped the production
of the next volume of lyrics that I want to notice. It is a fact I
believe not often dwelt on that George Crabbe's sourly anti-
traditional yet conservatively fashioned poem *The Village* ap-
peared in the same year, 1783, as the small volume of juvenile
poems, *Poetical Sketches*, printed and distributed to a few
friends by the young London engraver William Blake. These were
written, according to the Advertisement, between his twelfth and
his twentieth year. The earliest of them, that is, may have been
written about 1769, the year before the death of Chatterton.
The latest must have been written a little later than his twentieth
year, for there would seem to be debts to Chatterton's *Rowley*

10. To William Unwin, 24 November 1781.

Poems, 1777, and to his *Miscellanies*, 1778.[11] These poems, we remember, are miscellaneous, odd, rough-seeming, ragged, bold ("full of irregularities and defects," says the Advertisement)—a wider range of imitative experiments than anything we have so far consulted. They include rhythmic prose in the manner of Ossian (or of Chatterton's imitations of Ossian) and of the King James Bible; a nightmare pseudo-Gothic ballad, a mad song, and a song of frustrated love, all these in the manner more or less of Percy's *Reliques*; a large fragment of a Shakespearean history play, *Edward III*; a Miltonic prologue; a mythological poem in a sequence of variously approximate Spenserian stanzas; and, perhaps most impressive of all, opening the volume, a set of apostrophes to the four seasons, blended in a new and strangely lyric way from James Thomson, Milton, the *Song of Solomon*, and no doubt other sources. It is difficult to imagine what Dr. Johnson would have said of this volume of sub-cultural expressions if a copy had chanced to come into his hands. Blake took his liberties, right and left. One of the most obvious formal, if superficial, examples is that of the successive deviations in the Spenserian stanzas.[12] Here I should say the expressive effect is nearly zero. But it is not difficult to find, though it may require some tact to analyze, examples near the opposite end of the value scale. About twenty years ago Cleanth Brooks published in the *CEA Critic*[13] an essay showing how the song of frustrated love, "My silks and fine array," is a job of sweet-sad ritual cunning performed in variations upon Elizabethan lyrics of the Walsingham type which Blake's copy of Percy's *Reliques* at Wellesley College suggests that he knew very well. At about the same time, I myself made the observation, which has been, I believe, well enough received by the guardians of the field, that one deeply and freely romantic feature of the apostrophe *To Spring* is the remarkable fusion yet division of the imagery whereby the Biblical lover descends into and is blended with a native landscape, which also bears the image of his waiting bride. In a curious variant of the method, the fiery Apollonian tyrant King Summer descends upon the land, only to be invited to seek relief in a nap under an oak or a swim in a river.

The happy manner in which such mythic fusions join Miltonic

11. F. W. Bateson, *Selected Poems of William Blake* (New York, 1957), pp. 93-100.
12. The imitative manner of *Poetical Sketches* was first extensively studied, with a strong accent on detection of sources, by Margaret Ruth Lowery in her Yale doctoral dissertation, directed by C. B. Tinker, *Windows of the Morning* (New Haven, 1940).
13. Vol. 12 (October 1950), no. 9, pp. 1-6.

meter and syntax to make the freedom and originality of Blake
the youthful experimenter can, as it happens, be suggested *ab
extra* by contrast with a little-known poem which Blake's *To
Spring* seems in part to have inspired. William Stanley Roscoe
was the son of a Liverpool banker who in his spare moments
was an editor of Pope, a patron of the arts, and a friend of friends
of William Blake. The younger Roscoe's poem *To Spring, on the
Banks of the Cam*, written presumably in his youth, about 1800,
though published only in his *Poems* of 1834, combines the stan-
za of Collins's *Ode to Evening* with Blake's abruptly orotund
apostrophic opening.

> O thou that from the green vales of the West
> Comst in thy tender robes with bashful feet,
> And to the gathering clouds
> Liftest thy soft blue eye:
>
> I woo thee, Spring!

I do not undertake to prove or even adequately to illustrate the
thesis that Roscoe's poem is not a very good one. But it is not.
It can be consulted in Brooks and Warren's *Understanding Po-
etry*, or in the *Oxford Book of Victorian Verse*. It deserves, I
believe, special notice as perhaps the only instance of direct,
exemplary influence which can be claimed for Blake's half-
suppressed *Sketches*.[14]

More recently, Harold Bloom, in probably the most sustained
critical gaze yet directed upon Blake's *Sketches*, has observed
the "small . . . humanizing" scale of the two Spenserian epitha-
lamic apostrophes *To the Evening Star* and *To Morning*; the
"sexual paradise and trap" of the garden in the *Song* "How
sweet I roam'd"; conventional poetic diction turned on itself in
the "gently mocking" *To the Muses*; Shakespearean winter pas-
toral joined with the genial manner of Goldsmith in *Blind Man's
Buff*.

Blake's *Poetical Sketches* is a volume saturated with the Eng-
lish poetic tradition from the Elizabethan age through the
mid-eighteenth century, brimming with imitative exuberance,
and thus wildly and torrentially free. We might almost be
tempted to think in a careless moment that it is only accidentally,
crudely, and boyishly free. It would be difficult to think of a
single small volume more happily illustrative of the half-genetic,
half-critical argument I have been trying to push: that the ex-

14. Arnold Goldman, "Blake and the Roscoes," *Notes and Queries* 210
(May 1965): 178-82.

pressive freedom of eighteenth-century English poetry is born
only in virtue of the mimetic and repetitive tradition under
which the poets labored. This volume is surely, as Harold Bloom
would say, "premonitory" of the two strikingly original yet imi-
tative lyric collections which would follow before the end of
the century. Blake's *Songs of Innocence and of Experience* is
perhaps most readily located by a new reader in its superficially
traditional and formal aspects, the meters and the language of
childish songs, the "hymns unbidden." Its radical and explosive
originality lies at difficult depths. The emblematic character of
the form, as John Hollander says, is used to cover a shift in the
character of the content. The poems of Coleridge and Words-
worth in *Lyrical Ballads*, and especially those of Wordsworth,
seemed from the start, or were said from the start, and mainly
by Wordsworth himself, to be a conspicuous departure from all
that was expected of poems by a reader tamed in the eighteenth-
century popular tradition. "Every author, as far as he is great
and at the same time *original*," Wordsworth would later say,
"has had the task of *creating* the taste by which he is to be en-
joyed."[15] But Coleridge would qualify that. In the *Biographia*
he argued that a clamor of protest over *Lyrical Ballads* had been
aroused more by Wordsworth's extreme theoretical statements
than by the poems themselves. Within recent years an American
scholar, Robert Mayo, has demonstrated, I think, that in all the
superficials of both form and content, *Lyrical Ballads* was repre-
sentative of what had already grown to be a "persistent" minor-
ity segment of the magazine verse of the 1790's. Bereaved,
deserted, and vagrant females, mendicants of both sexes, old
soldiers, convicts, unfortunate rustics of every sort, are frequent
protagonists in those pages. Insanity and simplicity, picturesque
scenery, topographical meditation, humanitarianism, and senti-
mental morality are dominant motifs in poems which assume
the forms of ballad, "lyric," complaint, fragment, sketch, anec-
dote, expostulation and reply, occasional inscription.[16]

> Old Sarah lov'd her helpless child,
> Whom helplessness made dear,
> And life was happiness to him,
> Who had no hope or fear.

15. *Essay Supplementary to the Preface* (1815), seventh paragraph
from the end. The letter to Lady Beaumont of 21 May 1807, last para-
graph, attributes the same idea to Coleridge, in nearly the same words.
16. Robert Mayo, "The Contemporaneity of the *Lyrical Ballads*,"
PMLA 69 (June 1954): 486-522.

> She knew his wants, she understood
> Each half artic'late call,
> And he was ev'rything to her,
> And she to him was all.

Not a rejected Wordsworthian fragment from *Lyrical Ballads*—but part of a poem entitled *The Idiot* in the *Sporting Magazine* for October 1798.[17] When compared with earlier eighteenth-century primitives, Stephen Duck, Henry Jones, Ann Yearsley, or even Robert Burns, Wordsworth may seem to achieve his originality, as he claims, by the simple expedient of using a selection of the language of ordinary men—a plain, prosy middle sort of standard English—albeit informed by some special excitement. When he is compared with some of his more immediate contemporaries, however, this kind of originality largely disappears. Wordsworth's freedom and originality, whether in a poem of poetic diction, such as *Tintern Abbey*, or in his plainest ballad narrations, will be found ultimately to consist in the fact that he is a better poet than most of his contemporaries at most moments. He has "the original gift of spreading the tone." He writes with more force and interest, even with more "wit," if I dare use such a term. This is the essence of poetic freedom.

1968

17. Mayo, pp. 499–500.

Select bibliography of secondary works: Austin Warren, "The Mask of Pope," *Sewanee Review* (Winter 1946): 19–33 (also in his *Rage for Order* [Chicago, 1948]); Earl R. Wasserman, *Elizabethan Poetry in the Eighteenth Century* (Urbana, 1947); F. W. Hilles, ed., *The Age of Johnson: Essays Presented to Chauncey Brewster Tinker* (New Haven, 1949), Virginia Prettyman on Shenstone, Bertrand Bronson on Chatterton, W. K. Wimsatt on romantic nature imagery; R. S. Crane, ed., *Critics and Criticism: Ancient and Modern* (Chicago, 1952), Norman Maclean on theories of the lyric in the eighteenth century; Raymond D. Havens, "Assumed Personality, Insanity, and Poetry," *The Review of English Studies*, new series, 4 (January 1953): 26–36; Carroll Camden, ed., *Restoration and Eighteenth-Century Literature: Essays in Honor of Alan Dugald McKillop* (Chicago, 1963), Reuben Brower on Dryden and Pope, Geoffrey Tillotson on description in nature poetry, David Daiches on Burns, Ricardo Quintana on Collins, Aubrey Williams on Pope and Horace; Martin Price, *The Palace of Wisdom: Studies in Order and Energy from Dryden to Blake* (New York, 1964); F. W. Hilles and Harold Bloom, eds., *From Sensibility to Romanticism: Essays Presented to Frederick A. Pottle* (New York, 1965), A.S.P. Woodhouse on Collins, Ian Jack, Bertrand Bronson, and Frank Brady on Gray's *Elegy*, John Butt and Raymond Bentman on Burns's language, John Hollander on Blake's meters; Earl R. Wasserman, ed., *Aspects of the Eighteenth Century* (Baltimore, 1965), Maynard Mack on Pope and retirement literature, W. J. Bate on eighteenth-century poets and the "burden of the past."

IN PRAISE OF *RASSELAS*:
FOUR NOTES (CONVERGING)

Afterthoughts in Rasselas

Johnson most likely began to write *Rasselas* not long after Saturday, 13 January 1759, when he seems first to have heard of his mother's serious illness. A week later, on Saturday, 20 January, he wrote to the publisher William Strahan that he would deliver the book to him on Monday night, and that the title would be "The Choice of Life/or/The History of . . . Prince of Abisinnia." The several learned editors of *Rasselas* have, accordingly, not been inclined to take literally Johnson's later statement to Reynolds, as reported by Boswell, that he not only wrote *Rasselas* "in the evenings of one week," but "sent it to the press in portions as it was written."[1] In portions, as it was corrected during days subsequent to Monday, 22 January, perhaps.[2] It is not difficult to imagine revisions and afterthoughts even during the original week of rapid composition. One of the most obvious internal suggestions of such afterthought, or at least of a certain absent-mindedness during the course of writing, appears in the development of the character of the lady Pekuah. We hear of her first, momentarily, in the escape from the happy valley (chapter XV). "The princess was followed only by a single favourite, who did not know whither she was going . . . The princess and her maid turned their eyes toward every part, and, seeing nothing to bound their prospect, considered themselves as in danger of being lost in a dreary vacuity. They stopped and trembled." A second very brief allusion occurs in the next chapter (XVI), as they arrive at Cairo. "The princess . . . for some days, continued in her chamber, where she was served by her favourite as in the palace of the valley." Thereafter, for fourteen chapters (XVII–XXX), or during the whole first period at Cairo, including the trip to the cataract of the Nile to visit the hermit, we miss this personage altogether, until in chapter XXXI, at the great Pyramid, she reappears abruptly: ". . . the favourite of the prin-

---

1. *Rasselas*, ed. G. B. Hill (Oxford, 1887, 1954), pp. 22-25; ed. O. F. Emerson (New York, 1895), pp. xii–xv; ed. R. W. Chapman (Oxford, 1927), pp. ix–xv. A third part of the statement to Reynolds, that he "had never since read it over" has to be stretched to accommodate the fact that the second edition of *Rasselas*, following in June the first edition of April 1759, has about sixty emendations which bear the auctorial stamp (O. F. Emerson, "The Text of Johnson's *Rasselas*," *Anglia* 22 (1899): 497-509); ed. R. W. Chapman (Oxford, 1927), pp. xx–xxi; D. N. Smith, *Johnson & Boswell Revised* (Oxford, 1928), p. 13.
2. Chapman, p. xv.

cess, looking into the cavity, stepped back and trembled. 'Pekuah, said the princess, of what art thou afraid?'" In the first edition, this was the first introduction of the lady's name. For the second edition, Johnson went back and inserted this name after the word "favourite" in the sentence quoted above from chapter XVI. We remember that Pekuah, through her terror of the gloomy inside of the pyramid, remains outside and in chapter XXXIII is kidnapped by a band of Arab horsemen and becomes the central object of attention during six succeeding chapters (to XXXIX). She reappears thereafter, to the end of the story, in every family conversation (chapters XLIV, XLV, XLVII, XLIX); and in chapter XLVI, her interest in the stars, acquired while she was a prisoner of the Arab chief, is exploited when the ladies invade and civilize the mad astronomer. Once he had conferred a few colours upon this lady, Johnson found her a convenient enough addition to his *dramatis personae*. It is possible that, having in chapters XV and XVI, provided for her presence, he then forgot her, or even deliberately left her out of sight, for seventeen chapters. But it seems at least possible—to me it seems more likely—that he first conceived of the lady Pekuah as his travellers stood at the entrance of the Pyramid, and he bethought himself of Arab horsemen on the horizon and the opportunity to give his story an impetus towards action which at that juncture it badly needed. In that case, he went back (nothing could be simpler) and inserted the allusions to a "favourite" in chapters XV and XVI, and in the second edition the name Pekuah in chapter XVI.[3]

3. The second sentence referring to the favourite quoted from chapter XV would have required the addition of only three short words, "and her maid," and the change of three pronouns from singular to plural, to be transformed from a sentence originally referring only to Nekayah. At the end of the chapter we are told that Imlac "with great difficulty prevailed on the princess to enter the vessel." It is difficult to believe that Johnson wrote this sentence at a time when he had the fearful lady Pekuah well in mind.

In chapter VII, "The prince finds a man of learning," the first reference to Imlac is curiously abrupt, sounding as if he had already been introduced in some sentence or paragraph either earlier or later deleted. "This inundation confined all the princes to domestic amusements, and the attention of Rasselas was particularly seized by a poem, which Imlac rehearsed upon the various conditions of humanity. He commanded the poet to attend him in his apartment." Contrast chapter XIV, the first reference to Nekayah: "The prince, coming down to refresh himself with air, found his sister Nekayah standing before the mouth of the cavity." Another minor instance of absent-mindedness appears in the difference between chapter IX: "From Persia I passed into Arabia," and chapter XI: "From Persia . . . I travelled through Syria."

As Geoffrey Tillotson has already observed, Johnson through-
out *Rasselas* is preoccupied with the passage of time and pays
close attention to the number of days, months, and years which
measure out his story. At the age of twenty-six,[4] for example,
when he first becomes restless in his confinement, Rasselas lets
twenty months slip away in day-dreaming, then awakes and esti-
mates with chagrin that, since the active life of man, between
infancy and senility, amounts to no more than forty years, he
has just allowed a twenty-fourth part of his life to run to waste
($12 \times 40 = 480 \div 20 = 24$). In contrast to such numerical nicety,
the following curious sequence occurs in chapters XIX, XX, and
XXI. Rasselas and his friends hear of a hermit, famous for sanc-
tity, who lives near the "lowest cataract of the Nile." They set
out to visit him but stop during the "heat" of the [first] day at
the tents of some shepherds, whose barbarous conversation
proves disgusting to the princess (chapter XIX). Presumably they
do not linger for the afternoon or spend the night with these
shepherds. But: "On the *next day* [the italics are mine] they
continued their journey," says the first sentence of chapter XX.
Again they stop during the "heat" of the day, but this time at
the "stately palace" of a very prosperous gentleman. He entreats
them to stay. They do. And the "next day" he entreats them
again. They "continued," in fact, "a few days longer, and then
went forward to find the hermit." Then the next chapter (XXI)
begins: "They came on the third day, by the direction of the
peasants, to the hermit's cell." By the direction of the peasants?
Some might argue that this means simply "*the* peasants" of that
region. But this kind of slipshod phrasing is not like Johnson. It
appears to me all but certain that "peasants" is one of Johnson's
occasional quiet or pronominal "elegant variations." He means
the "shepherds" with whom they stopped at midday during
chapter XIX. After that, and "on the third day" after setting
out,[5] they came to the hermit's cell. It seems to me very likely
that the episode of the prosperous country gentleman is some-
thing which occurred to Johnson at some time after he had
written the sequence about the shepherds and the hermit (chap-

4. Geoffrey Tillotson, "Time in *Rasselas*," *Bicentenary Essays on
"Rasselas,"* ed. Magdi Wahba (Cairo, 1959), pp. 97–104. G. B. Hill,
ed., *Rasselas* (1887), p. 181, estimates, from the indications in chapters
XX–XXIII, that Rasselas is thirty-two years old at the time of his early
inquiries at Cairo.
5. The lowest cataract of the Nile, just below Assouan, is (or was be-
fore it was altered by the Dam) about 600 miles upstream from Cairo—a
fact which, on any interpretation of these chapters, does not help their
realism.

ters XIX, XXI), and that, wishing to get it in, he wrote it in where he could, but without noticing a slight derangement of the details of the itinerary. The stop with the shepherds is a brief episode which does not sidetrack the journey to the hermit. Chapter XX, on the downfall of a prosperous country gentleman, is an extended intrusion into that journey.[6] *Rasselas* is in a sense a travel story, but it is not on the whole a picaresque story.

The third example of narrative absent-mindedness which I wish to notice does, however, give us another exception to that rule. Chapter XL (immediately after the narrative of Pekuah's captivity with the Arab), begins: "They returned to Cairo ... none of them went much abroad. The prince ... one day declared to Imlac, that he intended to devote himself to science, and pass the rest of his days in literary solitude. 'Before you make your final choice,' answered Imlac, 'you ought to examine its hazards ... I have just left the observatory of one of the most learned astronomers in the world.'" For the space of five chapters (XL, XLI, XLII, XLIII, XLIV) Imlac continues a non-stop lecture upon the mad delusion by which the astronomer believes himself possessed of the power to control the seasons, bringing rain or sunshine to any part of the world as his conscience dictates. We discover that not only Rasselas but Nekayah and Pekuah are present during the whole conversation (chapters XLIII and XLIV). Then chapter XLV breaks into this sequence as follows: "The evening was now far past, and they rose to return home. As they walked along the bank of the Nile, delighted with the beams of the moon quivering on the water, they saw at a small distance an old man." But this does not really make sense. If we look back through the involvements of Imlac's long discourse on the mad astronomer, to the beginning of chapter XL, we remember that they are already at home and have been during the whole episode. (Looking back yet farther, a long way back, to chapter XXV, one might recall that during the first period at Cairo the prince and princess "commonly met in the evening in a private summer-house on the bank of the Nile." But this summer-house either was on the grounds of the main house rented and magnificently furnished in chapter XVI, or it was not. If not, if it was away from home, nothing in chapters XL-XLIV intimates that they have now gone there.) The episode of the mad astronomer has not been concluded. After chapter XLV, "They discourse with an old man," the long and dramatically

---

6. O. F. Emerson (*op. cit.*, n. 1) notices that this chapter is sufficiently self-contained to have been a late addition.

important chapter XLVI immediately resumes the story of the
astronomer, telling how he is visited by the ladies, Nekayah and
Pekuah, and under the softening influence of feminine conversa-
tion is gradually cured of his delirious fantasy. Chapter XLV,
devoted to the old man, a characteristically and passionately
Johnsonian projection of the bitterness of old age, is a stark
intrusion into the sequence about the astronomer. In its absent-
minded opening, it seems to me another of Johnson's after-
thoughts, so important that it had to go somewhere. Where else
would seem better when the other episodes were already in
sequence?

"Structure"

I have been urging genetic inferences and have not meant to
imply that the actual inconsistencies which I observe (with the
possible exception of Pekuah's long absence from the stage) are
in any sense aesthetic deficiencies. They do, however, appear to
me as complements of and accents upon a much larger and more
clearly observable character of the whole story—what I would
describe as its highly episodic, and hence very lumpy or bumpy,
structure. One recent critic of *Rasselas*, Professor Kolb, has said
that it is arranged in two main parts, one in the happy valley,
one after the escape.[7] Another critic, Professor Hilles, has dis-
cerned three main parts: (1) in the valley, chapters I-XIV; (2) the
escape and a period of relatively detached and orderly *observa-
tion* at and near Cairo, chapters XV-XXX; (3) beginning with
the abduction of Pekuah and the grief of Nekayah, a period of
greater personal *involvement* and, at the end, of more somber
experience, chapters XXXIII-XLIX.[8] In the chapters following
the episode of Pekuah's abduction (if I may expand this theme
a little), the mad astronomer is not merely observed, but con-
verted from his delirium and received into the family; even the
bitter old man comes home with them for a brief conversation.
A climax of experience and reflection is reached in the antepen-
ultimate chapters, with the visit to the Catacombs, Imlac's argu-
ment for the immortality of the soul, and Nekayah's conclusion:
"To me . . . the choice of life is become less important; I hope
hereafter to think only on the choice of eternity."

7. Gwin J. Kolb, "The Structure of *Rasselas*," *PMLA* 66 (1951): 702.
8. F. W. Hilles, "*Rasselas*, an 'Uninstructive Tale,'" in *Johnson, Bos-
well, and Their Circle*, Essays Presented to Lawrence Fitzroy Powell
(Oxford, 1965), pp. 111-13.

Nevertheless, I believe that the forty-nine chapters of the tale fall even more readily into another and more piecemeal pattern —more readily because with more aesthetic immediacy, more clearly segmented colouring. Thus: (1) chapters I-VI, the *unrest* of Rasselas in the valley, climaxed by the attempt at flying; (2) chapters VII-XV, the *story* of Imlac (surely too long in proportion to the whole book) and the implausible *escape* by tunnelling through the mountain; (3) chapters XVI-XXII, the first period at Cairo, *exploratory*, varicoloured, embracing the visit to the hermit; (4) chapters XXIII-XXIX, an extended *conversation*, on public and private life, on marriage and celibacy, between Rasselas and Nekayah; (5) chapters XXX-XXXIX, *adventures*: the Pyramids, abduction and recovery of Pekuah; (6) chapters XL-XLIX, return to Cairo and more *somber* experiences: the mad astronomer, the bitter old man, the Catacombs, the end. In each of these six segments, certain subdivisions can of course be seen. The first period in Cairo is notable for the rapid succession of separately sought-out episodes. The relentlessly continued conversation between the prince and his sister (chapters XXIII-XXIX) occupies the middle of the whole story as a prolonged central stasis or dead center. The sequence in which Pekuah is the focus of attention (chapters XXXI-XXXIX) is notable for the relative continuity of the adventure story. The visit to the Pyramids which begins this part, or ends the preceding, seems like a heavy punctuation mark (the accent of antiquity and the tomb), and this indeed is echoed in a second and similar punctuation, the visit to the Catacombs, which signals the end of the whole. The second period at Cairo, though it has fewer incidents than the first, is a sort of counterpart to the first, echoing its structure across the interval of the long conversation and the long adventure. Inside one episode in each Cairo period, a shorter and abruptly introduced intercalary episode, as we have seen, stands out like a special bump or knob in the grain of the story. The embittered and malignant old man looks out from his knot-hole or niche back across the chapters to the fearful and ruined country gentleman. But it is difficult to say just what is accomplished for the whole pattern by features of this sort. It is difficult, on the whole, to speak of the "structure" of *Rasselas* in a sense anything like that in which one speaks of the structure of a play by Shakespeare or of a novel by Fielding or Jane Austen. *Rasselas* has the kind of structure which satisfies, more or less, its modest requirements as a quasi-dramatic narrative—not the causal progression, the beginning, middle, and end of the Aristotelian "whole," but a structure of accumulation, something like that of a series of laboratory reports, or a series of chapters on animals sighted or taken, on a hunt across the veldt with gun or camera. "Eye Nature's walks, shoot Folly as it flies, And catch the Manners living as they rise."

Both Professor Kolb and, with less emphasis, Professor Hilles point out that the story, and especially the section dealing with the first period at Cairo, organizes a series of parallels and oppositions of human states and moral ideas: "prince and princess, male and female," "wise Imlac . . . naïve prince," "normal life . . . the happy valley," "urban life . . . rural," "epicurean . . . stoic," "shepherd, landlord, and hermit," "great and . . . humble," "youth and age, celibacy and matrimony . . . past and present."[9] There is nothing wrong with this kind of analysis. This kind of order, in some degree, may well be one of the requisites for the successful telling of such a tale. On the other hand, some such order is needed too in a moral essay or treatise, and maybe there it is needed even more. (It fits the conversation of the prince and his sister even better than their explorations.) We do not contrive a story for the sake of getting this kind of order, but perhaps the contrary, for the sake of relieving the threat of its rigors.

The Streaks of the Tulip

To put the matter conventionally and moderately, it is a paradox that a man who had Johnson's preference for both the homely and the abstract should undertake an oriental tale at all. Or better, it is a strangely fit incongruity that this tale, which both tries and refuses to be oriental, should contain as one of its most memorable exhibits a discourse on the art of poetry in which occurs the following sequence of assertions: (1) "I could never describe what I had not seen . . . I ranged mountains and deserts for images and resemblances, and pictured upon my mind every tree of the forest and flower of the valley." (2) "The business of a poet . . . is to examine, not the individual, but the species; to remark general properties and large appearances: he does not number the streaks of the tulip." (3) "He must be acquainted likewise with all the modes of life . . . and trace the changes of the human mind as they are modified by various institutions and accidental influences of climate and custom."

9. Kolb, pp. 707–08; Hilles, p. 112. These two essays are among the very few determined *critical* discussions of *Rasselas* I am familiar with. I have learned and have borrowed from both.

The local colour of *Rasselas*, the "oriental imagery" to the "charms" of which Boswell alludes, is not luxuriant. It is even very thin, and we may at moments wish it were thicker. It has a curiously deductive and even conjectural character—like the effort of a man who has read long ago a book of eastern travels for the purpose of translation, perhaps too has dipped into another book or two in the more recent past (see below, notes 22, 23).

The most conspicuous colour consists simply in the proper names of places, persons, and offices. We are "oriented" at the outset (chapter I) by the names "Abissinia," "Egypt," and "Amhara." Soon we follow Imlac (chapters VIII-XII) from "Goiama," near the "fountain of the Nile," by way of "the shore of the red sea," to "Surat," and to "Agra, the capital of Indostan," city of the "great Mogul," and thence to "Persia," "Arabia," "Syria," "Palestine," "many regions of Asia," "Egypt," "Cairo," and "Suez"—the latter names pre-establishing for us the route which will be followed by the fugitives from the valley a few chapters hence. Later, the sequence of adventure chapters (XXX-XXXIX) gives us "old Egyptians," the "Pyramids" (over and over), a "troop of Arabs," "Turkish horsemen," the "Bassa"[10] at Cairo, the "borders of Nubia," "the monastery of St. Anthony," "the deserts of Upper-Egypt," the "Arab's fortress" on an "island of the Nile . . . under the tropick."

"How easily shall we then trace the Nile through all his passage," says the aeronautical artist back in chapter VI. This is the first of altogether fifteen allusions by name to that great geographical feature and symbol. The escapees from the happy valley behold "the Nile, yet a narrow current, wandering beneath them." The hermit of chapter XXI lives "near the lowest cataract of the Nile." The "annual overflow" or "inundation" of the Nile is a leitmotif of chapters XLI-XLV, dealing with both the mad weather-maker and the sad old man. ("I rest against a tree, and consider, that in the same shade I once disputed upon the annual overflow of the Nile with a friend who is now silent in the grave.") In chapter XLIX, the Conclusion, a final "inundation of the Nile" confines the prince and his friends to reflection at home (as, long since, in the happy valley, Rasselas and Imlac had been brought together in "domestick amusements" forced upon them by an "inundation" from the lake). "No man," says the wise and aphoristic Nekayah, concluding an earlier chapter of conversation (XXIX), "can, at the same time, fill his cup from

10. A third Bassa. Two have been disposed of, along with a Sultan at Constantinople, murdered by Janisaries, in chapter XXIV.

the source and from the mouth of the Nile." But Johnson has come close to doing just this.

Another vehicle of exoticism may be identified here and there in a certain courtly, ceremonious, and archaic flourish of words —what Professor Hilles has called "the Grand Style," an aspect of the sublime.[11] This occurs a few times in the author's own voice, as in the opening of the first chapter: "Ye who listen with credulity to the whispers of fancy . . . attend." More often it is from the mouths of the characters—no doubt what the country gentleman of chapter XX detected as the "eloquence of Imlac . . . and the lofty courtesy of the princess." (It is Miltonic —like "Daughter of God and Man, immortal Eve.") As Rasselas saw the animals by moonlight, "'Ye,' said he, 'are happy . . . nor do I, ye gentle beings, envy your felicity'" (chapter II). "'Dear princess,' said Rasselas, 'you fall into the common error of exaggeratory declamation'" (chapter XXVIII). "'My dear Pekuah,' said the princess . . . 'Remember that you are companion of the princess of Abissinia'" (chapter XXXI). "Whoever thou art, that . . . imaginest happiness in royal magnificence, and dreamest . . . perpetual gratifications, survey the pyramids, and confess thy folly!" (chapter XXXII). Here Imlac echoes the rhythm of the narrator in the first sentence of the book. "'Illustrious lady,' said even the Arab outlaw, 'my fortune is better than I had presumed to hope.'" "'Lady,' said he, 'you are to consider yourself as sovereign'" (chapter XXXVIII, XXXIX). Probably the most full-blown instance in the book returns us, characteristically, to geography and to the mighty river. In chapter XXV, "The princess and her brother commonly met in the evening in a private summer-house on the bank of the Nile . . . As they were sitting together, the princess cast her eyes upon the river that flowed before her." And:

> "Answer," said she, "great father of waters, thou that rollest thy floods through eighty nations, to the invocations of the daughter of thy native king. Tell me if thou waterest, through all thy course, a single habitation from which thou dost not hear the murmurs of complaint?"

Certain other details of local colour are much less distinctive. At the start (chapter I) we are treated to "mountains," "rivulets," a "lake," "fish of every species," water falling "from precipice to precipice," "the banks of the brooks . . . diversified with flowers," "beasts of prey," "flocks and herds," "beasts of chase frisking in the lawns." We hear also of a "palace" with

11. Hilles, p. 113.

"squares or courts," "arches of massy stone," "upper stories," "private galleries," "subterranean passages," "columns," and "unsuspected cavities" closed with "marble." Such terms, so frequent throughout the work, whenever the argument seems to call for some evocation of physical decor, work as local colour mainly or only in conjunction with the proper names of places and persons which we have seen. It seems scarcely extreme to say that these combinations make the kind of local colour a schoolboy might supply. When I was in the eighth grade, we studied geography (which that year was Africa), and we had to write an imaginary journey through Egypt. I can still remember, approximately, one sentence of my composition—because it struck me at the time as so neatly yet richly executed. "Turning a bend in the Nile, we came in sight of the giant Assouan Dam."[12]

Certain other descriptive details are indeed more specially exotic. These, however, are scarce. I attempt the following approximately exhaustive list. In the "torrid zone"[13] of chapter I, we find the "monkey" and the "elephant." At the start of Imlac's travels in chapter VIII, we have "camels" and "bales" of goods. In chapter IX and again in XII, we have a "caravan," and in chapter X the "mosque of Mecca." In chapter XVIII, at Cairo, a "spacious building," with "open doors," housing a "school of declamation, in which professors read lectures," seems, in spite of its vagueness, much like a part of the ancient Alexandrian world. The shepherds in chapter XIX live in "tents." At the estate of the prosperous country gentleman in chapter XX, "youths and virgins" are "dancing in the grove" near a "stately palace."[14] In XXI, the hermit's "cell" is a "cavern" beneath "palm-trees." In XXX, as we begin to think of the Pyramids, we hear of "fragments of temples" and "choked aqueducts." In XXXII appear "galleries" and "vaults of marble"; in XXXIII, "dark labyrinths." The travel in the desert (chapters

12. Little did I realize that in turning that imaginary bend I must be very close to a spot once visited by Rasselas and Imlac. See above, note 5, and see below, note 26.

13. This phrase occurs again in chapter VII.

14. The opening paragraph of chapter XX, on the prosperous country gentleman, is a miniature projection in highly Johnsonian terms of an English landscaped park: "Shrubs diligently cut away to open walks," "boughs . . . artificially interwoven," "seats of flowery turf . . . raised in vacant spaces," "a rivulet . . . along the side of a winding path," "its banks . . . opened into small basins," "its stream obstructed by little mounds of stone." G. B. Hill, ed., *Rasselas* (1887), p. 179, has pointed out a parallel in Johnson's description in his *Life of Shenstone* of Shenstone's farm the Leasowes.

XXXI-XXXIX) gives us "tents"[15] (nine times), "camels" (three), "ounces of gold" (three),[16] "deserts" and "the desert," a "monastery," a "refectory," and a "prior"; in XXXVIII appear "carpets," "finer carpets," Pekuah's "upper vest" (with "embroidery"), "the lance," "the sword," "palaces," "temples," "granite," "porphyry"; in XXXIX, "the tropick," a "couch," "turrets," two special plums: "crocodiles" and "river-horses," "needlework," "silken flowers," and another plum: the "seraglio." In the final expedition, to the catacombs (XLVII-XLVIII), we have a "guard of horsemen," "sepulchral caves," a "labyrinth of subterraneous passages," "embalming" and "embalmed" bodies, "caverns."

A few ingenious manipulations of this slender exotic store, cunning jointures of it with the Johnsonian philosophic and plastic staple, stand out. In chapter I, just as I become mildly annoyed at "beasts of chase frisking in the lawns" and "the sprightly kid . . . bounding on the rocks," I am moderately diverted by "the subtle monkey frolicking in the trees, and the solemn elephant reposing in the shade." (No matter whether elephants would really be found in that mountain fastness.) By a somewhat different sort of conjunction, it seems to me, Johnson creates a moment of interesting local colour in chapter XXXIX, as Pekuah looks out on the "winding" river from her island prison: "The crocodiles and river-horses are common in this unpeopled region . . . For some time I expected to see mermaids and tritons, which, as Imlac has told me, the European travellers have stationed in the Nile."[17] And here let us quote too that moment of pregnant phrasing from chapter XXX: "The most pompous monument of Egyptian greatness, and one of the most bulky works of manual industry . . . are the pyramids." And from chapter XXXVIII, the Arab's observation to the lady Pekuah that

> buildings are always best preserved in places little frequented, and difficult of access: for, when once a country declines from its primitive splendour, the more inhabitants are left, the quicker ruin will be made. Walls supply stones more easily

15. "Women . . . weeping in the tents" (XXXII) may be said to have a specially oriental flavour.
16. Chapters XXXVII, XXXVIII, and XXXIX.
17. Donald M. Lockhart (*PMLA* 28 [1963]: 524; see below, note 23) shows the collocation of these four creatures on the upper Nile in Balthazar Telles, *Historia geral da Ethiopia a alta* (Coimbra, 1660), and in earlier atlases.

than quarries, and palaces and temples will be demolished to make stables of granite, and cottages of porphyry.[18]

By a slight extension of the idea of the exotic, perhaps we can bring in such learned words from the realm of *Mathematical Magick* as Johnson borrowed from his archaic dictionary source of that title,[19] or from other "philosophic" sources, and worked into chapter VI, the story of an attempt at the art of flying: "the tardy conveyance of ships and chariots," "the swifter migration of wings," "the pendent spectator," "volant animals," "the folding continuity of the bat's wings." And with these we come close to yet a wider category of somewhat notable descriptive phrases—all those, I should say, which, without including any word in any way exotic or bizarre, yet by some special energy of compression are likely to strike our attention or force on us the feeling that the description has "texture." In chapter I, the lake is "frequented by every fowl whom nature has taught to dip the wing in water . . . every blast shook spices from the rocks,[20] and every month dropped fruits upon the ground. All animals that bite the grass, or brouse the shrub . . . wandered in this extensive circuit." Such phrases as these may be looked on as Johnsonian substitutes for local colour.

A recent observer from the vantage point of Saudi-Arabia has expounded the extreme unrealism of the journey made by the princely party of fugitives, by ups and downs, through the nearly impassable tropical forests of the Abyssinian plateau, and then down the steep seven or eight thousand feet from the eastern escarpment to the narrow coastal plain and the port where they stayed several months. (This was probably Massawa, a typical Red Sea port, a "horrible place," lying under relentless sun, in saturation humidity.) No less dimly realized seem their "quick

18. Cf. Johnson in the *Western Islands* at St. Andrew's.
19. See Gwin J. Kolb, "Johnson's 'Dissertation on Flying,' and John Wilkins's *Mathematical Magick*," MP 47 (1949): 24–31; revised in *New Light on Dr. Johnson*, ed. F. W. Hilles (New Haven, 1959), pp. 91–106. Somewhere just to one side of this place in our scheme, perhaps we put such terms as "solstitial rains" and "equinoctial hurricanes" in chapter I, "celestial observations" in XXXIX, and the cluster of semi-technical terms that occurs in the chapters on the mad astronomer (XL–XLII): "constellations," "emersion of a satellite of Jupiter," "tropick to tropick," "dog-star," "crab," "equinoctial tempest," "equator," "axis of earth," "ecliptick of the sun," "solar system."
20. It seems to me at least possible that this remarkable phrase involves a typographical error. Why are spices shaken from the *rocks*? From plants, shrubs, and trees that grow among the rocks? One early traveller, Castanhoso, spoke of "honey from the rifts in the rocks." See J. R. Moore (note 23), p. 40.

and prosperous" coastal voyage [of twenty or thirty days] in a
primitive sailing dhow, their slow trip by camel caravan under
the desert stars to Cairo, and finally what must have been the
astonished arrival of this party of Coptic Christians amid the
teeming contrasts of a vast Islamic city.[21]

Johnson, we know, had long enjoyed some awareness of the
Abyssinian locale, for as a young man he had written and pub-
lished (1735) a translation from a French version of the seven-
teenth-century Portuguese Jesuit Father Jerome Lobo's *Voyage
to Abyssinia*.[22] Of recent years, the scholarship of sources has
been urging Johnson's debt to other writers on Abyssinia.[23]
Lobo, it is clear, could not have been his only source, for Lobo
said the prison of the princes was a rocky and "barren summit."
But the paradise on the Abyssinian hill was a commonplace—
"where Abassin kings their issue guard, Mount Amara—by some
supposed True Paradise, under the Ethiop line." One of the rea-
sons why Johnson was interested in Lobo's *Voyage* was that the
Jesuit missionary and diplomat himself was more interested in
human character and mores, the hardships and vicissitudes of

21. Louis E. Goodyear, "Rasselas' Journey from Amhara to Cairo
Viewed from Arabia," *Bicentenary Essays on "Rasselas,"* ed. Magdi
Wahba (Supplement to *Cairo Studies in English*, Cairo, 1959), pp. 21–30.

22. See Ellen Douglas Leyburn, "'No Romantick Absurdities or In-
credible Fictions,' The Relation of Johnson's *Rasselas* to Lobo's *Voyage
to Abyssinia*," *PMLA* 70 (1955): 1059–67.

23. John Robert Moore, "*Rasselas* and the Early Travellers to Abys-
sinia," *MLQ* 15 (1954): 36–41; Gwin J. Kolb, "The 'Paradise' in *Abyssinia*
and the 'Happy Valley' in *Rasselas*," *MP* 56 (1958): 10–16. (Kolb "redis-
covers" possible sources known to O. F. Emerson in his edition of *Rasselas*
[1895], pp. xxiv–xxviii); and Donald M. Lockhart, "'The Fourth Son of
the Mighty Emperor': The Ethiopian Background of Johnson's *Rasselas*,"
PMLA 58 (1963): 516–28. Lockhart's very learned and very clearly ex-
pounded article argues that Johnson, after an early interest in Ethiopia
represented by his *Lobo*, returned to the subject during his *Rambler* period
and undertook a heavy "project of documentation," a consultation of
"major sources for Ethiopian features." This programme "must have been
in progress and may even have been completed before 29 February 1752,"
when he published the first of the two *Ramblers* on Seged, Emperor of
Ethiopia—essays which have a "nearly identical bibliography" with *Rass-
elas*. He read not only Job Ludolph's *History of Ethiopia* (Latin, Frankfurt,
1681; English, London, 1682, 1684; "Ludolph's history of Ethiopia" in
the sale catalogue after Johnson's death), but other impressive texts, in-
cluding substantial passages in the Spanish of Luis de Urreta's *Historia
ecclesiastica . . . de la Etiopia*, Valencia, 1610. Whatever we may think of
this *PMLA*-ization of Johnson's working habits (which in effect supposes
deliberate heavy research not for *Rasselas* but for two *Rambler* essays),
Professor Lockhart makes it at least difficult to think that by 1752 Johnson
had not consulted some solid work on Ethiopia other than Lobo—
(Ludolph, at least, I should think).

the human adventure, than in exotic or fantastic colourations.[24]
Thus, Lobo reports of the crocodiles (which Pekuah saw from
the Arab's island fortress): "Neither I nor any with whom I
have convers'd about the *Crocodile*, have ever seen him Weep,
and therefore I take the Liberty of ranking all that hath been
told us of his Tears, amongst the Fables which are only proper
to amuse Children."[25] And Johnson, in a Preface to Lobo which
Boswell by quoting has made the best-known part of the book:

> THE *Portugese* Traveller, contrary to the general Vein of his
> Countrymen, has amused his Reader with no Romantick Ab-
> surdities or Incredible Fictions . . . He appears by his modest
> and unaffected Narration to have described Things as he saw
> them, to have copied Nature from the Life, and to have con-
> sulted his Senses not his Imagination; He meets with no *Bas-*
> *ilisks* that destroy with their Eyes, his *Crocodiles* devour their
> Prey without Tears, and his *Cataracts* fall from the Rock with-
> out Deafening the Neighbouring Inhabitants.[26]

Samuel Johnson—both Johnson the man and Johnson the trans-
lator of Lobo and the narrator of *Rasselas*—no doubt believes
that even the local colours, the geography, the flora, the fauna,
the architecture, and the costumes, of exotic places are far less
exotic than is commonly reported. Beyond doubt, he believes
that human living and human nature in Amhara or in Cairo are
far less exotic than is commonly supposed, are indeed essentially
the same as in London.

> THE Reader . . . will discover, what will always be discover'd
> by a diligent and impartial Enquirer, that wherever Human
> Nature is to be found, there is a mixture of Vice and Virtue, a
> contest of Passion and Reason.

General human nature is of course Johnson's theme—vice and
virtue, passion and reason. Why not then generalized local col-
our? The deliberate simplification, even complacent ignorance
about the actual colours of life in the supposed locale of John-
son's story, is a kind of counterpart and symbol of the general
human truth he would be getting at.

24. Leyburn makes this point very convincingly (p. 1067).
25. Lobo's *Voyage* (London, 1735), p. 104; Leyburn, p. 1066.
26. Lobo's *Voyage*, p. vii; Leyburn, pp. 1059–60; Boswell, *Life*, ed.
Hill-Powell, I.88. Cf. *Rasselas*, chapter XXI: "The hermit's cell . . . was a
cavern . . . at such a distance from the cataract, that nothing more was
heard than a gentle uniform murmur, such as composed the mind to pen-
sive meditation."

A Chorus of Sages

Various critical questions might be asked about *Rasselas*, but surely the main question must always be: What are we to make of the fact that the obvious element of morality is cast in the shape of an oriental tale? Or, what are we to make of the fact that the equally obvious oriental tale is invested with so much morality? The problem, or the task, of a writer who would tell a moral tale is, of course, to get the story and the morality together. He will have to do better than give us a close juxtaposition or rapid alternation of plot and sermon (programme and commercial plug), or a set of essays in a curiously wrought frame, a series of *Ramblers* inserted in a version of the *Arabian Nights*.[27] "We do not read *Rasselas* for the story," says Professor Hilles. "We read it for a view of life that is presented majestically in long sweeping phrases." But he immediately adds: "Diction, rhythms, character and plot are all of a piece."[28] So that he really has a warmer affection for the story (character and plot) than, for instance, Professor Kolb, who, while implying some distress at those critics who "have been content to praise the wisdom and ignore the narrative," at the same time (and on the same page) concludes "that the tale is not the principle which best explains . . . the book . . . the problem of happiness rather than the element of 'story' emerges . . . as the determinant by reference to which questions about the book's structure may be most adequately answered."[29] The structure is "didactic." And this seems to imply somehow that we can call it a "narrative," but not a "tale" or a "story."

In the second section of this essay, I have already given up the "structure" of *Rasselas* so far as that idea pretends to any

27. Any verbal or literary integration, if viewed from the outside, is a species of metaphoric (or symbolic) compression and projection.

William Kenney, in a useful survey, "Johnson's *Rasselas* after Two Centuries," *Boston University Studies in English* 3 (1957): 88–96, expounds objections often urged against three features of *Rasselas*: the unnatural *style*, the *pessimism*, the dubious or mixed *genre*. Kenney gives a good account of the nineteenth-century optimism which worked against *Rasselas*, and the more realistic attitude of our own age, which again favours it. My own reservations about *Rasselas*, difficulties, even objections, all relate to dramatic and organistic issues, and so embrace *style* and *genre*, as will be readily seen, but they do not reduce to these heads. By education, by long habit, and no doubt by inborn temperament, I enjoy a view of life antithetic to nineteenth-century optimism, and so I may claim to be a fundamentally receptive reader of *Rasselas*.

28. Hilles, pp. 114–15.
29. Kolb, pp. 699–700.

Aristotelian or organistic and dramatic implications. But then a story does not have to have *much* structure in order to be a story. It is a story if it has any characters and places at all, and if the characters do any talking at all and move about a little, from one place (or one state) to another. The story of *Rasselas* as such, a certain movement of certain persons in certain places —loosely constructed, vaguely characterized, largely undramatic or half-heartedly dramatic as it may be, unfictional fabric of a fiction that it is—has, nevertheless, some kind of imaginative bearing on the moral ideas. This is not an original thesis. "The eastern background," says Professor Kolb, "provides . . . the aura of strange and distant lands where human happiness is commonly thought to be complete and lasting; . . . reminding us of the superficial likenesses and essential differences between *Rasselas* and ordinary oriental tales with their happy-ever-after conclusions."[30] "The judgement of human life," says Professor Leyburn, "would leave a very different impression if it were presented stripped of such aesthetic distance as the regions of the Nile provide."[31] Oriental decor had been used in Augustan England for stories of adventure and fantasy (*Arabian Nights* and *Persian Tales*). It had well-established didactic uses too—as in *Spectator* and *Rambler* visions and apologues. An oriental spokesman could be used to throw a strange and skeptical perspective on Western mores (Montesquieu's *Persian Letters*, Goldsmith's *Chinese Letters*—just after *Rasselas*). The peculiar twist of Johnson's *Rasselas* is that he uses a sort of nominally or minimally exotic tale for the purpose of displaying the most homely human materials and of asserting a workaday perspective upon them.[32] The philosophy of *Rasselas* (Johnson's resistance to eighteenth-century "optimism") might readily enough become our theme now, but I am pushing, not the philosophy

30. Kolb, p. 703. Kolb quotes Robert M. Lovett and Helen S. Hughes, *The History of the Novel in England* (Boston, 1932), p. 125, in the opinion that the setting of the story in a "non-Christian part of the world" helps Johnson to "deal with man on a purely naturalistic level." But the main characters (taken historically) are Coptic Christians. (See above Mr. Goodyear and Professor Lockhart.) And they talk and think like Christians all through the story and especially in the Catacombs (chapter XLVIII).

31. Leyburn, p. 1067.

32. See, of course, Martha Pike Conant, *The Oriental Tale in England in the Eighteenth Century* (New York, 1908); Kolb, pp. 713ff.; Geoffrey Tillotson, "*Rasselas* and the *Persian Tales*," *TLS*, 16 November 1935, p. 534, and in his *Essays in Criticism and Research* (Cambridge, 1942), pp. 111–16. Tillotson and Kolb explore interesting parallels between *Rasselas* and certain adventuresome stories of unhappiness in *Persian Tales* Englished from the French by Ambrose Philips, *c.* 1714.

but the literary actualization of it, trying to improve the view
that it is important for Johnson's anti-rationalist and conserva-
tive purpose that he *should* have a story, of sorts, and a foreign
scene.

The Johnsonian substitutes for local colour, we have said, are
abstractive, at moments "philosophic," and all but invisible.
They may, for that very reason, have a broader spread than we
have so far mentioned. It was Johnson himself who observed of
Sir Thomas Browne that he "poured a multitude of exotick
words," and Johnson's friends Boswell and Arthur Murphy who
thought that Browne was a main source for Johnson's own
"Anglo-Latin" peculiarities. "How he differed so widely from
such elegant models [the Augustans] is a problem not to be
solved, unless it be true that he took an early tincture from the
writers of the last century, particularly Sir Thomas Browne."
Twenty-five years ago I ventured the opinion that Browne
"deserves the name 'exotick' which Johnson applies to him,"
but that this name would sit "curiously on Johnson himself."
"Where Browne uses remote terms to make us think of remote
things"—Pharaoh, mummy, golden calf, scorpion, and sala-
mander—"Johnson 'familiarizes.'"[33] That much is still true.
But, on the other hand, I will now undertake to argue that
Johnson's whole way of moral writing, what we may call the
Rambler style, is a form of moderate exoticism which did not
find its ideal setting until he wrote *Rasselas.* During the course
of producing his 208 *Ramblers*, Johnson tried out a number of
domestic settings of voices for the Rambler mood: the country
housewife and her kitchen (no. 51), Mr. Frolick the Londoner
in the country (no. 61), Quisquilius the curio-collector (nos.
82–83), Nugaculus the gossip (no. 103), Mrs. Busy (no. 138),
Captator the legacy-hunter (nos. 197–98). But in all such in-
stances, the more dramatic he makes the treatment, the more
the peculiar Rambleresque pomp of phrasing thins out. This hap-
pens even in the exotic setting of the Greenland idyll of Annin-
gait and Ajut (nos. 186–87). Perhaps it happens too with the
several oriental tales, including that of the Emperor Seged of
Ethiopia (nos. 204–05). Yet with the Emperor Seged, Johnson
was verging on the discovery of a curiously heightened affinity
between story and philosophic idiom. Perhaps the *Rambler* had
been all along a series of oriental apologues without the plot and
local colour?—the Rambler himself a kind of Abyssinian sage
without the name and the overt ethnic colouration? It was a

33. *The Prose Style of Samuel Johnson* (New Haven, 1941), pp. 117–
19.

strange language, that language of the Rambler in his own persona. Who really talked that way? Not Dryden or Addison, or Lord Chesterfield. Not really Johnson himself, except perhaps in the moments of his conversation when he was being the consciously pompous self-parodist or when Mrs. Thrale and Burney had come into the library at Streatham to "make" him "speak" a *Rambler*.[34]

The part of *Rasselas* which we remember best and carry away with us for allusion and quotation—the portable part—is beyond question the aphoristic moralism, the lugubrious orotundity. "We do not read *Rasselas* for the story." "Human life is everywhere a state in which much is to be endured, and little to be enjoyed." Who says this? Imlac, Rasselas, Nekayah, the Stoic philosopher, the hermit, the Arab, the mad astronomer, the old man? Any one of these, at the right moment, might say it. Actually, of course, we remember it is Imlac, near the end of his narrative of his own life (chapter XI)—the same Imlac who later, seated in one of the "most spacious chambers" of the great Pyramid, discourses so eloquently, in a vein of inverse romantic vision: "It seems to have been erected only in compliance with that hunger of imagination which preys incessantly upon life, and must be always appeased by some employment . . . I consider this mighty structure as a monument of the insufficiency of human enjoyments" (chapter XXXII). The same Imlac, who when the prince looks on a fissure in the rocks as a "good omen" of escape from the valley, replies—almost like a wound-up automaton, a speaking toy-philosopher: "If you are pleased with prognosticks of good, you will be terrified likewise with tokens of evil . . . Whatever facilitates our work is more than an omen, it is a cause of success . . . Many things difficult to design prove easy to performance."

"Marriage has many pains, but celibacy has no pleasures." Who says this? Any one of several characters might say it. Actually the speaker is the maiden princess Nekayah, in the course (chapter XXVI) of that lengthy and soon quarrelsome conversation with her brother about such profound issues: public and private life, youth and age, celibacy or marriage. The same princess who a few pages later, in the accents of a proto-Screwtape, "reckons" for us "the various forms of connubial infelicity . . . the rude collisions of contrary desire . . . the obstinate contests

34. In my *Prose Style of Samuel Johnson*, pp. 74–78, I assemble the main evidence both for and against the view that Johnson wrote as he talked. I am much more doubtful now than I was then that written prose is ever very close to conversation.

of disagreeable virtues, where both are supported by conscious-
ness of good intention) . . . " (chapter XXVIII).[35] The same
princess whom we have already heard, seated in the summer-
house by the bank of the Nile, utter her apostrophe to that
mighty "father of waters" who rolls his "floods through eighty
nations."[36]

The courtly and ceremonious discourse which we have already
noticed as a kind of local colour is only the most obvious in-
stance of a lofty and reflective idiom which plausibly pervades
nearly the whole of this oriental tale. (The notion of an oriental
sage, philosopher, poet, emperor, prince, is an easy one for us
to entertain. Who ever heard of an oriental buffoon or ninny?)
The *Rambler* idiom, Johnson's own idiom, if we like, an expan-
sion of homely human wisdom into the large perspective of
Latinate philosophic diction, is projected across time and
space, straight from London and Fleet Street, to cover appro-
priately, with a veil of the delicately exotic,[37] scenes which we
know, by a more than willing suspension of disbelief, are enacted
at places along the Nile from Amhara to Cairo.

The notion of *Rasselas* as a "comedy" (Johnson's "greatest
comic work") has been urged by two recent writers.[38] A third,
Professor Hilles again, thinks that they "overstress" the "comic
element." Probably they do overstress it. Professor Tracy sees
a "comic" (perhaps, rather, a "satirical") reduction of man's
fatuousness, shrewd laughter at the prince's chronic failure of
common sense, demolition of the poet Imlac's "grandiloquent
. . . rapture." Professor Whitley finds "pure comedy of ideas"
in the episodes of the first period at Cairo, "comedy of emotion
and behaviour," and "deflated oriental romance," in Pekuah's

35. R. W. Chapman's text (1927), following the second edition, 1759,
has "disagreeing virtues." But "disagreeable" appears at least as early as
the collected *Works* of 1787 (xi.78) and is so much more interesting that I
admit it.
36. "The character of the Princess is wanting in dramatic power. She is
sometimes Rasselas, sometimes Imlac, sometimes undisguised Johnson.
What she says is often very well said, but it might just as well, and often
even better, have been said by a man" (*Rasselas*, ed. Hill, 1887, 1954,
p. 31).
37. "The language they speak is language that no human being has ever
been heard to use." The opening sentence of the book is "incantation, ap-
plied at the outset to a never-never land" (Hilles, pp. 113-14).
38. Clarence F. Tracy, "'Democritus, Arise!' a Study of Dr. Johnson's
Humor," *Yale Review* 39 (1949): 305-10; Alvin Whitley, "The Comedy of
Rasselas," *ELH* 23 (1956): 63-65. Sheridan Baker, in an essay which
appeared after I had written my own ("*Rasselas*: Psychological Irony and
Romance," *PQ* 45 [1966]: 249-61) stresses the humanly internal or "psy-
chological" aspects of the ironic contrasts to romance idiom.

abduction, "dark comedy" in the later chapters about the mad astronomer and the catacombs. Probably we are on safer ground if we are content to say, with Professor Hilles, simply that the attitude prevailing in the story is not, as so often said, "pessimistic," not morose, not cynical, not even satirical; it is rather, gently "ironic" and "realistic." The "smile of the author is a sad smile."[39] Yes—though one may need to insist that it *is* a smile. With Professor Hilles, we must differ from certain critics who have supposed that a "tragic sense of life . . . informs it." It appears to me next to impossible that anyone should be moved either to tears or to shudders at any part of *Rasselas*. "In a short time the second Bassa was deposed. The Sultan [at Constantinople], that had advanced him, was murdered by the Janisaries." But that was, if not a long time ago, yet very far in another country. (The chapter, XVIII, where the Stoic philosopher mourning the death of his daughter is put in a position of nearly laughable contrast to his declamation of the preceding day is perhaps the only part of the whole book that verges on the uncomfortable.) "In a year the wings were finished and, on a morning appointed, the maker appeared furnished for flight on a little promontory: he waved his pinions a while to gather air, then leaped from his stand, and in an instant dropped into the lake."[40] There we have the characteristic motion of the story as action—the immediate and inevitable plunge, so inevitable and so confidently foreseen as to warrant not the smallest flourish or comment.[41] "'I . . . resolve to return into the world tomorrow' . . . He dug up a considerable treasure which he had hid among the rocks, and accompanied them to the city, on which, as he approached it, he gazed with rapture" (chapter XXI). At many moments the comic smile of the narrator is turned directly on one or another of his characters. "'But surely, interposed the prince . . . Whenever I shall seek a wife, it shall be my first question, whether she be willing to be led by reason?'" (chapter XXIX). More often, however, or in general, the smile of this narrator envelops in a less direct way, in a more reticent parodic spirit, the whole of his own Abyssinian tale. He is very close to the endlessly meditative and controversial nature of each of his personae. What does the narrator think of his own

39. Hilles, pp. 115-19.
40. G. B. Hill's remark in 1887 that "Johnson is content with giving the artist a ducking. Voltaire would have crippled him for life at the very least; most likely would have killed him on the spot" remains as valid as ever (*Rasselas*, ed. Hill, 1887, 1954, p. 165).
41. "The end . . . is immediate, flat and final" (Tillotson, *Essays in Criticism and Research*, 1942, p. 116).

"Tale" when he gives his chapters titles such as these: "The prince continues to grieve and muse," "A dissertation on the art of flying," "Imlac's history continued. A dissertation upon poetry," "Disquisition upon greatness," "Rasselas and Nekayah continue their conversation," "The dangerous prevalence of imagination," "The conclusion, in which nothing is concluded"?

In real life, Johnson sometimes indulged in a complacent self-consciousness and amusement at his own inflations. His moments of self-parody are celebrated. In his essays too, *Ramblers* and *Idlers*, a sort of shackled playfulness often parodies the solemn parade. A shadow of grimace accents some restrained contrast between gravity of diction and homeliness or meanness of sentiment.[42] In *Rasselas*, the Johnsonian speaker has translated himself into a realm of sober fantasy where the grim smile, the sad smile, the wan smile, can be more or less constant. Probably it was some feeling like this about the tale that prompted Voltaire to say that its philosophy was *aimable*.[43] Indeed there are profoundly reflective and even solemn moments—and they occur increasingly in the later chapters—at the Pyramids, in the conversation about the astronomer's madness, in the confrontation with the savagely embittered old man, and finally at the Catacombs, in the contemplation of death and immortality. But the last seems to me the only place where it may be impossible to find a smile. Here the initially dominant tone is metaphysical sobriety ("as thought is, such is the power that thinks; a power impassive and indiscerptible"), and this deepens at the end to theological solemnity ("The whole assembly stood a while silent and collected . . . 'To me,' said the princess, 'the choice of life is become less important: I hope hereafter to think only on the choice of eternity'"). But this is an exceptional moment, not the ground tone of the book and not its conclusion. The conclusion, in which nothing is concluded, reverts to the basic plan.

It is not possible to smile sympathetically at nothingness without a degree of participation. Johnson's way of laughter is not the high-comedy way of the wit and his butts, but a quieter way of partly encumbered rehearsal and laboured formulation. Martin Price has deftly alluded to the "gently preposterous oriental setting" of Johnson's tale, "the self-mocking formality of its dialogue, the balance and antithesis of characters as well

42. See my *Philosophic Words* (New Haven, 1948), pp. 115–21; *The Prose Style of Samuel Johnson*, pp. 61, 76.
43. Hilles, p. 115; Boswell, *Life*, II.500, quoting Voltaire's letter of 16 May 1760 to a French translator of *Rasselas*.

as dialogue, and the circularity of its total structure."[44] All this is the *imagination* of Johnson's quasi-oriental and ceremonious no-tale—"the wine of absurdity," or absurdity mitigated only in its own rich self-contemplation. In our day, Albert Camus has explained absurdity in Kantian terms as "the division between the mind that desires and the world that disappoints."[45] Johnson's *Rasselas* has much in common with modern versions of the absurd—with a *Godot* or a *Watt*. One main difference, which may disguise the parallel for us, is that the modern versions of the descent take place at a level which is, to start with, subterranean, the very sub-cellar or zero level of modern man's three-century decline from the pinnacles of theology and metaphysics. Johnson's descendental exercise, with its saving theological clause in the Catacombs, takes place at a level still near the top of the metaphysical structure. It is of course all the richer for this. In the "endgame" played at the modern level, a nearly complete numbness and boredom is roused only as occasional stabs and jolts of obscenity reach a buried nerve. In the more spacious and better lighted areas available to Johnson, there was still eloquence—an eloquence profound and moving as it verges continually on a smiling absurdity.

1968

44. Martin Price, *To the Palace of Wisdom* (New York, 1964), pp. 316–17.
45. Paul West, *The Wine of Absurdity* (State College, Penna., 1966), pp. [ix], xii, 57. See the same author's "Rasselas: The Humanist as Stoic," *English* 13 (1961): 182–85.

JOHNSON'S DICTIONARY

Samuel Johnson's *Dictionary of the English Language* was pub-
lished in two folio volumes by a combination of London book-
sellers on April 15 just 200 years ago.[1] It is a big book—big
enough to furnish materials for a number of different studies.
Today I wish to talk about it both as a certain kind of lexi-
cographic feat and in virtue of that as a record and revelation
of a certain mind and personality. On account of the latter bias
it is inevitable that I shall not say everything of a technical and
philological nature that it is possible to say about the Dictionary;
it is even likely that I shall neglect some of the main things that
historians of lexicography and the English language might wish
to hear said.

What kind of bigness does Johnson's Dictionary have? We dis-
cover, perhaps with some surprise, that it was not the biggest
English dictionary of its era in the sense of listing and defining
more words than any other. Johnson's Dictionary lists about
40,000 words. But the folio *Dictionarium* of Nathan Bailey
(Johnson's nearly immediate predecessor and one of his finding
tools in his own work) had in the edition of 1730 listed about
48,000 words and in that of 1736, about 60,000. The revision of
Bailey by Joseph Nicol Scott which appeared in 1755 as a rival
to Johnson's second edition, went as high as about 65,000
words. There are other respects too in which Johnson's Dictio-
nary was less extraordinary for its era than one might have
thought. And these respects the scholars of the neutralizing and
levelling habit of mind have recently been adducing with some
gusto. It may not be altogether clear, for instance, that Johnson's
selection of the words that make up his 40,000 was more
judicious—that is, more prophetic of English linguistic develop-
ment or more influential on that development—than the lists of
Bailey or other contemporaries. And it must all along have been
fairly obvious that Johnson was not the first to write a history
of the English language, or a grammar, or a preface to a dic-
tionary, and that his efforts under the first two of these heads
were even somewhat perfunctory. His etymological notions were

1. This paper was originally delivered as a lecture on April 15, 1955, at
the opening of an exhibition entitled "Johnson's Dictionary" in the Yale
University Library.
Parallels to several parts of the paper and further documentation are
to be found in my *Philosophic Words* (1948), and in my articles and notes
on Johnson's Dictionary appearing in the *Times Literary Supplement*
(1946), *Review of English Studies* (1947), *Modern Language Review*
(1948), *ELH* (1948), *Johnsonian News Letter* (1950), and *Studies in
Philology* (1951).

unlearned by modern standards, and in places even comic. His attempts to discourage some words by applying a kind of linguistic weedkiller, or notation of censure, were not very successful; even in his Preface he reports his loss of faith in that campaign. Johnson was not the first to write definitions of English words nor the first to subdivide and number his definitions. In short, and to use the phrasing of the recent scholarship, Johnson wrote his Dictionary in an age when "many men, at work on different undertakings, were thinking in similar ways." And both in his history and grammar and in his Plan and Preface, and presumably in all the rest of the work, he proceeded under the handicap of being rather "fully . . . aware of tradition."[2]

A single respect remains in which Johnson must be credited with a large measure of originality. He was the first English dictionary-maker to collect and insert substantial illustrations of his meanings—authorities or testimonies from the wealth of documents in which the English language had been achieved and preserved. With respect to the use of authorities, simply considered, it is true, however, that certain anticipations of Johnson's method may be pointed out. These appear on the Continent, in Italian, French, Spanish, and Portuguese dictionaries, and especially in the revised *Vocabolario* of the Italian Accademia della Crusca issued in 1729. And once again we have our warning from the recent scholars. It would be "hardly wise" to view Johnson's Dictionary as the first English dictionary of its kind, a conspicuous transcendence of all earlier English dictionaries in the feature of its quoted authorities, the fulfilment of a demand which Englishmen had been voicing for nearly two hundred years. We are only "wise" if we try to see Johnson's Dictionary in an international perspective and to assimilate it as far as possible to Italian and French models. For Johnson's "announced intention" was to "rival the academies." That is, he refers several times to both the Italian and French academies in his Plan and in his Preface, and this is important—even though the authorities who composed the French Academy were content to rest on their authority and furnished their *Dictionnaire* with no illustrations.[3] But I am not sure I understand this line of argument.

2. Gwin J. Kolb and James H. Sledd, "Johnson's *Dictionary* and Lexicographical Tradition," *Modern Philology* 50 (1953): 184. Shortly after the present paper was read, Professors Kolb and Sledd published *Dr. Johnson's Dictionary: Essays in the Biography of a Book* (1955), in which the article here cited reappeared as the first chapter.
3. Kolb and Sledd, "Johnson's *Dictionary*," pp. 173-74, 184, 193.

I remain content to argue that Johnson's Dictionary has an extraordinary character and enjoys a unique position in virtue of its numerous, varied, and substantial illustrative passages and the framing of these by his discriminations and definitions. There are four contemporary accounts, including Johnson's own in his Preface, of how he made his Dictionary. The biographer Hawkins says that Johnson began with a copy of Bailey's folio, using it as a list of words in which he interleaved definitions and illustrations when they had been discovered in his various authorities. Boswell's statement that words were "partly taken from other dictionaries, and partly supplied by [Johnson] himself," that they were "written down with spaces left between," and that Johnson then filled in the etymologies and definitions, seems a safe enough account of a certain phase of the work. But Boswell is not very clear about the authorities, seeming actually to suppose that these were copied by the printers of Johnson's Dictionary directly from the books which Johnson had marked with his black lead pencil. Later Bishop Percy in a reminiscence of talks with Johnson gives a more plausible testimony. As Johnson "himself expressly described" the matter:

> He began his task by devoting his first care to a diligent perusal of all such English writers as were most correct in their language, and under every sentence which he meant to quote, he drew a line, and noted in the margin the first letter of the word under which it was to occur. He then delivered these books to his clerks, who transcribed each sentence on a separate slip of paper, and arranged the same under the word referred to. By these means he collected the several words and their different significations; and when the whole arrangement was alphabetically formed, he gave the definitions of their meanings, and collected their etymologies from . . . writers on the subject.[4]

Here is a report which has the accent of substantial truth. Johnson himself in his Preface reported that "the deficiency of dictionaries was immediately apparent." "When they were exhausted" (and I take this to mean: when a brief skirmish had revealed their almost total unfitness for his purpose), "what was yet wanting must be sought by fortuitous and unguided

4. ". . . taken from the third edition of Dr. Robert Anderson's *Life of Johnson*, published in 1815. . . . recorded by Percy, in 1805, in an interleaved copy of the second edition" (*Johnsonian Miscellanies*, II: 208, 214).

excursions into books, and gleaned as industry should find, or chance should offer it, in the boundless chaos of a living speech." Let us set to one side any thought about the mechanical difficulties which we may well suppose would have arisen through the attempt to interleave Johnson's copious illustrations in Bailey's one-volume folio—and set aside also any speculations about the actual assemblage of copy in the eighty large notebooks which are mentioned by Boswell in another place. The idea that is essential to a comprehension of Johnson's feat is that he read his authorities, at least in large part, first.[5] He embarked on a huge program of reading English poetry, drama, prose essays, history, biography, science, and arts. He then arranged his collection of words alphabetically, matched the list thus obtained against other dictionaries, mainly Bailey, and wrote in some words that he had missed—the occasional words that appear in the Dictionary with only the tag *Dict.* or *Bailey* or *Ainsworth* or *Phillips* appended.

The one thing it is absurd to suppose Johnson did is that he began working through Bailey or any other dictionary alphabetically, departing on excursions through English literature for each illustration as the need arose. This, as Bishop Percy remarks, "would have taken the whole life of any individual." Try to imagine Johnson at his task of single-handed reading for the Dictionary, and you will see, or feel, that the essential and operative principles in the enterprise were precisely his own great powers as a reader—his strength and tenacity, his initial familiarity with English usage, his comprehension of what his plan implied, and his continuing and cumulative capacity to remember what he had already done and what he had yet to do. Imagine yourself halfway through Johnson's program of reading for the Dictionary, arriving at the page of Bacon's *Natural History* which lies open in the exhibition outside this room today. Which of the words and passages on the page would you mark in black lead pencil for your amanuenses to copy? Which would you pass over? By what norms would you make your selection? How many minutes would you need to reach your decisions on one page? It is my impression on reading the tentative, brief, and scattered remarks on authorities which Johnson makes in his Plan of a Dictionary, published in 1747, that at that date he had barely begun his reading, or perhaps had not yet begun it at all. His elaborate and eloquent reflections on the topic in his

5. "Johnson has four Amanuenses still employ'd in his English Dictionary; but their Business will soon be over; for they have almost transcrib'd the Authorities" (Thomas Birch to Philip Yorke, 6 August 1748, British Museum, Add. MS 35, 397, fol. 140. Courtesy Professor James L. Clifford).

Preface (written seven years later) testify to the magnitude, the
novelty, and the richness of the experience when he actually en-
countered it, as well as to its supreme importance for the making
of the Dictionary.

I therefore extracted from philosophers principles of science;
from historians remarkable facts; from chymists complete
processes; from divines striking exhortations; and from poets
beautiful descriptions.

If the language of theology were extracted from *Hooker* and
the translation of the Bible; the terms of natural knowledge
from *Bacon*; the phrases of policy, war, and navigation from
Raleigh; the dialect of poetry and fiction from *Spenser* and
Sidney; and the diction of common life from *Shakespeare*,
few ideas would be lost to mankind, for want of English
words, in which they might be expressed.

The chief glory of every people arises from its authors . . .
I shall not think my employments useless or ignoble . . . if
my labours afford light to the repositories of science, and add
celebrity to *Bacon*, to *Hooker*, to *Milton*, and to *Boyle*.

Johnson's reading of the authorities first was a shrewd, an
energetic, a daring stroke. The most conspicuous result was that
he got the Dictionary done. Look for a moment at Johnson's
Dictionary as a practical and economic venture, a piece of book-
maker's engineering, and you find it a signal instance of that
sanity, perspective, balance, and sense of proportion for which
Johnson's whole career is so notable. Consider the meaning of
his complacent statement to Boswell: "I knew very well what I
was undertaking—and very well how to do it—and have done it
very well." Or of the somewhat too confident boast, in mid-
stream, about the single Englishman and three years against
forty Frenchmen and forty years. One of Johnson's humble
amanuenses, a Scot named Macbean, later began to compile a
geographical dictionary, provoking from Johnson the comment:
"I have lost all hopes of his ever doing anything properly, since
I found he gave as much labour to Capua as to Rome." John-
son's own way was exactly the opposite. It is true that as the
work proceeded he had to make certain retrenchments. One of
these, as he complains in his Preface, was the "detruncation"
and even the complete sacrifice of numerous flowers of expres-
sion which were part of his original collection. Another was the
minimizing and slighting of references which begins in the Dic-
tionary, so obviously, after the letter A. But on the whole John-

son set out with a strategy admirably fitted to his aims and to the mechanics of research which were at his disposal, a workable set of rules, well calculated to bring a single master reader and a staff of amanuenses in nine years to the conclusion of even so large a task. The job was done with economy of effort, confidence, rapidity. If it was also in some senses haphazard, incomplete, even careless, any other policy, under the conditions which governed the enterprise, would have been quixotic. Johnson had the good sense to see that, given the generosity of his major vision, some deficiencies were inevitable. He had the courage to proceed without scruple.

And here I think it may be appropriate if I insert a few words in recognition of those London booksellers who were Johnson's immediate patrons in the Dictionary project and who made it possible not only that a Dictionary, but that this particular kind of Dictionary, should be compiled. W. Strahan, J. and P. Knapton, T. and T. Longman, C. Hitch and L. Hawes, A. Millar, and R. and J. Dodsley (thus runs the roster on the title page of the first edition)—with their business addresses in New Street, in the Strand, at the Crown in Ludgate Street, at the Ship and at the Red Lion in Paternoster Row, at Tully's Head in Pall Mall—these sponsors of the Dictionary were in their own way members of an English academy, and in their alliance with Johnson, who supplied the learning of the academy, they contrast with the continental academies in a manner closely tied in with the spirit of sturdy eccentricity which the English during that age were cultivating with so much satisfaction. What a literary academy might have done for England was to be recited more than a century later by Matthew Arnold in his anachronistic essay on "The Literary Influence of Academies." The reason why there was never an English academy is somewhat violently betrayed by Johnson himself in his Dictionary Preface. "If an academy should be established for the cultivation of our style," he begins to speculate, but immediately adds, "which I, who can never wish to see dependence multiplied, hope the spirit of *English* liberty will hinder or destroy." "The edicts of an English Academy," he wrote later, in his *Life of Roscommon*, "would probably be read by many, only that they might be sure to disobey them."

Johnson seems to have had a strong sense of the personal character of his undertaking, his personal proprietorship. Let me pursue for a few moments one of the most traditional themes of Johnsonian Dictionary celebration—that of the numerous whimsical and licentious manifestations of his personality which the lexicographer permitted himself. Here again of course I encounter the frown of the levellers, who want to tell me that even in Johnson's day dictionary-making was a sober thing, that the lexicographer had "few opportunities for originality, few temptations to eccentricity, and every inducement to follow the beaten track."[6] But here again I would urge Johnson's sense of proportion, his insight into the nature of the specific thing he was doing, and its real decorum. A century and a half later, if he had been one of the staff working on the new *Oxford English Dictionary on Historical Principles*, certain things might not have been possible. Modern scholarship sometimes seems to want to read Johnson as if he had been a member of such a staff. An elaborate article in *PMLA* was once devoted to arguing that Johnson's account of "oats" in the Dictionary was not a joke on the Scots (because the joke has sources, and because such trifling would have been out of place in a philological monument). But Johnson himself said later that he "meant to vex them." And in his own Dictionary, I ask, why not? Boswell alludes to Johnson's "capricious and humorous indulgence" of his own "opinions" and "prejudices." Johnson's Scotch critic Lexiphanes Campbell said it was a "very facetious dictionary"—"witty," "personal," "political," "national," and "patriotical," "in a word, everything but what it ought to be." A long list of the curiosities in the Dictionary—the jests against Whig, patron, dedicator, favourite, pension, or excise, the audacities, delinquencies, loyalties, and mellow moments—have long ago become common property, to be looked up, if we forget them, in Courtney's *Bibliography*, in Hill's footnotes to Boswell, in the more neglected *Leisure Moments in Gough Square* by Alfred Stringer. A few other matters of this sort I believe I myself may have been the first to discover, and as news of such discoveries does not travel very fast, I may still share with the shade of Johnson some kind of proprietorship.

Under the head of satire and insult, for instance, Johnson would not only write a definition of "oats" that said something about horses in England and men in Scotland, but he would cut up a metaphysical satire by John Cleveland, *The Rebel Scot*, and insert twenty-seven pieces of it in his Dictionary, at least thirteen of them good, cleanly pointed anti-Scot jibes, the more amusing, or annoying, perhaps, because planted mostly under quite innocent words. Thus, under *proselyte* and again under *twilight*.

6. Sledd and Kolb, "Johnson's Definitions of *Whig* and *Tory*," *PMLA* 57 (1952): 882.

> He that saw hell in's melancholy dream,
> And in the *twilight* of his phancy's theme,
> Scar'd from his sins, repented in a fright,
> Had he view'd Scotland, had turn'd *proselyte.*

Or consider the case of Lord Bolingbroke. Bolingbroke had written deistic essays and at his death had left "half a crown" to a "beggarly Scotchman" to publish them. Bolingbroke used Gallicisms. And it has been often noticed that his name appears coupled with a linguistic censure under the word *Gallicism* in the Dictionary. But other ways occurred to Johnson too. Thus under the word *irony* he would write simply: "A mode of speech in which the meaning is contrary to the words: as, *Bolingbroke was a holy man.*" And under the word *sophistically*, he would take a friendly passage in a letter from Swift to Pope, something about the difference between Swift's poverty and Bolingbroke's wealth: "I must observe that my Lord Bolingbroke, from the effects of his kindness to me, argues most sophistically. The fall from a million to a hundred thousand pounds is not so great, as from eight hundred pounds a year to one." Johnson would take this and trim it down to four words, which it seems safe to say few readers have ever understood as *not* referring to philosophic or political argument. "*Sophistically*: With fallacious subtilty."

> Bolingbroke argues most sophistically.
>
> —Swift

In the eighteenth century Horace Walpole could write: "It would have been a very extraordinary work if he had inserted all the words he has coined himself, but he had unluckily excluded himself, as he confined his authorities to our Standard authors." We of course know better than that. We know that Johnson would quote himself in the Dictionary, sometimes overtly, sometimes under cover of the tag "anonymous." In a spurt of curiosity a few years ago I counted altogether forty-eight of these self-quotations.[7] Some of them show Johnson's memory at work in the characteristically free way of a poet, as when a line quoted from *Irene*[8] does not follow the printed

---

7. William R. Keast, in *Notes & Queries*, new series, 2 (1955): 292-93, and 3 (1956): 262, adds three more. The same writer's "The Two *Clarissas* in Johnson's *Dictionary*," *Studies in Philology* 54 (1957): 429-39, is one of the most curious revelations yet made concerning Johnson's use of a contemporary source.

8. Mouldring arches, and *disjointed* columns.

text nor yet the manuscript now in the British Museum, but is a
tidying up of the latter. And at least some of the quotations
marked "anonymous" I should suppose to represent a real mo-
ment of uncertainty on Johnson's part as to their authorship.
As a kind of support and complement to this theory, let me
adduce the couplet quoted under the word *island* from Pope's
Essay on Man:

> Some safer world in depths of woods embrac'd,
> Some happier *island* in the wat'ry waste,

to which Johnson affixes his own name: *Johnson*. Certain
phrases—something about a "secret island in the boundless
main," "some happier place"—in two passages of Johnson's
London (a poem quoted twice by title and five times anony-
mously in the Dictionary) do a great deal, it seems to me, to
promote the suspicion that in that quotation from Pope over
Johnson's name the sympathy between the minds of the two
poets was for a moment perfect. Let me insist that for me this
notion has not the faintest derogatory implication.

But what I shall call the "best" instance of Johnson's self-
quotation in the Dictionary is a different sort of thing. The
word *dissipate* in the Dictionary is unique in that under it John-
son quotes himself two times. And behind that juncture a person
with a pinch of good will may read the following story: In the
spring of 1738 appeared Johnson's *London*. Here, following his
Juvenalian model, he produces the "injured" and complaining
character Thales, who is about to leave London for the rural
retirement of Wales and bids farewell to a sympathetic friend. A
little more than a year later it must indeed have seemed a curious
parallel (as if, to use the sceptical words of Boswell, "the event
had been foreseen") when Johnson himself said a fond farewell
to his friend the down-at-heels and chronically injured poet
Richard Savage as the latter was about to set out toward a last
and unsuccessful attempt at readjustment in the retirement of
Wales. Savage "parted" from Johnson "with tears in his eyes."
Johnson himself wrote a *Life of Savage* a few years later and
tells us that circumstance. In the Dictionary under the transitive
verb *dissipate*, sense 2, "To scatter the attention," Johnson
quotes:

> This slavery to his passions produced a life irregular and
> *dissipated*.
>
> —*Savage's Life*

And immediately below, under sense 3, "To spend a fortune,"
he quotes:

> The wherry that contains
> Of *dissipated* wealth the poor remains.
> —*London*

I suggest that in this collocation of materials we have Johnson's casually erected and semi-private testimony to the fact that in what was for him a peculiarly poignant instance, life had been the realization of poetic vision.

Certain other examples of softer sentiment in the Dictionary are very well known. Let me conclude this section of my paper by quoting two of them, with some attempt at a gloss upon the second. Both touch the theme of home-coming. Under *Grubstreet*, after the abrasive definition:

> originally the name of a street in Moorfields in London, much inhabited by writers of small histories, dictionaries, and temporary poems; whence any mean production is called *grubstreet*,

he throws in two lines of Greek from the *Palatine Anthology*, which mean approximately:

> Hail! Ithaca! after struggles and after bitter trials,
> Gladly do I approach thy threshold.

Then there is the word *lich*, a dead body, and *Lichfield*. . . . ("The earth that's nature's mother is her tomb; What is her burying grave that is her womb.") A strong blend of interest attaches to the very etymology and history of the name, and upon these Johnson dwells for a moment, before the sudden intrusion of a Latin apostrophe which leaps to the paradoxically united opposite of feeling.

> *Lich*, a dead carcase, whence *lichwake*, the time or act of watching by the dead; *lichgate*, the gate through which the dead are carried to the grave, *Lichfield*, the field of the dead, a city in Staffordshire, so named from martyred Christians. *Salve magna parens.*

But it is now time to shift our attention and attempt to say something about certain more essential features of the Dictionary, the peculiar and richly interesting texture of its illustrations and definitions as these appear from page to page, from A to Z. One main principle to be observed is that Johnson regularly chose passages not only because they were good examples of certain meanings but because they were in themselves interesting. In his Plan he had promised "such sentences as, besides

their immediate use, may give pleasure or instruction, by con-
veying some elegance of language, or some precept of prudence
or piety." After the abbreviations and eliminations, which in
the course of his work had been forced upon him, he reflected
in his Preface that he had yet "spared" some passages which
might "relieve the labour of verbal searches, and intersperse
with verdure and flowers the dusty desarts of barren philology."
This policy was noted and censured as a lexicographical fault by
his American successor Noah Webster. It may not be an econom-
ical pattern of lexicography. But the very objection of Webster
serves to point up the difference between the Dictionary of
Johnson and all others.

Johnson's Dictionary—as a reader knowing the character and
literary taste of the author might indeed have hoped—is, for one
thing, embellished by numerous aphorisms, anecdotes, thumb-
nail dramas, biographical glimpses, drawn from Bacon, for
instance, from Shakespeare, from Ben Jonson, from Knolles,
from Camden, from L'Estrange, from Swift.

As a cock was turning up a dunghill, he espied a diamond:
Well (says he) this sparkling foolery now to a *lapidary* would
have been the making of him; but, as to any use of mine, a
barley-corn had been worth forty on't.

—L'Estrange

And must they all be hang'd that swear and lie?
. . . . Every one.
. . . . Who must hang them?
. . . . Why, the honest men.
. . . . Then the liars and *Swearers* are fools; for there are
liars and *Swearers* enow to beat the honest men, and hang
them up.

—Shakespeare

Thou hast most traitorously corrupted the youth of the
realm in erecting a *Grammar School*.

—Shakespeare

A philosopher being asked in what a wise man differed from a
fool? answered, send them both *naked* to those who know
them not, and you shall perceive.

—Bacon

Hope is a good *breakfast* but it is a bad supper.

—Bacon

Sir Henry Wotton used to say, that criticks were like *brushers*
of noblemen's clothes.

—Bacon

Cromartie after fourscore went to his country-house to live *thriftily*, and save up money to spend at London.

—Swift

An old lord of Leicestershire amused himself with mending *pitchforks* and spades for his tenants gratis.

—Swift

(Johnson's marked copy of Bacon's *Apophthegms* and *Ornamenta Rationalia* shows that he originally selected many more examples of this kind than actually appear in the Dictionary after his retrenchments.)

Again, Johnson's Dictionary is generously planted with miniature expressions of literary theory and of critical judgement—from Sidney's *Defense*, from Ben Jonson's *Timber* (a work otherwise largely neglected during the eighteenth century), from Dryden, from Swift, from Addison—the shapers of the English critical tradition before the time of Johnson himself.

Spenser, in *affecting* the ancients, writ no language; yet I would have him read for his matter, but as Virgil read Ennius.

—Jonson

After Chaucer there was a Spenser, a Harrington, a Fairfax, before Waller and Denham were in being; and our numbers were in their *nonage* 'till these last appeared.

—Dryden

Nineteen in twenty of perplexing words might be changed into easy ones, such as occur to ordinary men.

—Swift

Since phrases used in conversation contract meanness by passing through the mouths of the vulgar, a poet should guard himself against the *idiomatick* ways of speaking.

—Addison

Again, the Dictionary is fortified on almost every page by morality and religion—by passages from the whole range of the Old and New Testaments, from the sermons of South, Sprat, Tillotson, Bentley, Atterbury, and other divines, from such devotional manuals as *The Decay of Piety* and *The Government of the Tongue*.

Slothfulness casteth into a deep sleep, and an idle soul shall suffer hunger.

—Proverbs, XIX, 15

Let atheists and *sensualists* satisfy themselves as they are able; the former of which will find, that, as long as reason keeps her ground, religion neither can nor will lose hers.

—South

And once again, the Dictionary is a magazine of contemporary science—though it has to be admitted that here one encounters certain rather severe limitations. The technical articles, extracted from Chambers' *Cyclopedia* and from various other lexica, seem to be inserted somewhat at random and, though often curiously associated with other details, are not on the whole among the Dictionary's clearest triumphs. Under the word *electricity*, for example, there is in addition to a brief, out-of-date technical definition also a short original essay in which Johnson sketches the recent rise of electrical theory, from the beginnings by Stephen Gray (the Charterhouse inmate who had been a friend of Johnson's friend the blind poetess Anna Williams) up to the wave of activity with lightning rods stimulated by Cave's publication in 1751 of Franklin's *Experiments and Observations*. Much comes out if we look into the background of that Dictionary entry. But it is one of the Dictionary's personal revelations, rather than a part of any systematic effort at science.

The most impressive scientific feature of the Dictionary is the wealth of illustrations drawn from the prose of the seventeenth- and eighteenth-century physical, chemical, mechanical, and medical essayists—from Bacon, for instance, from Browne, Boyle, Newton, Ray, Derham, Arbuthnot, Cheyne, and a crowd of others. The first volume of the Dictionary, from A to K, contains about 10,000 illustrations from such authors, which is about one in five of all the illustrations in the volume. Some of these passages, falling even in Johnson's day under the head of fantastic science (science fiction), are part of the lighter side of Dictionary reading.

Bellerophon's horse, fram'd of iron, and placed between two loadstones with wings expanded, hung *pendulous* in the air.
—Browne's *Vulgar Errors*

That cold country where discourse doth freeze in the air all winter, and may be heard in the next summer, or at a great *thaw*.
—Wilkins' [*Mathematical Magic*]

But, to speak more broadly, Johnson's numerous scientific illustrations show us a world of physical "philosophy" in conjunction with a great variety of other things—with poetry, with history, with moral philosophy and religion, with the homeliest parts of everyday life. Look up the word *digger*, for instance, in Johnson's Dictionary, and you find Robert Boyle in the mines studying the effect of the atmosphere on candles. Look up *druggist*, and Boyle is in a shop buying nitre; look up *drugster*, and the same scientist appears again, buying turpentine; look up *distiller*, and he sends for spirit of salt. Look up some of the many concrete and makeshift expressions for shades of sensory experience which were beginning to expand the English vocabulary in that era—*brownish, bluishness, greenish*, for instance— and you find Boyle, Newton, or the geologist Woodward.

One of the most persistent strains of higher meaning which run through the Dictionary is the union of the scientific and religious. Six mighty works of the physicotheological school, Ray's *Wonders of God in the Creation*, Grew's *Cosmologia Sacra*, Derham's *Physico-Theology*, Burnet's *History of the Earth*, Bentley's *Sermons on the Boyle Foundation*, Cheyne's *Philosophical Principles*, and works of a similar tenor like More's *Antidote against Atheism* and Hale's *Primitive Origination of Mankind*, provided Johnson with succinct arguments for insertion under the most widely varied, concrete, and commonplace words.

The reason of the motion of the balance is by the motion of the next wheel, and that by the motion of the next, and that by the motion of the *fusee*, and that by the motion of the spring; the whole frame of the watch carries a reasonableness in it, the passive impression of the intellectual idea that was in the artist.

—Hale

The wise author of nature hath provided on the rump two glandules, which the bird catches hold upon with her bill, and squeezes out an oily pap or *liniment*, fit for the inunction of the feathers.

—Ray

Johnson's Dictionary is an eighteenth-century tabloid *speculum*—a *Speculum Historiale, Naturale*, and *Doctrinale*. As John Ray had seen the wonders of God everywhere in the Creation, Johnson's readers found the same wonders everywhere in the variegated realm of discourse of which his Dictionary was the alphabetized reflection.

I have heard it argued that Johnson's reading for the Dictionary is hardly to be counted as first-rate reading, that it would not have made the kind of impression on his mind that we can consider an influence. To this I would object the principle—for which I feel sure the psychologists must have a name—that casual attentiveness, the tension of some fairly easy routine job, is often very productive of side discoveries and inspirations. Not drowsy boredom and not the clenched effort of a conscious frontal assault on a difficult puzzle, but the mind running easily alert—turning a stick on a lathe and thinking a variety of thoughts, looking for words in a book and noticing all sorts of passages *en route*. This comes strictly under the head of Johnson's intellectual biography.

One very nice report on this side of his biography has recently appeared—perhaps the only pointed instance so far. A good many of the scientific arguments concerning the possibility of "volant or flying automata" that make up Johnson's "Dissertation on the Art of Flying," chapter VI of *Rasselas*, appear to be derived from one of the most venerable scientific sources of the Dictionary, Bishop John Wilkins' *Mathematical Magick: Or the Wonders That May Be Perform'd by Mechanical Geometry*, published first in 1648.[9] Other instances I think might be more or less readily developed. Such essays in the *Rambler* and *Idler* as those on the English historians, the history of translations, the sufficiency of the English language, exhibit fairly clear evidence of Dictionary reading. How many passages in Johnson's *Lives of the Poets*, published twenty-five years after the Dictionary, were drawn not from new reading but from the capacious storage of his memory? A great deal of research into his conversations and later writings might be undertaken and might not yield conclusive results. But it seems at least clearly on the side of plausibility to speak of Johnson's long labor on the Dictionary, from his thirty-seventh to his forty-sixth year, as one of the great episodes, the last great episode, in the formation of his mind. From this he emerged the terrifying arbiter and universal cham of the mature years with which we are most familiar.

But to return to the Dictionary: It seems to me that at least three main principles have to be borne in mind in order to appreciate the most seriously original character of Johnson's performance. That character is essentially a literary and imaginative character, and the principles are: (1) that his discriminations of meanings and definitions grow out of and are determined empirically by the materials gathered from his actual reading; (2) that these discriminations and definitions, at their best and most interesting, which comes often enough, are metaphorically

---

9. The phrase "volant or flying automata" is from Wilkins' definition in Book II, chapter VI, quoted by Johnson in the Dictionary *s.v. volant*. Chapter VI of *Rasselas* speaks of the "structure of all volant animals."

structured; (3) that there is often a close relation in the Dictionary between metaphor and the scientific or "philosophic" materials to which we have been alluding.

The metaphoric principle in Johnson's Dictionary may be more or less implicit and elliptical in places, and it may spread out into various broadly associative patterns. Consider, for example, the elaborately rounded treatment of the word *swan*, where a natural and historical account from Dom Augustin Calmet's *Historical, Critical, Geographical and Etymological Dictionary of the Holy Bible* is followed by three quotations from Shakespeare:

> And I will make thee think thy swan a crow,

a comment from Peacham on the drawing of the swan, a quotation from Dryden, and a concluding description from Locke of "the idea which an Englishman signifies by the name swan." Or consider such words as *lentil* and *thigh*, where the treatment moves in only two examples from the realm of Miller's *Gardeners Dictionary* and Quincy's *Lexicon Physico-Medicum* to the "ground full of lentils" in II Samuel and Jacob's thigh out of joint in Genesis. I persuade myself, however, to pass over a number of variations on my theme—curious matters concerning science and everyday life in that age of Boyle, Newton, and Arbuthnot, or science and burlesque in that age of Scriblerus— and to conclude my argument with a brief emphasis upon the kind of arrangements which appear in the Dictionary under words of the scientific or "philosophic" vocabulary itself—the big Latinate abstractions which were so congenial to Johnson as a prose stylist. I estimate that he includes about 3,000 of these in the Dictionary. Under the letter A we are likely to find the most explicit and full examples of almost any character of the Dictionary we may be discussing. We are taking then a somewhat select, but not unfair, example when we look at the word *accelerate* and note that it has a primary physical sense ("It is generally applied to matter, and used chiefly in philosophical language"), and that this sense is illustrated by five quotations, from the scientific writings of Bacon, Glanville, Newton, and Arbuthnot, and from the philosophic poet James Thomson. It has a secondary sense (". . . it is sometimes used on other occasions"), and this sense is illustrated from Bacon's *History of Henry VII* and from Isaac Watts's *Improvement of the Mind*. Or take the word *adhesion*. The definition of sense 1 of this word embodies a special distinction:

1. The act or state of sticking to something. *Adhesion* is

generally used in the natural, and *adherence* in the meta-physical sense: as, *the adhesion of iron to the magnet*; and *adherence of a client to his patron*.

An illustration from Boyle and one from Locke refer to the ad-hesion of particles of matter; one from Prior is more widely applied:

—Prove that all things, on occasion,
Love union, and desire adhesion.

Then the definition of the second sense, which has already been indicated.

2. It is sometimes taken, like *adherence*, figuratively, for firmness in an opinion, or steadiness in a practice.

The same want of sincerity, the same adhesion to vice, and aversion from goodness, will be equally a reason for the rejecting any proof whatsoever.

—Atterbury

The relation between such Dictionary materials and Johnson's own mind and character as a prose stylist may be specially illus-trated in the fact that of the thirty-five Dictionary quotations which he acknowledges to be from his own writing, eleven are for the metaphoric or psychological meaning of philosophic words. The word *dissipate* which we have already seen illustrated from Johnson in its second and third meanings (psychological and social) has of course also a first meaning, physical and scien-tific, illustrated from the geologist Woodward, the botanist Ray, and the poet Thomson. The word *transmute*, to take another example, after being illustrated in its alchemical sense from Raleigh and Ray, has a line from *The Vanity of Human Wishes*:

Patience, sov'reign o'er *transmuted* ill.

Johnson remembers his own work to complete a metaphoric pattern with an example which his original excursions into Eng-lish literature have by chance failed to provide.

In a few other instances, he apparently cannot remember the example from his own writing, or perhaps has not *yet* written it. The prime Johnsonian words *fugacity*, *suavity*, and *volatility* are illustrated in the Dictionary under their physical senses from Boyle, Brown, and Bacon, but under their second or psycho-logical senses there is an absence of illustration which cannot better be filled than by turning to Johnson's main creative writing of the Dictionary years, the *Rambler*. Here we find that poets lament "the fugacity of pleasure," good humour is defined as "a constant and perennial . . . suavity of disposition," and the author speculates "whether a secret has not some subtle volatility."

Both in his Plan of a Dictionary and his Preface Johnson lays some stress on the liability of scientific terms to undergo the metaphoric process.

As by the cultivation of various sciences a language is amplified, it will be more furnished with words deflected from their original sense; the geometrician will talk of a courtier's zenith, or the eccentrick of a wild hero, and the physician of sanguine expectations and phlegmatick delays.

We may say—or at least we shall not be challenged by modern linguistics if we do say—that metaphor through the ages shows a characteristic direction of reference, from the physical towards the social, psychological, and spiritual. And this was one of the main assumptions upon which Johnson the dictionary-maker proceeded. Where his predecessor Nathan Bailey and others, in accord with their technical bent and in a way that emphasized only the more recent chronology of word histories, made the philosophic or physically scientific meaning, when they gave it, a special instance of a more general meaning, Johnson, as Latinist, etymologist, and literary philosopher, conceived a more remote history of words and a basically correct order of physical or "primitive" and of psychological or secondary meanings. In his Preface he explains that there are even some words (for instance, *ardour* and *flagrant*) where, in the absence of any known examples of the "primitive" meaning, he has extrapolated or supposed that meaning from known examples of the secondary.

The metaphoric movement of language from physical to psychological need not, of course, be specially related in all cases to scientific ideas or words. But there were good enough reasons why a certain special relation between metaphor and science did prevail during the age of Johnson.[10] During the period when most of the sources of the Dictionary were written—and indeed for a considerable time before that—the preferred vision of the physical universe had been a scientific one, and its language was

10. In his *Plan of a Dictionary* Johnson uses the word *arrive* and, perhaps by an accident in the composition and transcription of drafts of the *Plan*—cf. W. R. Keast, *Philological Quarterly* 33 (1954): 341–46—also the word *ground* in his main account of the relation between "primitive" and metaphoric meanings. The examples are synthetic, however, and when these nonphilosophic words actually make their way into the Dictionary, though the treatment is ample and informative, neither the definitions nor the examples lay any stress on a metaphoric pattern.

the language of scientific experiment and speculation, that is, "philosophic diction." Many of the most novel and ample opportunities for metaphor arose during this period out of the very words by which science was altering the known contours of ordinary physical reality and the trend of any educated man's thoughts about that reality. The very Latinism of the vocabulary enhanced it with deep etymological vistas and luminous intimations of meaning. And this went well with a scientifically thoughtful and ambitious way of looking at things. Again, this scientific way was a way mainly oriented upon and endlessly repetitive of the Galilean and Cartesian philosophy—that radical division, and hence complete, if rather chilly, reflection, between the outer and the inner of human experience, matter and spirit. The scientific image of the universe was an image that required and promoted a special idiom of mechanical and chemical metaphor for the analysis of the spirit, the introspections of the moral and religious mind.

I have been arguing, in brief, that the history of science and of scientific words in English for the century and a half before he wrote his Dictionary provided Johnson with one of his best opportunities, perhaps his best opportunity, for illustrating the metaphoric structure of language, that he took this opportunity, and that his general interest in metaphor and his capacity for dealing with it were among a few main reasons why he wrote the first English Dictionary that gives a lively reflection of the modern English language. In this feat he became a champion among English lexicographers in his day and for some days to come, and at least a noteworthy figure on the broader horizon of international lexicography.

                                                              1955

III

POETRY AS POEMS

BATTERING THE OBJECT

> *Hamlet*: To what base uses we may return,
> Horatio! Why may not imagination trace the
> noble dust of Alexander till 'a find it stopping
> a bunghole?
> *Horatio*: 'Twere to consider too curiously,
> to consider so.
> —*Hamlet* v.i

The question about the correct, or most plausible, object of literary study blurs today into the question whether such a question can be correctly asked. The best short statement of this modern problem that I know appears near the end of Murray Krieger's book *The Tragic Vision*. From a richly elegiac thirteen pages lamenting the demise of American "formalist" criticism, I select a few eloquent enough sentences.

> Organicism and inviolability of context being matters of kind and not of degree, poetry must be seen as a form of discourse in some sense nonreferential even as it must be in some sense referential to be a form of discourse at all.

> This dilemma seems to me to represent the crucial point, if not the dead end, reached by modern criticism.

> Future theorists who will want to preserve the gains of . . . these critics and who will not want to see them washed away into the common stream of Platonic theory will have to find a way to keep poetry's contextual system closed; to have the common materials which enter poetry—conventions of word meaning, of propositional relations, and of literary forms—so transmuted in the creative act with its organic demands that they come out utterly unique. [pp. 236–37]

These passages stress the problem of distinguishing the poem as a separable and knowable object amid the welter of our complex experience both real and verbal, rather than the complementary or closely dependent problem with which Krieger in this book—arguing "Manichaean" versus "Platonic" choices—is mainly concerned, that of the truth and value of the conceptual patterns necessarily implicated in the structure of the knowable object. The former problem, that of knowledge of the object (or in loftier language, epistemology), is what I am here directly concerned with.

The development of this little knot of ideas has been no less

slow, roundabout, and gradual than that of most ideas. But for
our present purpose, I believe only four critical moments need
be distinguished. The first two of these are separated from each
other by about a century. The third and fourth, following hard
upon the second, are occurring simultaneously today. It is on
these that I will mainly dwell.

I

The modern idea of the art work as a separately existent and
in some sense autonomous or autotelic entity is closely tied to
the idea of a vital organic form. A squirrel running in a tree and
the rooted tree are more respectable and convincing *things* than
a chunk of crumbling clay or even a hard piece of rock broken
off a mountain side. That much is Aristotelian. But the modern
status and emphasis of the idea was achieved only in the era of
Romantic art and nature theory. The full image of organic form
in poetry had its seedbed and first growth in the tropical rain-
forest of eighteenth-century *naturphilosophie* and early scientific
accounts and drawings of living forms, the biological world of
Kant, Goethe, Schelling, Coleridge, and Keats. Organicism was
a literary content, a very material subject matter (as in Erasmus
Darwin's *Botanical Garden*), for several decades before it be-
came the rarefied metaphysics of a theory of aesthetic knowl-
edge and form. Coleridge, with an eye intent both on living
nature and on Shakespeare, specified five characteristics of
biological form and hence implicitly, and in part explicitly, of
the art work. He said in effect that works of art, like living
organisms, were wholes (not assemblages of parts—"The parts
are nothing"). Art works grew like living plants, assimilating
diverse elements into their own substance. They were shaped
from within, not by external pressures or moulds. The parts
were interdependent ("interinanimating").[1] This has remained a
classic and much respected account. Certain locally brilliant
parts of poems (couplets or soliloquies), the modeller's clay, the
sculptor's stone and chisel, the noise of the typewriter or the
smell of cooking, the moulds of bronze statues (even like those

1. The evidence in Coleridge's *On Poesy or Art*, Shakespeare lectures,
Table Talk, *Philosophical Lectures*, and *Treatise on Method* has recently
been reassembled by Philip C. Ritterbush, *The Art of Organic Forms*
(Washington, 1968), pp. 19–21. In his book-length introduction to this
catalogue of an exhibition of modern pictures and sculptures (Odilon
Redon, *c.* 1905—Catharine Homan, 1968), Ritterbush argues, interestingly,
that the universal of organic form is nowadays being realized by both sci-
ence and art at the submicroscopic level.

of sugar cookies and aspic jellies), the interdependence of two children on a seesaw—notions such as these may stir, if we let them, some questions about that metaphoric complex. But it will be scarcely on these grounds that we care to prolong the discussion.[2]

II

The practical position elaborated by the American New Critics in essays of the late nineteen-thirties and the forties had been earlier asserted with great dramatic force and a tenacious strategy by I. A. Richards in the first part of his *Practical Criticism* (1929), a sort of machine or trap constructed out of experiments he had undertaken at Cambridge—upon poems with students, and upon students with poems. It was an implication, though scarcely a demonstration, of Richards's book that a good poem could be distinguished from a bad one by resolute examination of its internal relations, joined from outside only by a "sincere" response of the reader's whole personality. The thirteen anonymous, untitled, and undated poems selected for display (along with choice betrayals, "protocols," by his students, and a limited number of sly intimations by Richards himself) may begin to assume, if one revisits them in the context of today's debates, somewhat the appearance of a collection of small mammals, birds, and insects, with perhaps a fossil, a stick, or a stone thrown in for good measure, each exposed under a vacuum jar, with instructions to pupils from a presiding scientist: "Examine thoroughly and determine which are alive." Yet they did not look that way to an interested young generation of academics in the nineteen-thirties. Perhaps they do not altogether look that way now. Not many, I imagine, of the most resolute external-contextual critics today would maintain that under the artificially purified conditions of Richards's experiment they would honestly be unable to discern any difference in point, tone, poetic entity (and poetic value) between the first stanza of Richards's Poem IV.

> There was rapture of spring in the morning
> When we told our love in the wood.
> For you were the spring in my heart, dear lad,
> And I vowed that my life was good.

2. See the issue discussed in the idiom of general aesthetics by Richard Peltz, "Ontology and the Work of Art," *JAAC* 24 (Summer 1966): 487–99; and in response to Peltz, Patrick Æ Hutchings, "Works of Art and the Ontology of Analogy," *Philosophical Studies* 16 (1967): 82–103.

and the first four lines of his Poem III,

> At the round earth's imagined corners blow
> Your trumpets, angels, and arise, arise
> From death you numberless infinities
> Of souls, and to your scattered bodies go.

III

Given the extreme vulnerability of father figures, the instructions of Freud, and the consequent awareness that has prevailed in the academic world of our time, it was not to be expected that the stance of the American New Critics, even at its most convincing, could turn into anything like a stasis, or that their ideas could enjoy anything like so long a reign as those of the preceding entrenchment of historicism. The explosion of the academic population in the postwar period and the consequently appalling escalation of publishing efforts have worked towards the same revolutionary result. New persons, new professional generations, need new platforms. Pound's injunction to the poet has been found equally cogent advice for the ambitious critic. Positive programmes have to be ushered in by protests too, which may be the louder and more easily defined part of the doctrine. Critics under fifty years of age today are very likely, on one occasion or another, to have voiced their distress at the wave of Alexandrian pedantries, the merely mechanical applications of "Anglo-Saxon formalism," that have followed on the vogue of the New Critical theory. It would appear that exegesis is "our Whore of Babylon, sitting robed in Academic black on the great dragon of Criticism, and dispensing a repetitive and soporific balm from her pedantic cup."[3]
In a report on a symposium of young scholars held at Yale University a few years ago, we encounter the complacent announcement that "native formalism" and its chief antagonist of but yesterday, the archetypal system of Northrop Frye, no longer "figure centrally" in wise deliberations. There is hostility to neither. But their lessons can be taken for granted. The next inspirations will come from Europe. The director of the symposium was a member of the Yale French department. Most of the participants were "European trained" or at least were teachers in departments of romance language or comparative literature. The commentator whom I have been quoting was a

3. *MLN* 81: 556.

professor of English, J. Hillis Miller. We have Miller's report in another place, at about the same moment, on what has come to be known as the "Geneva School"[4] of French criticism, whose heritage runs back immediately through the *Nouvelle Revue Française* and certain nineteenth-century English figures to Romanticism—and is ultimately, I should think, Longinian. "Consciousness of consciousness," the critic's consciousness of the author's consciousness, in an identical transparency—this makes or is criticism. It is union of subject with another subject, spiritual activity—almost angelic. The *work* of literature as objectified by Aristotelian conceptualism is only an opaque obstacle. Nothing less than a whole consciousness, diffused through a whole canon of expressions, both the complete and the fragmentary, the deliberate and the accidental, will assuage that yearning for communion. At the same time (and paradoxically, in spite of a necessary self-effacement on the part of the critic in the presence of his author), criticism is the pursuit of the critic's own spiritual adventure (as in days gone by, with some differences, for Anatole France and for Oscar Wilde). It is a secondary artistic act, a genre of creative literature, faithful to the native Swiss tradition of meditation, reverie, confession, in the manner of Rousseau, Sénancour, Constant, Amiel, Ramuz.

In a volume of studies in nineteenth-century English literature, *The Disappearance of God*, Hillis Miller had already put example before the precepts delivered apropos of the Yale Symposium of 1965. In a preface to a paperback edition (1965) of this work he elaborated:

> ... it appears possible that European ways of doing criticism ... may present themselves to Americans as alternatives to the creation of another indigenous criticism ... assimilating the advances of European criticism in the past twenty years, but reshaping them to our peculiarly American experience of literature and its powers.

"If literature is a form of consciousness," his original hardback preface had expounded, "the task of the critic is to identify himself with the subjectivity expressed in the words, to relive that

4. J. Hillis Miller, "The Geneva School," *Critical Quarterly* 8 (Winter 1966): 305–21. The critics of the Geneva orientation are Marcel Raymond (b. 1897), Albert Béguin (1901–1957), Georges Poulet (b. 1902), Jean Rousset (b. 1910), Jean Starobinski (b. 1920), Jean-Pierre Richard (b. 1922). Poulet and Starobinski have held posts at the Johns Hopkins University, 1952–1957, 1954–1956. See another account by Laurent Le Sage, "The New French Literary Critics," *The American Society Legion of Honor Magazine* 37 (1966): 75–86.

life from the inside, and to constitute it anew in his criticism."
A concluding long chapter of *The Disappearance of God*, on
Gerard Manley Hopkins, is perhaps the book's most ample
illustration of the Genevan method transplanted to the literary
experience of the USA. Poems, devotions, undergraduate notes,
journals, letters, essays, "late" and "early," are pulverized and
reassembled in a mainly *a*-chronological dialectic. We inspect
the reconstruction of a mind—one specially isolated in acute
consciousness of the "taste" of itself, yet restlessly yearning
through the manifold inscapes and instresses, the metaphors,
the rhyming and chiming, of a diversely dappled world of words
and poetry, towards the harmony of a sense of immanence of
God in nature and the human soul. The emphasis is recurrently
and emphatically on the manifold. The helter-skelter, the stac-
cato and dappling of the Hopkins experience, the stippling of
the fragmentary record, make him an ideal example for this kind
of exposition by shredding or atomization. A fine mist of the
mind of Hopkins is generated. A critic of some old-fashioned
biographical school (from whose clutches modern American
critical discourse, by the way, was liberated by no other than
the New Critics) might well complain that here we are given
very little shape or line of a life, or even of any mental career,
very little contour, episode, approach, or climax. This sort of
shape by shapelessness no doubt bears some relation of counter-
part to the orthodox Genevan inattention to the author's own
achieved poetic shapes. "Glory be to God for dappled things . . .
Praise him." This one exquisite curtal-sonnet *Pied Beauty* is
examined with considerable loving care, for the critic looks on
it as a kind of synopsis or emblem of the Hopkins rhyming con-
sciousness. It seems equally a good emblem, in its asserted mean-
ing, if not in its cunning form, of the critical method being
demonstrated.

Murray Krieger is another American professor who of recent
years has been watching the Geneva critics very closely and sym-
pathetically—though with a good deal of artful capacity to resist
them. Two of his most recent lectures, addressed to a Johns
Hopkins University Humanities Seminar in the spring of 1968,[5]
dilate on that notion of the poem as a conceptual obstruction
arising between the critic and the pure consciousness of the au-
thor. The dissolution of such a mediate entity, all too successfully

5. *Mediation, Language, and Vision—and the Reading of Literature*,
Lectures I and II, at the Johns Hopkins University, May 1968, type-
script. I am profoundly indebted to Professor Krieger for his kindness
in letting me read these lectures before publication—in *Interpretation:
Theory and Practice*, edited by Charles S. Singleton (Baltimore, 1969).

promoted by critics of the Genevan inclination, is a very narrowly averted outcome towards which Krieger's own dialectic has often led him in spite of himself. He points in passing to the extreme impatience of the American Ihab Hassan, who in his flight from the poetic object nearly but not quite asserts the nihilism of silence. (Here too might have come a distinguished voice of silence from Cambridge, England, that of George Steiner, and here also that of Susan Sontag, New York dissenter from *Interpretation.*) At heart Krieger does not want this destruction. And now again, as in his *Window to Criticism* (1964), he invokes the last-minute miraculous analogy of a closed poetic room of "mutually reflecting mirrors" opening (presto!) so many windows back to outside reality. Or he has a newer formula: The poem is both "discourse" and "thing" and as such "is motion and is in motion. Yet it is motion in stillness, the stillness that is at once still moving and forever still."[6] Thou still unravished bride of quietness! The extreme anti-mediators of the Geneva School, chief among them Georges Poulet, have dwelt much on the theme of "time," that Bergsonian interior dimension in which consciousness, the human dynamism, has its true being and movement—in contrast to those coldly spatialized objective mediations into which Platonists and New Critics, formalists all, would harden poems.

The more narrow the escape from the flux of time, as Murray Krieger sees it, the better. One can earn one's right to the poem as entity only by first confronting and accepting its literal nonentity. Those who are not brave enough to run that risk and whose skill is hence never really tested make up the numerous and diverse ranks of the critics who nowadays more than ever indulge in over-mediation or materialization of the poetic object. The point seems well taken. We can repeat the distinction along national and cultural lines. Here, in this garden of the definable mediate categories, though Krieger politely refrains from urging it, are to be located the present very flourishing crop of American home-grown disguises of the poetic object. The debate of the late nineteen-fifties in America between the old New Critical assertors of the poem and the new archetypists and mythopoeists and their demi-allies the demonic visionaries (a kind of Pyrrhic victory for the latter, in that they gained much ground but were

6. Krieger develops this idea at greater length in his essay "The Ekphrastic Principle and the Still Movement of Poetry; or *Laokoön* Revisited," in *The Poet as Critic*, ed. Frederick P. W. McDowell (Evanston, Illinois, 1967), pp. 3-25; reprinted in Krieger's *The Play and Place of Criticism* (Baltimore, 1967), pp. 105-28.

consumed in their own heat) has been followed among younger critics by a phase of frenzied bolting and grabbing for the most tangible and durable equipment in sight on the historical shelf. In this new era one book urges the revolutionary argument that the long-overlooked and only correct key to the reading of Chaucer lies in medieval rhetoric, and another finds the same key in a so-far unsuspected deep affinity of Chaucer for the geometry of medieval architecture.[7] Another book, written in a vein of super-annotation which the author's mentor the Hopkins Professor Earl Wasserman has had much to do with developing, demonstrates that Pope's Horatian poems ought to be read, image by image, not only in the perspective of Horatian satire and epistle but in that of Renaissance commentary on Horace— *Horace moralisé*.[8] "There is no rational and methodological concept, no attempted translucent universal," I have ventured in another essay, "which is not capable of being transformed, and very quickly, into an opaque historical gimmick." Let me add now that there is no opaque gimmick or dead piece of critical history which is not capable of a galvanic revival when rediscovered by a seminar in search of vehicles, and perhaps by scholars too intent on the future to have been vividly aware of a former demise. One will think now especially of the recent programmes for literary "genre" (shades of Brunetière, Babbitt, Croce!), which spring up like chestnut saplings round the venerable blighted grey trunk of the Chicago School of Neo-Aristotelianism. Genre, which was once a classical norm for censures and exclusions, which has always been a needed part of the literary historian's descriptive vocabulary, and which under New Critical auspices has recently been usefully invoked as a part of a poet's language or frame of reference enabling his own expressive departures, is now rediscovered in German handbooks and becomes a part of liberal historical perspective and critical method and as such a norm for explanations, inclusions, and critical tolerance. Samuel Johnson's *History of Rasselas* has characters who speak throughout like philosophical puppets and pompous pedants, and yet it is a successful tale and—as most of us would say—justly celebrated. How does Johnson bring off this stylistic feat? The answer is to be found in the fact that

---

7. Respectively, Robert O. Payne, *The Key of Remembrance: A Study of Chaucer's Poetics* (New Haven, 1963), and Robert M. Jordan, *Chaucer and the Shape of Creation: The Aesthetic Possibilities of Inorganic Structure* (Cambridge, Mass., 1967).

8. Thomas E. Maresca, *Pope's Horatian Poems* (Columbus, Ohio, 1966). See G. S. Rousseau's trenchant review of this book, *Philological Quarterly* 47 (July 1968): 407–09.

Rasselas is not a novel but an apologue. An apologue had its own rules, and these provided for and led to the expectation of abstractive and moralistic language.[9] A group of young scholars centering at the Chicago Circle branch of the University of Illinois have recently begun the publication of a journal entitled *Genre*. They have sponsored a forum on genre at the 1967 Modern Language Association meeting in Chicago; and they have published (no. 3, July 1968) a symposium on a new treatise on hermeneutics, *Validity in Interpretation* (1967), by Professor E. D. Hirsch, of the University of Virginia. In a long chapter of this book Donald Hirsch spirals around the term "genre" a series of momentary concepts, excluding the fixed broad definitions of the traditional literary genres and moving towards a plane *just* above and all but identical with the unique meaning of each work—or perhaps in fact identical with that and tautological. Hirsch thinks he can keep the "genre" apart from each work but close enough so that he can operate a rule that correct interpretation depends on knowing the genre. I doubt that he can. I think that in all broader (and usual) senses of the term "genre" we discover the genre of a work by being able to read it, and not vice versa. I cite this instance of Hirsch's reasoning because it seems to me to be, like Krieger's, one of the more subtle and valiant (though I think mistaken) current attempts to lay hands on, without destroying, the poem's delicate mediate status between poet and reader. Under bushes in the garden behind an old house near my office lies a small slab of stone bearing the inscription:

LOTTERY

NOV. 25, 1889.

LOVING

FELLOW-CREATURE

About midway of my interpretation of this document (starting from the bottom) I conjecture the genre in the broad sense; this helps with the rest of the interpretation; and this in turn leads to near certainty about the genre in a broad sense and to a highly plausible conjecture about a more narrow sense. If a dog was acquired in a lottery and named for that reason, it might well be

---

9. Sheldon Sacks, *Fiction and the Shape of Belief: A Study of Henry Fielding with Glances at Swift, Johnson and Richardson* (Berkeley, 1964), esp. pp. 49–60. René Wellek, "Genre Theory, the Lyric, and 'Erlebnis,'" *Festschrift für Richard Alewyn* (Köln, 1967), pp. 392–412, reviews two modern German revivals of genre method—Emile Staiger, *Grundbegriff de · Poetik* (1946) and Käte Hamburger, *Logik der Dichtung* (1957).

that the date of the birth was not known. [Lottery was actually a pet monkey; see *Yale Alumni Magazine* 34 (1971): 40.]

IV

The third moment in our modern history of the poem as entity, that of reaction and rejection which we have just seen, has been simultaneous with a fourth, a phase of the last fifteen or twenty years which emerges with a continuing activity of the old New Criticism (as in Cleanth Brooks's manorial *William Faulkner: The Yoknapatawpha Country*, 1963) and which has been strengthened by developments in post-Bloomfieldian American linguistics and more recently by arrivals from a second tradition of Continental criticism, identifiable most readily, if so far somewhat vaguely, under the name of "structuralism."

The contemporary Parisian vogue or energy called "structuralism" is a manifold: "structuralism" is anthropological, it is psychological, it is linguistic, it is (in perhaps its least developed extension) critico-literary. Literary structuralism descends along fairly obvious lines from the Russian formalism of the World War I era (expounded for the English-speaking world by Victor Erlich in 1955.),[10] and from the immediately postwar Prague Linguistic Circle.[11] Today it is increasingly enveloped and merged with general linguistics. Neither the Slavic background and authority nor the marked literary bent of the most eminent of contemporary linguists, Roman Jakobson, are to be seen as accidents. "Formalism" having been converted into a bad thing by Marxist censures, the term "structuralism" has evolved into the acceptable European equivalent. Even some critics of Genevan or Baltimorean orientation incline towards some kind of "structure" (or "structuralism"). They look on these as better terms than "form" (or "formalism"), because "structure" can be reconciled with temporal experience and hence with the essentially romantic subjectivism and dynamism of the human consciousness, whereas "form," as we have seen, is spatial and external conceptualization.[12] For Murray Krieger, even "struc-

10. Victor Erlich, *Russian Formalism: History-Doctrine* ('S-Gravenhage, 1955). And see Tzvetan Todorov, *Théorie de la littérature: Textes des Formalistes russes reunis, présentés et traduits* (Paris, 1955)—with a *Préface, Vers une Science de L'Art Poétique*, by Roman Jakobson.
11. Paul L. Garvin, *A Prague School Reader on Esthetics, Literary Structure, and Style* (Washington, 1955) (an anthology of translations from the Czech).
12. See Hillis Miller in *MLN* 81: 562, 569–70.

turalism" is too much like New Critical formalism and is hence an enemy, one of the "over-mediators."[13]

At this point I interject a few homespun observations—about objects of study, their contexts, and their status.

We know that literary study sometimes focuses (1) on an age or an aspect of an age, an audience or a genre (baroque, pastoral, bourgeois, tragic, paradoxical), or (2) on an author considered etiologically as the explanation of his works, or (3) on the author just as a sufficiently interesting personal object in himself (as in most literary biography), or (4) on the author as a pure translucent consciousness revealed in the canon of his works (as in the Geneva-Hopkins criticism), or (5) on the literary work itself (what we are driving towards), or (6) on some sort of parts or passages of literary works (the figures and tropes of classical rhetoric, the elemental symbols of Bachelard, the album-reading for spiritual motifs by Croce). It is no doubt never feasible or desirable to legislate anybody's preference among such objects. It may be possible, however, to observe some differences of status among them. The author Shakespeare or the author Proust, I find myself compelled to assume, is a better entity than any biography of him or any aspect of his biography, a better entity than either the age he lived in, the genre of any one of his works, or any one of his works itself—better a fortiori than the collection of his works. For authors, like the rest of us, are capable of absent-mindedness, of emotional off-balance, even of obtuseness, of inferior moments, of being young and callow, of growing old and weary, garrulous, repetitious. It is their extraordinary capacity for transcending these usual human limitations at certain intense moments of their living and working—i.e., in their individual and separate works—which makes them great authors. These remarks are intended to converge by analogy upon the question what kind of entity is enjoyed by the literary masterpiece. "Imperial Caesar, dead and turn'd to clay, Might stop a hole to keep the wind away." But our critics who are most scrupulously worried about the kind of status they can grant a poem (without making it something "objective," "spatial," merely mediatory), are never, so far as I have read, much worried about the Caesar or the Napoleon problem. We run now into an area where it is very easy to be charged

---

13. Lecture I at Hopkins, 1968 (see note 5 above). Krieger's idiom often seems to accuse poetry and criticism of an identical sin, or to imply that poetry in the end *is* whatever criticism finds itself forced to make of poetry. Structuralism is an "over-mediator" in the sense that it would make poetry an over-mediator.

with merely indulging in metaphors. Yet I have noticed that the
very person who objects most earnestly to spatial metaphors for
the poetic entity (the urn or the icon) is likely enough to reach
for the metaphor when his own crisis arrives. These critics write
at moments with the air of a person finding things where they
are not lost, pouncing triumphantly upon or insistently explain-
ing difficulties that have always been evident and which have
actually been the source of tension and interest in the metaphors
that the theorists have contrived to circumvent them. Murray
Krieger, for instance, is one who certainly demands of the
theories of others a degree of literalism which he himself is far
from being able to achieve in those "magical" mirror-and-win-
dow or time-and-space moments of his own dialectic.[14] That
Genevan and Bergsonian theme of conscious duration is one of
the most receptive to metaphor and most demanding of it—
boundless metaphoric quicksilver of the external world drawn
into the vortex of the spirit's self-awareness. "Lips that meet,"
"an abyss that fills up to the brim," "the beat of a wing," "a
firebrand," a "sheet of water," a "shadow," the "chase," the
"catch," the "folds" and "windings" of our nature, "the
agility of the soul," "the suppleness of thought"—what image
can be imagined that could not be summoned into the utterly
valid spectrum of metaphors which express the time conscious-
ness for Pascal in only three pages of a study by Georges
Poulet?[15] As an English writer once said in a much simpler
classical context: "Time is, of all modes of existence, most ob-
sequious to the imagination."

A poem is an utterance which bids for, or at least often re-
ceives, attention for its excellence. That is to say, it is contem-
plated and can be criticized and judged; it is hypostatized as an

14. *Cf.* my review of Krieger's *A Window to Criticism* (1964) in
Modern Philology 64 (August 1966): 71–74. One does not begrudge Krie-
ger his time-and-space manipulations, so long as they are not taken too
literally and triumphantly as a magic solution of any critical problem. An
important service recently performed by Professor Marshall McLuhan and
his associates (despite certain obscurities and oversweep in the theory, as
I see it) has been their manifold (electronic) recapture of the ancient truth
that not every kind of "space" and "environment" is visual. My own pref-
erence is to urge that some kinds of order and concept are neither visual
nor spatial. The current simple dichotomy between temporal dynamics
and spatial rigidity is a complacent vulgar error. See Marshall McLuhan and
Harley Parker, *Through the Vanishing Point: Space in Poetry and Painting*
(New York, 1968), esp. pp. 238–67.
15. *Studies in Human Time*, trans. Elliot Coleman (Baltimore, 1956),
pp. 84–86. Cf. my review in *The New Scholasticism* 32 (October 1958):
523–36.

object, and metaphorically as a spatial object. We can ask what kind of rights the poem has to be considered an object, or what kind of protection it has for its limits and structure. And I would urge, at least, that we ought not to talk as if the poem had to meet some kind of impossible angelic or metaphysical standard of absolute entity—or else be considered as nothing at all. It would seem silly to expect of the poem a kind of hardness and self-sufficiency which the best entity we know directly—its author the human person—himself does not have. I am thinking of context, of course—not internal, or verbal, in Krieger's main sense, but the external envelopment, both verbal and real, which under the drive of our historical studies has in modern times tended to pull the poem apart or absorb it atomically into the boundless.

We might slide off here into an emphasis on the ecology[16] or mutually modifying relation of organism and environment—and this would suit very well in a discussion of the creative force of vision in poetry or the continually renewing reciprocity between poems and tradition, as in the formula of Eliot. But I am saying something easier than that Eliot's *Waste Land* alters either the modern landscape or that of Homer. One part of mutual modification is selection. True, there is a sense in which the whole of the environment (that is to say, the universe) must tolerate the organism. We read that if the earth's magnetic field ever dwindles towards a reversal of direction, as no doubt it can, certain harmful solar electrons and protons will get through and may well cause mutations in the human species. Yet as I hike through the primeval forest, it is the needle on my wrist that responds directly to the magnetic field, and not my own bones, though these, luckily for me, are pulled by the earth's gravity.

A man's momentary states of mind, his moods, his conversations may be even closer to the analogy we seek. Our moments protect themselves—sometimes against very urgent outer forces or against establishments of very long standing. It is possible to be driving a car on a familiar but somewhat monotonously featured road, and at a given moment not to know whether or not we have yet come to a given village. Professor A, about sixty years old, is walking across the campus on a Saturday morning and encounters Professor B, about sixty-eight years old, recently retired, on his way to some hours of fruitful work in the library. Professor A, smiling ruefully: "I am on my way to the oral examinations." Professor B, cheerfully: "I am sorry for you."

16. Cf. Harry Berger, Jr., "The Ecology of the Mind," *The Review of Metaphysics* 17 (September 1963): 109-34.

The context which explains this flicker of an exchange is the fact that for about fifteen years past these two professors have often sat together on tedious oral boards on Saturday mornings. A further context, we may be surprised to learn, is that much earlier, about thirty years earlier, Professor B had sat on the oral board of *A*, then himself a candidate for the Ph.D. But that earlier incident, sunk to a level of stratification where it could now be revivified only by a pointed conversational effort, is not present to the mind of either professor on this Saturday morning. It would utterly spoil their joke.

Let us recall one small curious moment of the eighteenth-century—that when Mrs. Malaprop gets off her expression "as headstrong as an allegory on the banks of Nile." There is something which Mrs. Malaprop does not know, but which the audience of London ladies and gentlemen do have to know in order to get the laugh. Not allegories, but alligators, close their incisive jaws on the banks of rivers. But wait. There is something else that perhaps none of those Londoners knows—though it could be learned approximately in Johnson's *Dictionary* or in chapter XXXIX of *Rasselas*. As critics no doubt we ought to tell them or their present-day surrogates, our students. Alligators (short, broad snout, dark colour) are found in Florida or China. The kind of large saurian found on the banks of the Nile is the crocodile (long, sharp snout, greyish or greenish colour). Doesn't this enlargement of context have some bearing on Sheridan's joke on Mrs. Malaprop? Emphatically not. We had better not ever mention it again.

"Where," asks Hillis Miller, "does the context of a poem stop?" Where indeed? Where does it begin? What paths through the ambient does it take? At what immediate or at what remote reaches of the stratification of the abstractive sheathing of environment does the context resonate? The internal structure of the poem plays a strong role in all this. There was a student once who wrote a paper saying that a couplet by Alexander Pope, ". . . no Prelate's Lawn with Hair-shirt lined,/Is half so incoherent as my Mind" (*Epistle* I. i. 165–66) ought to be read in the light of a couplet in another poem by Pope: "Whose ample Lawns are not asham'd to feed/The milky heifer and deserving steed" (*Moral Essays* IV. 185–86). Since I believe in the force of puns and all sorts of other verbal resemblances in poetry, I do not know quite how to formulate the rule of context by which I confidently reject that connection.[17] But I seek first ineluc-

17. A structural linguist might say that the range of meanings associated

table confrontations, only later, if at all, rules. The result of the
boundless and atomically even absorption of poem in context
which Hillis Miller conceives is best conveyed in his own sen-
tences. The poem's "relations to its surroundings radiate outward
like concentric circles from a stone dropped in water. These
circles multiply indefinitely until the scholar must give up in
despair the attempt to make a complete inventory of them. . . .
as he proceeds in his endless quest, the poem . . . gradually fades
into the multitude of its associations. . . . Instead of being a
self-sufficient entity, it is only a symptom of ideas or images
current in the culture which generated it."[18]

The study of language in the classical Western tradition—
vocabulary, grammar, rhetoric—has all along of course been
structural. There was literally nothing else it could be. The reason
why contemporary linguistic studies deserve in some special
sense to be called "structural" lies in the great advances they
have made in the study of "relations," in analysis and general-
ization, in the definition of linguistic entities smaller than
words, and, perhaps most important of all for literary criticism,
in the recognition of a wide range of implicative (iconic and
diagrammatic) powers of language. This is formalism in the
strictest sense. We arrive at a conception of language, not as a
random or merely spontaneous accumulation of unconnected
conventions, but as an emergent system of analogical and
interlocking relations of expressiveness. This holds not only for

with *lawn* (grass) is not "actualized" in the passage containing *lawn*
(cloth).
   "All very true, no doubt," says I. A. Richards about a student remark on
a word in Marvell's *Garden*, "but not anything that the semantic texture of
the language will allow the two lines to mean or that the rest of the poem
will invite us to understand here. Surely a teacher-to-be should have a bet-
ter sense than this of what is and is not admissible in an interpretation.
What can have been happening to cause this alarming condition, this reck-
less disregard of all the means by which language defends itself?" ("Poetic
Process and Literary Analysis," in *Style in Language*, ed. Thomas A. Se-
beok, New York, 1960, p. 23).
   The so-called poetry of "inclusion" expounded by the early Richards has
never, of course, included more than a few snatches of all there is (the uni-
verse).
   18.   In a note to his article, Hillis Miller refers to a then forthcoming,
now published, essay of his which celebrates the doctrine of absorptionism
at greater length ("Literature and Religion," in *Relations of Literary
Study: Essays on Interdisciplinary Contributions*, ed. James Thorpe, New
York, 1967). I am not sure I understand how this ultimately unavoidable
dispersion is consistent with Hillis Miller's avowed devotion to the "novel
and unique beauty" of each author to which we have already referred. If
the poem fades, why doesn't the author too—in what his essay calls "the
gray dusk of historical and para-historical generalizations"?

the structural logic of given individual expressions,[19] but for
patterns of whole languages lying in dictionary and grammar
and considered as potentials for individual expressions.[20]
It is a little more than thirty years since I. A. Richards, adapt-
ing some features of Leonard Bloomfield's analysis of "root-
forming morphemes," propounded the extremely persuasive
and significant rhetorical doctrine that hidden mimetic powers
of words in a given language (the theme of Plato's *Cratylus*) re-
side neither in "verbal magic" (favourite notion of belletristic
criticism) nor in simple or direct onomatopoeic powers, but in
networks of pervasive intimation—both syntactic (or present
and actually heard) and paradigmatic (contextually implicit
equivalents of words in a text).[21] This is a convenient juncture
for the observation that the elusive word "structure" as it is
employed in the contemporary vogue is perhaps most elusive in
that it is used (sometimes almost simultaneously) to refer to
what we may describe broadly, with respect to any given
object of attention, as both internal and external structure, the
two conceived as mutually reflective—in language, "syntactic"
structure (along the line of contiguity in the utterance) and
"paradigmatic" structure (in the dimension of the enveloping
linguistic context).[22] There is a slender but important difference

19. For instance, the parallels (*parisosis, homoioteleuton*) observed by
classical rhetoric and even nowadays a muted resource of some expository
writing.
20. Such specially morphemic or mutually mimetic word families, for
instance, as *sister, brother, father, mother*, or such expressive patterns as
phonemic crescendo in comparative and superlative degrees of adjectives—
big, bigger, biggest: altus, altior, altissimus. See Roman Jakobson, "Quest
for the Essence of Language," *Diogenes* 51 (1965): 21-37.
21. In the same year as Richards' *Philosophy of Rhetoric*, 1936, ap-
peared also perhaps the earliest of the American textbooks in the new
mode, Brooks, Purser, and Warren's *Approach to Literature*, first pub-
lished by the Louisiana State University Press, now by Appleton-Century-
Crofts, and in its fourth revision.
22. *Hal had his hat.* A syntactic rule of the language forbids us to say
Hal hat his had. But this rule can be applied in this instance only in the
virtue of the phonemic structure of the English language, in which the
voiceless dental *t* is significantly distinguished from the voiced *d*.
    Such systems as Cambridge anthropology and Frye's archetypes are larger
instances of "structuralism" for those who push the mythic *exo*-structure
of stories and their societal values. See Geoffrey Hartman's brilliant essay
"Structuralism: The Anglo-American Venture," in *Structuralism, Yale
French Studies 36–37* (October 1966), esp. pp. 151-52.
    Internal structure too can, of course, be viewed in larger ways than the
verbal and lyric which I am about to use as a convenient exhibit. See, for
instance, Malcolm Bradbury, "Structure," *Novel: A Forum of Fiction* 1
(Fall 1967): 45-52: Tzvetan Todorov's collection *Théorie de la Littérature*;

between truism and the Saussurian observation that making sentences consists in a simultaneous act of selecting words (from ranges of similar or "equivalent"—and at the same time more or less antithetic—alternatives) and of combining these in associative and causal sequences or contiguities. Roman Jakobson in a suggestive essay of 1956, "Two Aspects of Language and Two Types of Aphasic Disturbance," shows how these two essential language aspects are related not only to the classic figures of metaphor (similarity) and metonymy (contiguity) but to two kinds of *aphasia* or pathological splits in speech performance—elliptical racing along contiguous sequences and manifold clutter of loose equivalences. At a conference on "style in language" held at Indiana University in 1958, Jakobson in his "Closing Statement: Linguistics and Poetics" ventured this bold compression: *"The poetic function projects the principle of equivalence from the axis of selection into the axis of combination.* Equivalence is promoted to the constitutive device of the sequence." The pronouncement seems specially relevant to the metrical aspect of poetry (a formality which no doubt enables much else),[23] and Jakobson proceeds to make the metrical application at some length. A person interested in the poem as an object involved in transactions with both a verbal and a real external context might observe that this account implies that poetry is a very highly concentrated compression of external structure into internal.[24] In the same masterly paper, during the

and such essays by Todorov himself as "Les Catégories du récit littéraire," *Communications* 8 (1966): 125-51; "Le Récit primitif" and "Les Hommes-récits," *Tel-Quel: Science/Littérature* 30, 31 (Summer, Autumn, 1967): 47-55, 64-73.

Not critical "truth," but internal coherence or validity of the *critical* structure (corresponding to a similar value in literature) is the emphasis of Roland Barthes, an editor of the influential structuralist organ *Communications*; see his clear statement "Criticism as Language," *Times Literary Supplement*, 27 September 1963, pp. 739-40. The structuralist critic reaches out for frames of reference for his coherencies in various places—sociological, psychoanalytic, and anthropological. See Barthes, *Critique et vérité*, Paris, 1966, a brief polemic against Raymond Picard of the Sorbonne, and the somewhat distracted hints concerning the Parisian scene in a *Times Literary Supplement* front article, 23 June 1966.

23.   In a native version of this situation which I once contrived ("Verbal Style: Logical and Counterlogical," *PMLA* 65 [March 1950]: 5-20), metric "parallel" was the artifice which enabled various kinds of verbal equivalence (alliterations, agnominations, near paronomasias) to appear on the axis of contiguity without the effect of accident and illogicality which often marks their appearance in prose.

24.   "In poetry," says Jakobson later in the same paper, "not only the phonological sequence but in the same way any sequence of semantic units strives to build an equation. Similarity superimposed on contiguity imparts

course of an argument illustrating the pervasiveness of the
poetic "function" in many types of language use, Jakobson
throws out the following analysis of a political slogan:

"I like Ike" /ay/layk/ayk/, succinctly structured, consists of
three monosyllables and counts three diphthongs /ay/, each
of them symmetrically followed by one consonantal phoneme,
/ ..l..k..k/. The makeup of the three words presents a varia-
tion: no consonantal phonemes in the first word, two around
the diphthong in the second, and one final consonant in the
third.... Both cola of the trisyllabic formula 'I like/Ike'
rhyme with each other, and the second of the two rhyming
words is fully included in the first one (echo rhymes), /layk/
—/ayk/, a paronomastic image of a feeling which totally en-
velops its object. Both cola alliterate with each other, and the
first of the two alliterating words is included in the second:
/ay/—/ayk/, a paronomastic image of the loving subject en-
veloped by the beloved object.

That was a humorous capsule—perhaps the largest illustration of
a linguistic analysis we can afford to transplant. But far from
the largest available. Imagine a discourse of this tenor, in its
whole range (from the consonantal phonemes *l* and *k* to the lov-
ing subject enveloped by the beloved object), amplified and
subtilized fifty- or a hundred-fold in an essay of sixteen pages
written by Jakobson in collaboration with the anthropologist
Lévi-Strauss and devoted entirely to the structural exposition of
a French sonnet.[25] Charles Baudelaire's *Les Chats* (*Les Fleurs
du Mal* LXVI) asserts a fusion of romantic passion and visionary
contemplation in the image of those ambivalent little household
pets (*puissants et doux, orgueil de la maison*), mythologized
through the superimposed image of sphinxes sunk in their end-
less desert dreams. The cat-sphinxes, as I understand it, are in a
sense both enveloped by and in turn envelop and unify the two
kinds of humans who love them. (*Les amoureux fervents et
les savants austères/Aiment également... /Les chats....*)

---

to poetry its thoroughgoing symbolic, multiplex, polysemantic essence
which is beautifully suggested by Goethe's 'Alles Vergängliche ist nur ein
Gleichnis' (Anything transient is but a likeness). Said more technically,
anything sequent is a simile. In poetry where similarity is superinduced
upon contiguity, any metonymy is slightly metaphorical and any meta-
phor has a metonymical tint."
    25. "*Les Chats* de Charles Baudelaire." The article, except for an intro-
ductory note by Lévi-Strauss ("On s'étonnera peut-etre ..."), has little of
an anthropological slant and reads like a pure burst of fireworks from the
critico-linguistic faculty of the Russian master.

"I like Ike." Imagine further this essay having such an impact as to provoke from an American professor of French, Michael Riffaterre, a counter essay of forty-three pages—or it may seem perhaps largely a complementary essay—rehearsing this sonnet again, almost phoneme by phoneme, in terms no less refined and elaborate—from the title ("The definite article and the plural lead us to expect a precise and concrete description: against such a back-drop, the spiritualization of the cats will be more arresting") to "a global, summative apprehension" of a "sequence of synonymous images, all of them variations on the symbolism of the cat as representative of the contemplative life." Our aim has been to show how the different structures of the poem interact, say Jakobson and Lévi-Strauss, ". . . donnant ainsi au poème le caractère d'un objet absolu." To this Riffaterre assents emphatically.[26]

The combined and partly convergent efforts of the three structuralists do make an impressive case for the linguistic and ideational entity of the sonnet. It remains only to observe that the literary critic who welcomes this kind of argument may run some risk of finding it in the end somewhat too impressive. At the end of his own interpretation, Riffaterre believes that he has "covered every aspect of the text." And he has some abusive words for the literary scholar of the "humanist stripe," who has "always assumed that grammar failed because it was incomplete." "The linguist," he says, "sees all the data." This is good modern structural linguistic doctrine, that linguistics can write a grammar for all the aspects of poetry, even for the metaphors. On the other hand, it would scarcely occur to any linguistic critic, I suspect, to say that even the combined relentless analyses of Jakobson–Lévi-Strauss and Riffaterre provide, for a person unacquainted with the text of Les Chats, sufficient instruction for writing out the text. So far as one could approximate this feat, the reason would be the numerous quotations from the text carried by the critique. The humanist literary critic, in reaching out to avail himself of the linguistic defense of the literary object, should, I believe, be in no great danger of succumbing to this tyranny of the exhaustive theoretical claim.

26. "Describing Poetic Structures: Two Approaches to Baudelaire's Les Chats." Riffaterre writes a jealously assertive account of the screening powers of Baudelaire's text in its reception of the rest of French language and the canon of his poetry. He makes the keen observation that structure of symbols (an invariant pattern of variant materials) is more relevant than simple content. So Baudelaire's two poems entitled Le Chat (Fleurs XXXIV and LI) seem less relevant to Les Chats than the prose poem La Chambre double, with its symbolism of furniture.

The alternative, as some no doubt would urge, may appear to be a ticket with Poulet or Hillis Miller in their voyage into boundless consciousness. Having been very willing to avoid that journey and to notice, on the contrary, the structuralist testimony in favour of the poetic object, I report in conclusion my persisting, perhaps paradoxical, but I think not perverse, conviction that the critic who wishes to retain his humanism and his identity as a literary critic will have to persevere in his allegiance to the party of Coleridge and Croce. These philosophers knew that no rules either of language or of poetry will ever be formulated which speakers and poets, responding to the manifold of actual life with the abandon of catachresis and metaphor, will not rejoice in violating, and that the same logic applies for the critic in his exploration of the uncatalogued and uncataloguable past.[27] This should seem no more implausible to the critic than his intimate experience that he can recognize his own person and distinguish himself from Julius Caesar, while at the same time he is convinced that no science, either anatomical or psychological, has charted or is likely to chart his person exhaustively.

1968

27. F. W. Bateson, in "Linguistics and Literary Criticism," in *The Disciplines of Criticism*, uses the insufficiency of the Saussurian *circuit de la parole* to urge similar arguments against the totalitarian linguistic claim. See also David Lodge, *Language of Fiction* (1966), pp. 49–69, discussing stylistics and linguistics, and Harry Levin, *Why Literary Criticism Is Not an Exact Science* (Cambridge, Mass., 1967).

Bibliographical Note

The ontological or "internal" approach to literary art and the counter approaches converge from the whole literary horizon. Some of the essays collected in my *Verbal Icon* (Lexington, Kentucky, 1954) touch earlier phases of holistic or internal "contextualist" criticism in modern English studies. Here I list a few works which survey recent developments and some which have contributed most directly to the shape of the argument I here attempt.

Section I: Murray Krieger, *The Tragic Vision: Variations on a Theme in Literary Interpretation* (New York, 1960) and *A Window to Criticism: Shakespeare's "Sonnets" and Modern Poetics* (Princeton, 1964) survey essential difficulties for this criticism. Ingo Seidler, "The Iconolatric Fallacy: On the Limitations of the Internal Method of Criticism," *JAAC* 26 (Fall 1967): 9–15, shows some recent parallels between two largely independent national areas of debate, the American and German; Edgar Lohner, "The Intrinsic Method," in *The Disciplines of Criticism: Essays in Literary Theory, Interpretation, and History* edited by Peter Demetz et al. (New Haven, 1968), expands the perspective to take in Russian and Czech formalism and even French *explication* since 1902. Lee T. Lemon, *The Partial Critics* (New York, 1965), chapters V and VI, surveys the same difficulties as Murray Krieger. And see Graham Hough, *An Essay on Criticism* (1966), especially chapters III and XXII, on formalism and the "metaphor" of "organic form."

In section III, expounding current notions of "context" as external, the boundless milieu of the literary work, I refer to the symposium on literary criticism held at Yale in 1965. Six articles from it appear in *MLN* 81 (December 1966): see especially Geoffrey Hartman, "Beyond Formalism" and J. Hillis Miller, "The Antitheses of Criticism: Reflections on the Yale Colloquium." I go on to refer to J. Hillis Miller's "The Geneva School," *Critical Quarterly* 8 (Winter 1966): 305–21; see also A. E. Dyson's editorial welcome in this issue; Miller's book *The Disappearance of God: Five Nineteenth Century Writers* (Cambridge, Mass., 1963); and Sarah N. Lawall, *Critics of Consciousness: The Existential Structure of Literature* (Cambridge, Mass., 1968), with chapters on six Geneva critics and one on J. Hillis Miller.

For my reference in section IV to developments in post-Bloomfieldian linguistics, see, e.g., Archibald A. Hill, "Linguistics since Bloomfield," *Quarterly Journal of Speech* 41 (October 1955): 253–60; "An Analysis of *The Windhover*: An Experiment in Structural Method," *PMLA* 70 (December 1955): 968–78; and "'Pippa's Song': Two Attempts at Structural Reading" in *Readings in Applied English Linguistics*, edited by Harold B. Allen (New York, 1958). At the end of this section, I discuss structuralism; see *Structuralism, Yale French Studies* 36–37 (October 1966), on structuralism in anthropology, psychoanalysis, linguistics, and literary criticism, with valuable annotated bibliographies—and especially the essays by André Martinet, "Structure and Language"; Geoffrey Hartman, "Structuralism: The Anglo-American Adventure"; and Michael Riffaterre, "Describing Poetic Structures: Two Approaches to Baudelaire's *Les Chats*." Also see Roman Jakobson and Claude Lévi-Strauss, "Les Chats de Charles Baudelaire," *L'Homme* 2 (1962): 5–21; Jakobson's "Two Aspects of Language and Two Types of Aphasic Disturbance," *Fundamentals of Language* ('S-Gravenhage, 1956), pp. 64–72 (reprinted as "The Cardinal Dichotomy in Language" in *Language: An Enquiry into its Meaning and Function*, edited by Ruth Nanda Anshen, New York, 1957); and his "Closing Statement: Linguistics and Poetics," in *Style in Language* edited by Thomas Sebeok (New York, 1960), the proceedings of a conference held at Indiana University in 1958. The contextual relations of the "intensional" poetic object are discussed in terms of English philosophy of language by John Casey, *The Language of Criticism* (1966), especially pp. 1, 12, 27–28, 100, and 162.

ORGANIC FORM: SOME
QUESTIONS ABOUT A METAPHOR

The metaphor is ancient, and most of the questions have been asked before, many times. That I should write an essay of about twenty pages pretending to say anything worth while upon such a classic theme requires a courage that I derive largely from the support of two scholars who have recently written on it—one, Philip C. Ritterbush, a historian who has made himself an expert guide in that tropical rainforest of eighteenth-century romantic nature philosophy and early scientific "representation" of living form, in which some of our most cherished modern notions about both science and poetry had their seedbed and first growth; the other, G. N. G. Orsini, an idealist aesthetician and critic of imposing authority. It is not my aim to expound very much history, either of science or of aesthetics. I take history as an object that is before us, almost palpably, upon the table, and I choose my own exhibits. A first one that I call attention to I take from a play by Molière, *Don Juan, or the Feast with the Statue.* The agile valet Sganarelle in one of his several running debates with his atheistic master, bursts into teleology:

> Can you perceive all the contrivances of which the human mechanism is composed without wondering at the way the parts are fitted with one another? These nerves, these bones, these veins, these arteries, these . . . this lung, this heart, this liver, and all the other organs. . . . My argument is that there is something mysterious in man which, whatever you may say, none of the philosophers can explain. Is it not wonderful that I exist and that I have something in my head which thinks a hundred different things in a moment and does what it wills with my body? I wish to clap my hands, to raise my arms, to lift my eyes to heaven, to bow my head, to move my feet, to go to the right, to the left, forward, backward, to turn. . . .
> (He falls down whilst turning.)
> *Don Juan.* Good, so your argument has broken its nose.
>
> [*Don Juan*, III, i]

A centuries-old Aristotelian and scholastic commonplace— "What a piece of work is a man"—is good enough material here for a hamstrung sprint of servile boldness, a bumbling theology. Larger versions of organicism appear in the same era with a kind of cool solemnity, as in the cosmic unity, the social and ethical harmonies, which critics nowadays celebrate and annotate from

the whole Western tradition in the *Essay on Man* of Pope or
his *Windsor Forest.*[1]

A quicker pulse, a new accent of excitement, marks, I believe,
my second exhibit—if not a subtlety and coolness equal to that
of either Molière or Pope.

> What Beaux and Beauties crowd the gaudy groves,
> And woo and win their vegetable Loves.
> ·
> The love-sick Violet, and the Primrose pale,
> Bow their sweet heads, and whisper to the gale;
> With secret sighs the Virgin Lily droops,
> And jealous Cowslips hang their tawny cups.
> How the young Rose in beauty's damask pride
> Drinks the warm blushes of his bashful bride.
>
> BOTANIC MUSE! who in this latter age
> Led by your airy hand the Swedish sage,
> Bade his keen eye your secret haunts explore
> On dewy dell, high wood, and winding shore;
> Say on each leaf how tiny Graces dwell;
> How laugh the Pleasures in a blossom's bell.
> How insect Loves arise on cobweb wings,
> Aim their light shafts, and point their little stings.[2]

The author of these heroic couplets, the grandfather of Charles
Darwin, tells us in a footnote that he is drawing upon "Linneus,
the celebrated Swedish naturalist," and in an advertisement to
the volume, he says that "The general design ... is to inlist
Imagination under the banner of Science; and to lead her vota-
ries from the looser analogies, which dress out the imagery of
poetry, to the stricter ones, which form the ratiocination of
philosophy." The enlistment of the imagination and the looser
analogies were a more successful part of the program than the
stricter analogies. "Eighteenth-century naturalists," Dr. Philip C.
Ritterbush instructs us, "denied or overlooked every distinction
between plants and animals that they might have been expected
to consider."[3] The frontispiece of a German edition of Alex-
ander von Humboldt's *Journey to the Equatorial Regions of the*

---

1. See, for example, Earl R. Wasserman, *The Subtler Language* (Balti-
more, 1959), chap. 4.

2. Erasmus Darwin, *The Botanic Garden* (1789-1791), 4th ed. (London,
1799), Part II, *The Loves of the Plants*, ll. 9-10, 15-20, 31-38. Cf.
Philip C. Ritterbush, *Overtures to Biology* (New Haven, 1964), pp. 162-
265.

3. *Overtures*, p. 156.

New World (1807), transplanted as frontispiece of Ritterbush's *Overtures to Biology* (1964), shows us an Apollonian figure, the spirit of poetry no doubt, unveiling an Asiatic Artemisian statue, appropriate emblem of the mysterious fecundity of nature; the title of Goethe's *Elegie* on the growth of plants (*Die Metamorphose der Pflanzen*, 1799) is inscribed on a tablet lying at the feet of the multimammiferous goddess. Such celebrations were surely not harmful for the development of Romantic nature poetry. At the same time, a degree of confusion in poetic theory may have been a concomitant, even an inspiration, of the poetry. It is perhaps significant that the English Romantic poet who described nature (that is, English landscape) the most often and the most lovingly—Wordsworth, of course—had in his theoretical essays little to say about organic form. Yet, by and large, the prevalence of nature, especially landscape and botanical nature, in English poetry during about two centuries does suggest a kind of latent equation in the poetic mind: Themes or images of organic life in poetry confer upon that poetry the poetic life of organic form. Coleridge, the most important translator of German organic idealism to the English scene, could speak, or seem to speak, both for and against that equation, and in the same essay. "If the artist copies the mere nature, the *natura naturata*, what idle rivalry."[4] On the other hand, it did seem to him that the visible image of nature was in a special way "fitted to the limits of the human mind." Natural forms, in a very natural way, yielded moral reflections; nature was thought, and thought nature. That was the "mystery of genius in the Fine Arts."[5] This might be illustrated by many passages of description and simile in the poetry of both Coleridge and Wordsworth or of Shelley. But, as Bernard Blackstone has pointed out, there is no English Romantic poet better than Keats for showing us the genial swell of organic forms, the unfolded buds, the ripening fruit, the loaded blessing of the vines, the swollen gourd, the plumped hazel shells, and for making such images symbolize a transcendent experience of beauty—even beauty like that of a Grecian Urn. The first volume of Erasmus Darwin's *Botanic Garden* opened with engravings of flowers, and the second volume concluded with engravings by William Blake of the Portland vase.[6]

What then of organic form in visual art? The notebooks of

4. *Biographia Literaria*, ed. J. Shawcross (London, 1939), II: 257 ("On Poesy or Art").
5. *Biographia Literaria*, II, 253-254, 258.
6. Ritterbush, *The Art of Organic Forms* (Washington, 1968), pp. 19-20.

Goethe and a crowd of other Nature Philosophers and sci-
entists and their treatises and textbooks are lavish with both
pictures and scientific "representations" or modules of or-
ganic life. But these no doubt served little enough any aes-
thetic purpose. The "meticulously veined leaves" painted
under the Pre-Raphaelite hand lens of Millais, or Ruskin
sprawled out drawing a square foot of meadow grass on a
mossy bank,[7] are more valid indexes to our theme, and no less
the vegetable curves of Art Nouveau at the end of the century—
Hector Guimard's sinuously framing metallic green tendrils and
leaves for Paris Métro station portals, for instance, one of which
we can see today in New York, in the sculpture garden of the
Museum of Modern Art. Let a recent historian of that era in art
have the last word about this: "Up from the sidewalk there
sprang a profusion of interlacing metal, bouquets of aquatic
plants, luminous tulips, gorged with the rich disturbing sap of
Paris, its cellars, and subsoil."[8] The date was about 1900, at
about the same date the Parisian aesthete Gustave Geffroy wrote
the following encomium upon a flower: "*A flower*— . . . Free
and growing out of the earth, or captive in a vase, it presents an
artist with the perfect example of the universal creative force—
in it he may find form, colour and even expression, a mysterious
expression composed of stillness, silence, and the fugitive beauty
of things which are born only to die in the same moment."[9]

And this brings us to the art exhibition put on by Dr. Ritter-
bush at the Museum of Natural History in Washington, D.C.,
during June and July of 1968—*The Art of Organic Forms*: cells,
globules, curves, filaments, membranes, tentacles, emulsions,
gelatins, pulsing fluids, capillary action, liquid diffusions, amoe-
boid shapes, nascent protoplasmic entities,[10] all this and more
concentrated in seventy-two paintings, graphics, and sculptures
of our own century: Odilon Redon, for instance, *Au Fond de la
Mer*, c. 1905; Paul Klee, *Male and Female Plants*, 1921; Wasily
Kandinsky, *Capricious Forms No. 634*, 1937; Max Ernst, *Prenez*

7. *The Art of Organic Forms*, p. 23. René Wellek (*A History of Modern
Criticism*, III [New Haven, 1963], 140), speculates that Ruskin's liking for
organistic theory influenced his distaste for Dutch painting and classical
landscapes.
8. Maurice Rheims, *The Age of Art Nouveau*, trans. Patrick Evans (Lon-
don, 1966), p. 14, cf. p. 95, plate 114.
9. No doubt to be found somewhere in Geffroy's eight volumes of *La
Vie artistique*, 1892-1903. I quote from Martin Battersby, *The World of
Art Nouveau* (New York, 1968), p. 145. Cf. Rheims, *Art Nouveau*, p. 212.
10. *The Art of Organic Forms*, pp. 83-84.

garde au microbe de l'amour, 1949; Pavel Tchelichew, *Itinerary of Light*, 1953. Matta's *Le Vertigo d'Eros*, 1944, at the Museum of Modern Art, supplies the mysterious greenish ektachrome frontispiece of the *Catalogue* of this remarkable exhibition. The thesis of many of these artists and of their critics, expressed in essays and catalogue notes, is that such submicroscopic life forms symbolize the secret life of the creative human spirit.

We have been skirting a sophism: namely, the notion that the representation of biological forms in a work of verbal or visual art implies something about the presence of organic or artistic form in that work.[11] An idealist historian and philosopher such as G. N. G. Orsini will not wish to linger long in discussion of that issue. Nevertheless, its recurrent presence, even as a hint or as a half-committed fallacy, throughout the now long stretch of the modern organistic era, justifies its being noted and put aside with some deliberateness at the start of a discussion that aims at the center of the critical question of organicism. The issue is perhaps more easily defined in literary art, perhaps more nicely subject to confusion in visual art. Consider the following paradox. If the picture is overt enough, say a Currier and Ives print of watermelon vines, trumpet flowers, and humming birds, it presents organic forms, but I think none of us will be likely to argue that it thereby *has* high artistic form. Move the picture, however, through several shades of abstractionism, say through Art Nouveau sinuosities to pure or supposedly pure nonreferential curves, and then to the golden-section compositional style of Piet Mondrian or the "illusionary modulations," *Despite Straight Lines*, of Josef Albers.[12] We reach a stage where, so far as the picture has content, it is a geometric content. But this too is a geometric form, for geometry is all form. Form and representational content coincide perfectly. So in a sense this must be artistic form, and hence, by idealistic definition, it must be organic form. Yet it is not life form, but rather crystal form, as Dr. Ritterbush would say, or mere lifeless mechanical form, as A. W. Schlegel and Coleridge and many another Romantic would say.[13] So by a line of reasoning that starts with biological imagery we arrive at the conclusion that

11. *The Art of Organic Forms*, p. 86.
12. Josef Albers, *Despite Straight Lines* (New Haven, 1961), p. 10.
13. "These results require the use of ruler and drafting pen and establish unmodulated line as a legitimate artistic means. In this way they oppose a belief that the handmade is better than the machine-made, or that mechanical construction is anti-graphic or unable to arouse emotion" (ibid., p. 16).

organic form can occur in visual art only by not occurring at either terminus of a spectrum running from realistic representation to extreme abstraction.

If we believe that a poem grows in the mind like a plant (which is what Coleridge and the others did believe, or at least assert), and if we notice that the poem which emerges from the mind does not in fact look very much like a plant, and that furthermore (as we have been saying) the poem may or may not contain vegetable imagery, then as we ponder and expound our doctrine of growth and form, it may well be the perhaps more profound, but certainly less inspectable, part of the doctrine, the accent on the genetic, that we assert with the most energy. And thus it was in fact with Coleridge. A few of his most striking and deliberate statements about organic form occur in his notes for a general lecture on Shakespeare, which editors rightly place in the context of yet other notes for lectures on Shakespeare's power as a poet, his imagination, his judgment so happily wedded with his genius. Here Coleridge executes a double step away from any possible implication that organic form consists in vegetable imagery. He moves the discussion into the fully human and dramatic arena of Shakespeare's plays and his *Venus and Adonis*. At the same time he is recurrently inclined to depart from the poems themselves and to search the organic depths of the mind of the great maker. This is Coleridge's well-known leaning. Wordsworth was content to illustrate the concept of "imagination" in poems and passages of poems, especially in his own. Coleridge, as he himself explains in the *Biographia*, essayed the further radical task of tracing the poetic principle to its seat in the psychology of the poet.

Five properties of plant life (according to the clear exposition by Meyer Abrams)[14] enter into the analogy between plants and poems to be construed from Coleridge's several treatises, notes, letters, and conversations. (Coleridge both draws in part upon a German source, A. W. Schlegel, and in turn becomes archetypal for a moderate English tradition. Many passages in the first two volumes of René Wellek's *History of Modern Criticism* testify to the preoccupation of the romantic Germans with organic form, and also to their extravagance.[15] The five properties or principles of organic form, in the order arranged by Abrams, are (1) the WHOLE, the priority of the whole; without the whole

14. Meyer Abrams, *The Mirror and the Lamp* (London, 1953), pp. 170–76.
15. See, for instance, II:48, 358: A. W. Schlegel, in his Berlin Lectures, said that Euripides was the "putrefaction of Greek tragic form."

the parts are nothing; (2) GROWTH, the manifestation of growth in the "evolution and extension of the plant"; (3) ASSIMILA-TION; the plant converts diverse materials into its own substance; (4) INTERNALITY; the plant is the spontaneous source of its own energy; it is not shaped from without; (5) INTERDE-PENDENCE, between parts and parts, and parts and whole; pull off a leaf and it dies.

These somewhat overlapping or merging principles are all in effect equivalents of the single principle that we may call "Organic Form." The five, I believe, might be readily synthesized into fewer, or into one; or they might be analyzed into a larger number. They have a close affinity for, or near identity with, a sixth; the favorite Coleridgean concept of the tension and reconciliation of manifold opposites which it is the peculiar power of artistic genius to accomplish.[16] All of these principles as expounded by Coleridge blend a measure of poetic structuralism, or objective doctrine concerning poetic form, with a measure of geneticism, or psychological doctrine, concerning the author's consciousness or unconsciousness. The second principle, or that of GROWTH, especially invites the genetic accent. As I have the authority of Orsini on my side, I will not take upon myself the full burden of the argument against what I have fallen into the habit of referring to as the "intentional" or the "genetic" fallacy. "It is only to the finished product," says Orsini, "that we can apply the concept of organic unity."[17] I assent emphatically. Let me add, however, one observation. There is at least one respect in which the physical organism, either growing plant or animal, is immeasurably surpassed by the human poetic consciousness. I mean, in its capacity for self-revision, rearrangement, mending. Plants renew leaves and flowers; animals moult in several ways; a lobster can lose a claw and regrow it; the human body heals cuts and regrows a finger nail. But there is no action of any physical organism that remotely approaches the power of the human mind to revise and recast *itself*, constantly to reaffirm or to cancel its own precedent action, in whole or in part. We confront here self-involution, a spiritual power. (The world soul, says Plotinus, looking to its consequent dreams up

16. René Wellek, "Coleridge's Philosophy and Criticism," in *The English Romantic Poets: A Review of Research*, ed. T. M. Raysor (New York, 1950), pp. 109, 113, argues the close connection for Coleridge between the organic principle and that of polarity of opposites; he thinks too sharp a distinction between the two is drawn by Gordon McKenzie, *Organic Unity in Coleridge* (Berkeley, 1939).

17. G. N. G. Orsini, "The Organic Concepts in Aesthetics," *Comparative Literature* 21 (Winter 1969): 5.

the physical universe; looking to its antecedent it reflects the ideas of the nous.) As if a tree could move one of its own branches from the bottom to the top, or on looking itself over could change from an oak to a pine. What we call the "finished product," the poem, is a moment of spiritual activity, hypostatized, remembered, recorded, repeated. The human psyche makes the poem out of itself, or offers a remembered action of itself as the poem. Thus it differs notably from the tree, which does not offer anything, but simply appears, as the necessary product of the process which is itself.

The Romantic analogy between vegetable and poetic creation tended to assimilate the poetic to the vegetable by making the poetic as radically spontaneous as possible—that is, indeliberate, unconscious. Some theorists clearly affirmed this. Shakespeare created his Hamlet "as a bird weaves its nest."[18] A poet, urged Schiller, should *be* a plant.[19] An alternative which we have come close to noticing when we alluded to the eighteenth-century nature philosophers, was to draw plant life closer to human consciousness. According to one generous analogical view, plants *were* conscious. Coleridge, as Meyer Abrams has shrewdly pointed out, enjoyed the kind of classical sanity that compelled him to reject both solutions. Shakespeare's judgment was equal to his genius. He never wrote anything without conscious design.[20] On the other hand, "the man would be a dreamer, who otherwise than poetically should speak of roses and lilies as *self-conscious* subjects."[21] The inside history of literature as recorded in the testimonies of authors themselves is full of their awareness that the process by which they have arrived at the mental and verbal act presented as a poem has not necessarily, or even usually, been identical with that act as finally achieved. The moment presented as the poem is a contrived moment. This is so even on the supposition that the author achieves his sonnet in one perfect first draft. For he reviews it and accepts it and puts it out as a poem. No matter how spon-

18. Wellek, *History*, III: 166 (Emerson); cf. II: 290 (Kleist); II: 217 (A. W. Schlegel).
19. Abrams, pp. 168–74; 202–08.
20. Abrams, pp. 364–65. It was still possible for Walter Pater to read the general emphasis of Coleridge's *dicta* on organicism in the opposite way. He thought that Coleridge made the artist "almost a mechanical agent"; poetry "like some blindly organic process of assimilation" ("Coleridge," *Appreciations* [London, 1898], p. 80). And indeed see "On Poesy or Art," *Biographia*, II: 258: "There is in genius itself an unconscious activity; nay, that is the genius in the man of genius."
21. Abrams, p. 173 and note pp. 364–65.

taneous and lucky in one sense, in another sense it is also artificial. Few poets have, like the French inspirationalist Charles Peguy, looked on their first impulses as so literally inspired that the least revision of a first draft was an aesthetic sin. "A line will take us hours maybe," says Yeats. "Yet if it does not seem a moment's thought,/Our stitching and unstitching has been naught."[22] He knew that the hours of stitching and unstitching were a normal part of "Adam's Curse." And with a somewhat different emphasis: "Verse, 'tis true," argues Dryden, "is not the effect of sudden thought; but that hinders not that sudden thought may be represented in verse." "A play is supposed to be the work of a poet."[23]

And so we come to the third of three issues which I am trying to define—not whether the poem presents biological imagery; and not whether the process of its growth in the mind resembles the growth of a tree; but whether the poem itself, the hypostatized verbal and mental act, looks in any way like an animal or a vegetable. In section 65 of the *Critique of Judgment* Kant observes, and few besides Orsini seem to have noticed it,[24] that a work of human art differs from a natural organism in that the latter is self-organizing, that it can repair itself when damaged, and that it reproduces itself. I have already suggested that under its genetic aspect (as the creator's mind in act) the verbal work of art rivals and even surpasses the natural organism in the capacity for self-correction. We have seen that Coleridge, with his strong inclination to the genetic, claimed internality, or self-organization, as one of the characters of the poetic organism. But our theme now is the poem as presented or objectified act—as poetic object. Plato said a composition should have an organized sequence of parts, and that it ought to be *like* a living being, with foot, body, and head.[25] And Aristotle said that it ought to be a unity, like an organism.[26] But we might ask of Plato: What are the foot, body, and head of a poem? Or of Aristotle: What are the beginning, middle, and end of a squirrel or a tree? Or: Professor Orsini recites for us the rude question of an imagined objector: "What corresponds to

22. "Adams's Curse," *The Collected Poems of W. B. Yeats* (New York, 1959), p. 78.

23. John Dryden, *Essays*, ed. W. P. Ker (Oxford, 1900), I: 102, 114: *Essay of Dramatic Poesy and Defence of the Essay*.

24. G. N. G. Orsini, *Coleridge and German Idealism* (Carbondale, Illinois, 1969), pp. 160–62.

25. Plato, *Phaedrus*, 265.

26. Aristotle, *Poetics*, VIII. 4; XXIII. 1.

the stomach in a tragedy?" Such conceptions, he remarks wisely, are carrying the simile too far. He argues indeed that the simile (or metaphor) of physical organic life is not essential to the concept of aesthetic organic unity.[27] The aesthetic unity is generated by the Kantian *a priori* synthetic idea, the human reason's glorious power of nonempirical creative unifying vision.[28] The art work, says Orsini, has indeed, and literally, an organic form, a synthetic unity in multiplicity. The merely physical organism enjoys this character only by metaphoric extension and hence in a less exact degree.[29] Thus he would reverse the usual direction of the metaphor. One will readily nowadays think of certain senses in which he may be right about the physical organism. Nowadays a batch of amoebas is chopped up and the parts are reassembled, more or less higgledy-piggledy, as I understand it, and a new set of amoebas emerges—"synthetic."[30] The human body, we read with queasy feelings, fights hard to reject the benevolently transplanted kidney or heart. Yet even this obtuse archaic organism (our body), struggling to carry out the Coleridgean rules, can be coerced for a certain time, even an extended time, into entertaining and being sustained by alien organs. And thus it succeeds in looking a little more than we might previously have thought possible like a machine with interchangeable parts.

The aesthetic organicist, therefore, in his dealing with poems, will no doubt do well to appeal but cautiously to that analogy with the all too ragged physical organism. He may well be content to confine his appeal to a very purified post-Kantian version of the aesthetic properties: the individuality and uniqueness of each aesthetic whole, the priority of the whole to the parts, the congruence and interdependence of parts with parts and of parts

27. Orsini, pp. 4–5, 27. Cf. Wellek, *History*, I: 9, 18, 26 (the romantic emphasis upon biology); IV: 70–71 (Brunetière adopting biological evolutionary concepts too literally); Meyer Abrams, "Archetypal Analogues in the Language of Criticism," *University of Toronto Quarterly* 18 (1949): 313–27; Graham Hough, *An Essay on Criticism* (London, 1966), chap. 22, "Organic Form: A Metaphor."

28. The reference is to Kant's *Logik*, chap. 1, par. 3 (Orsini, pp. 2–3, 4, 17). This kind of unity embraces also mental activities other than the aesthetic—e.g. philosophical, political, scientific, technological (Orsini, p. 26). Though the idealist aesthetician must guard against the sin of "intellectualism" in defining the unifying motifs of aesthetic works (Orsini, pp. 9–10), he is ready to extend the purified concept of "organic" unity into the areas of the highest abstractionism. This, I should say, involves Plotinian and Crocean problems about how to distinguish Art from the whole remaining horizon of being and of human knowing.

29. Orsini, p. 27.

30. *New York Times*, 13 November 1970, p. 1.

with the whole, the uniqueness and irreplaceability of parts and their nonexistence prior to the aesthetic whole or outside it.[31] Surely these are ideas against which no literary critic is likely to rebel—none at least whose knowledge of critical history extends far enough backward for him to appreciate the embarrassments for criticism created by the more extreme versions of legislation according to the classical literary kinds or of evaluation according to the classical ornamental rhetoric, or of explanation according to economic, sociological, or other historical categories, or according to any theological, anthropological, or psychological archetypes. If we had never known any romantic interest in life forms, if we had never heard of organic form, we should today be under the necessity of inventing it. We might well be dedicating this very volume to a struggle to invent and proclaim some doctrine of Romantic organicism. Given, however, the very well-established theory as we do know it, and given its several main articles of doctrine, such as we have been reciting, I confess my opinion that both the metaphor and the literal idealist doctrine invite some not unreasonable questions.

If the leaf is detached from the tree, it dies. Still we may press it between the pages of a book and treasure it years later. It has that kind of superiority to certain parts of other and higher organisms, say an ear cut from a vanquished bull by a matador, a human finger cut off and preserved in formaldehyde. The German metaphysical humorist Jean Paul speaks in a typically enough Romantic idiom when in his *Vorschule der Aesthetik* he alludes contemptuously to the traditional right of book-reviewers to pluck the feathers of the "jewelled humming-bird."[32] Jean Paul is confident too that "the spirit of a work like the *Iliad* is manifest both in the whole and in the smallest syllable."[33] Load every rift with ore," said Keats to Shelley. And even Coleridge, with a hedging glance at a Kantian distinction, uttered this well-known half-betrayal: A poem proposes to itself "such delight from the *whole*, as is compatible with a distinct gratification from each component *part*."[34]

31. Orsini, pp. 17, 10-11.
32. *Vorschule* (1804-1813), Second Preface, par. 11, in *Sämtliche Werke*, ed. Eduard Berend, Part I, vol. 11 (Weimar, 1935): 11. I am indebted to the translation by Margaret Cardwell Hale, forthcoming from the Wayne State University Press.
33. Chap. 86, p. 311. The quotation is from Mrs. Hale's close paraphrase of Jean Paul's fragmentary chapter.
34. *Biographia*, II: 10 (chap. 14). He was hedging less carefully when he said that poetry permits a "pleasure from the whole consistent with a consciousness of pleasure from the component parts," and that it com-

Few of us, I suppose, have had the experience of finding a hummingbird's tail feather. But I have found many blue jay feathers, and pheasant feathers, and glossy black crow feathers, all of which I thought were beautiful and put in my hat or lapel or preserved for a while at home in a vase. No doubt there is an implicit sustaining context within which we admire such relics, and the same is true for certain fragmentary, sketchy, or partly abstracted representational forms of art—for instance, a single fleeting leg in a sculpture entitled "Runner" by Leon Underwood.[35] We admire these in the context of a habitual consciousness of their relation to the rest of the visible surface of a bird or a human body. And these surface contexts too have beyond them an interior context, where interdependence or mutual need of parts is very great; it is peremptory or absolute. These we know about, and no doubt the fact has aesthetic significance. Still we do not need to see these things; we do not want to see them. The ancient haruspicators were bent on no aesthetic purpose. Elizabethan or Augustan lovers might hope to see themselves imaged through a window in a lady's bosom, or to look more cynically at the "moving toy shop" of her heart, silks, ribbons, laces, gewgaws.[36] But when Humbert Humbert in Nabokov's *Lolita* longs in effect to eviscerate his nymphet, to kiss her insides, heart, liver, lungs, kidneys, we have already, some chapters before this, begun to enjoy a dawning comprehension that he is a madman.[37]

I am trying to emphasize one dimension of gross differentiation between physical organism and poetic organism and thus to reinforce the opinion I have already expressed that it is easy to push the analogy between them too far. We know there is not any part, detail, or aspect of a poem which we cannot at least try and wish to see in relation to all the other parts and the whole. The poem is all knowable; it is all knowledge, through and through. It is transnoetic, an act or a possible act of a self-reflexive consciousness. (In this respect, certain other kinds of art, stone statues, for instance, have a status different from that of either a poem or a person. A flaw at the center of the marble does not become known unless the statue is destroyed. Still the

municates "from each part the greatest sum of pleasure compatible with the largest sum of pleasure of the whole" ("Definition of Poetry," *Shakespearian Criticism*, ed. T. M. Raysor, I: 148).

35. R. H. Wilenski, *The Meaning of Modern Sculpture* (London, 1932), plate 18 (facing p. 133) and p. 160.

36. Murray Krieger, *A Window to Criticism* (Princeton, 1964), Part II; *The Rape of the Lock*, I: 100; and Pope's *Guardian* 106.

37. Vladimir Nabokov, *Lolita* (New York, 1955), p. 167.

statue *is* solid and opaque and is conceived aesthetically in that way. Shelley's remark about the impurity of all the arts other than verbal poetry was more accurate than the more extreme unifying idealisms.) And so we might at first think that the absolute idealist doctrines—no life in the part without the whole, no substitution of one part for another, and the like—if purged of too much contact with the unhappy biological metaphor and applied *literally* (as the idealist says) to poems, might hold up much better. I think this is in fact not true. I am not urging a paradox, but only one further confrontation with reality. I mean that in some respects the poem as organic unity will come off rather worse without the crutch, or the distraction, of the physical comparison.

The head of many a marble statue has survived truncation—and has been admired for centuries in a garden or a museum. Necessity in the relation of parts to parts and of parts to whole differs very widely with different arts and with different parts. Go into a movie by Antonioni or Fellini just in time to see the last few flickers, and you will likely experience a nearly maximum loss of meaning and aesthetic quality in a part deprived of its whole. Arrive at the beginning of the movie, or read the first chapter of almost any novel, and you will likely have the opposite experience. If the high aesthetic doctrine of the whole were true, we would never sit out even a very good movie or a very good play, never finish reading a novel or a poem. We recognize and enjoy the trenchancy or the delicacy of Augustan couplet wit before we finish the first page of any one of the major poems in that mode. We recognize and reject the sentimental inflation, the witless couplets, of Erasmus Darwin's *Loves of the Plants* on reading a very few lines. The reader unsophisticated by aesthetic theory has a constant and not always unhappy tendency to escape the tyranny of title pages, chapter, act, and scene headings, even the tag of the *dramatis persona*. The wider stretches of poetry are often, like life, a kind of spread-out and general, or atmospheric, or virtual, context for local episodes of the most intense aesthetic quality. Many couplets by Alexander Pope are better poems in their own right than Ezra Pound's miniature image *In a Station of the Metro*. Matthew Arnold's "touchstones" do not offer a viable method of criticism, but his conception of them is far from absurd. A very different spirit, in a far distant era, the Roman neoplatonist Plotinus, spoke words of wisdom against the Stoic notion that symmetry is one of the necessary conditions of the beautiful. Think, he says, what that doctrine leads us to. "Only a compound can be beautiful, never anything devoid of parts. . . . Yet beauty in an aggregate demands beauty in details; it cannot be constructed out of ugliness; its law must run throughout."[38]

We are told by the Kantian aesthetician, solemnly, that the interdependence of parts in the organically unified poem is so close that to remove any part is to "damage" the whole (to damage it badly, we suppose), and that no part is replaceable by any other conceivable part.[39] But how can we ever be sure about either of these propositions? Many poets continue to revise their poems assiduously, to remove parts, to add others, to replace others, even to the last gasp of their Death-bed editions. Alexander Pope's intended order of satiric portraits in his moral Epistle *Of the Characters of Women* remains conjectural today. It apparently remained unclear to him (and to Warburton) what the ideal order was. Some of the portraits apparently have been lost.[40] Editors, compositors, critics, theatrical producers, and actors make many inspired changes in works, either on purpose or accidentally. (Richard Burton has turned his back on the audience, lurked in the shadows, and mumbled the soliloquies of *Hamlet*—in effect, actor against the play.) Even a dunce, Lewis Theobald, introduced into Shakespeare an emendation that for two centuries has been gratefully accepted. Startling examples of this kind, from the annals of textual editing, from critical speculation, from innocent appreciation directed to a corrupt text, have been assembled in a recent article by James Thorpe, who was pushing the case for the author against the printer's devil and his associates.[41] We need have no quarrel with this cause. We are aiming here, not at genetic or textual problems, but at a confrontation with certain perhaps embarrassing aesthetic dubieties. Five-act plays and epic narratives are often lumpy—in ways that producers of plays can cope with but which

38. *Enneads*, I. vi. 1.

39. "In the unified object, everything that is necessary is there, and nothing that is not necessary is there. . . . If a certain yellow patch were not in a painting, its entire character would be altered, and so would a play if a particular scene were not in it, in the place where it is. . . . In a good melody, or painting, or poem, one could not change a part without damaging (not merely changing) the whole" (John Hospers, "Problems of Aesthetics," *Encyclopedia of Philosophy* [New York, 1967] I: 43–44, quoted by Orsini, pp. 1–5).

40. Frank Brady, "The History and Structure of Pope's *To a Lady*," *Studies in English Literature, 1500-1900* 9 (Summer 1969): 439–62: "*To a Lady* is no immutable 'organic' whole."

41. "The Aesthetics of Textual Criticism," *PMLA* 80 (1965): 465–82. Cf. Fredson Bowers, "Textual Criticism," *The Aims and Methods of Scholarship in Modern Languages and Literatures*, ed. James Thorpe (New York, 1963), p. 24.

reading aestheticians may have to blink. The authors are masters of episodes and scenes. Think of the partition of the kingdom by Hotspur, Glendower, and Mortimer in the First Part of *King Henry IV*, of Justice Shallow's nostalgia for the good old days at Clement's Inn in the Second Part of the same chronicle play. Think of the closing books of the *Odyssey*. Think of the Doloneia or nighttime slaughter of the scout in Book X of the *Iliad*—perhaps genetically intrusive, as scholiasts for centuries have suspected—in any event a hypertrophic development, but a cherished one.[42] A professor of aesthetics, Catherine Lord, has argued that too close a degree of organic unity necessarily defeats the episodic and multifarious nature of such extended literary works.[43] An advanced speculatist in Renaissance studies, Harry Berger, notices the "conspicuous irrelevance" of descriptive detail, the "perverse insistence on the digressive elements," with which Spenser roughens and gives character to the otherwise too smooth and logical lines of allegory in Book II of *The Faerie Queene*.[44] It is my own heretical belief that a good chess problem, viewed according to the idealist organistic norm, has a more fully determined and hence more perfect structure than even a sonnet by Shakespeare. A hallmark of linguistic expression, as linguists are now telling us, is a certain surplus of information. The *Hopscotch* novel, with a hundred expendable chapters to be inserted at intervals as the reader wills,[45] and other sorts of open-ended or multiple-choice fictions are now a well-established feature of the literary scene. Such terms as "indeterminacy," "irrelevance," and "nonstructure" and studies devoted to *Strains of Discord* begin to appeal to the critics. We need not be partisans of all these kinds of innovation in order to carry on our dialogue with Coleridge and Professor Orsini.

In saying all this, we are, of course, subscribing without reserve to the Kantian proposition recently cited by E. D. Hirsch[46] that

42. Cedric Whitman, *Homer and the Heroic Tradition* (Cambridge, Mass., 1958), pp. 283-84, 353.

43. Catherine Lord, "Organic Unity Reconsidered," *JAAC* 22 (Spring 1964): 263-68. Note 17, p. 268, quotes Hans Eichner: ". . . Shakespeare is the very last dramatist whose plays one would normally describe as integrated wholes" ("The Meaning of 'Good' in Aesthetic Judgments," *The British Journal of Aesthetics* [October 1963], p. 316, n. 3).

44. Harry Berger, *The Allegorical Temper: Vision and Reality in Book II of Spenser's Faerie Queene* (New Haven, 1957), chaps. 5-7; esp. pp. 122-23, 128.

45. Julio Cortázar, *Hopscotch*, trans. from the Spanish (*Rayuela*) by Gregory Rabassa (New York, 1966).

46. Kant, *Critique of Judgment*, §21; E. D. Hirsch, "Literary Evaluation as Knowledge," *Contemporary Literature* 9 (Summer 1968): 328.

we must confront and interpret the aesthetic object in our best frame of mind. Whatever is ideal (if it is not in fact clearly chimerical) is what in fact the work is and says. This extends (in the absence of other kinds of factual evidence) to textual arguments about intentions. What makes clearly better sense always has the superior claim. Hamlet, as F. W. Bateson has sensibly affirmed, yearned not that "this too, too sullied flesh," but that "this too, too *solid* flesh would melt, thaw, and resolve itself into a dew."[47] The Wife of Bath, as Talbot Donaldson, manifesting both textual erudition and concern for poetic meaning, has been the only editor to conclude, speaks of human organs of generation having been created not by a "perfectly wise wight," but by a "perfectly wise wright"—*a conditore sapientissimo*, as the wife's source St. Jerome had put it. And we are convinced, not because the key word happens to occur in three "bad" manuscripts among the total of fifty-two, but because this is the only reading that makes good sense.[48]

The direction in which my argument has been pointing must be clear. Examples of less than complete organicity such as I have cited could be multiplied indefinitely and indefinitely varied. But I seem to hear the neo-Kantian idealist voices murmuring: "Enough of this. You are talking of imperfections. The organicist doctrine applies only to aesthetic perfection, and perfection in this world is hard to come by."[49] And I answer: Just so. But I think of passages in Plato where he seems to be voting in favor of poetry, or at least in favor of poetic inspiration, if only that inspiration will produce something like the beautiful wisdom of philosophy. The poets as we know them, Homer and the tragedians, are a mad gang of corrupters. They are outside the pale. I myself have been speaking of English poetry as we know it—of Shakespeare, for instance, or Pope. A doctrine of organicity, if it means an exceedingly subtle, intimate, manifold (and hence dramatic and imaginative) "interinanimation" of parts in a poem, must surely be one of the modern critic's most carefully defended doctrines. Yet if he faces the facts, he will at the same time find the organic structure of the poem, perhaps paradoxically, a notably loose, stretchable, and adjustable kind of organic form. A "loose" conception of poetic organicism is, in short, what I am arguing for. The time has perhaps arrived in

47. "Modern Bibliography and the Literary Artifact," in *English Studies Today*, ed. G. A. Bonnard (Bern, 1961), pp. 67-70.
48. E. Talbot Donaldson, *Speaking of Chaucer* (New York; 1970), pp. 115, 119-21, 125-28.
49. Orsini, p. 3.

the dialectic of literary theory when we gain little by repeating the organistic formulas. We can perhaps gain more now by trying to test and extend the more precise schemata that are at our disposal for describing the organization of poems. Some advances, along with perhaps some merely ingenious exercises, in modes of grammatical exegesis are being shown these days by critics of the "structural" inclination, and notably by those of the orientation toward Paris. Brilliant exercises, for instance, have been broadcast by Roman Jakobson and a few associates. Sonnets by Baudelaire, Sidney, Shakespeare, a song by Blake along with its illumination, verses by two painters, the *douanier* Rousseau and Paul Klee, are subjected to extremes of analysis under the rigorous structural technique, and they yield no doubt some subliminal secrets of "the grammar of poetry and the poetry of grammar." A similarly progressive, a finely tempered and well-assured idiom of analysis is demonstrated in a recent book (1968) by an American scholar, Barbara Herrnstein Smith. The title will suggest something of the special insight: *Poetic Closure: A Study of How Poems End.*[50] Stephen Booth's *Essay on Shakespeare's Sonnets* is an even more recent adventure (1969) which, despite what to my mind is an overemphasis on the reader's "experience" of a sonnet (in addition to the sonnet itself), takes a more or less rewarding interest in such logical and grammatical commonplaces as "Unity and Division, Likeness and Difference," and in such various multiple occurrences of pattern as "Formal, Logical, and Syntactical," "Rhetorical," "Phonetic," and "Lexical."[51]

Taken together, these two books exhibit an ingenious array of structural commentary upon English lyric poems—Elizabethan, Metaphysical and Cavalier, romantic, and post-symbolist. Explication of poems is, to my mind, one of the termini of literary criticism. It should rarely, if ever, be reported or reexplicated in anybody else's essay. It suits my purpose of the moment very well, however, to take some notice of the theoretical or speculative idiom employed by Barbara Herrnstein Smith.

> A poem or a piece of music concludes. We tend to speak of conclusions when a sequence of events has a relatively high degree of structure. [p. 2]

If, on the other hand, there have been no surprises or disap-

---

50. Barbara Herrnstein Smith, *Poetic Closure: A Study of How Poems End* (Chicago, 1968).

51. Stephen Booth, *An Essay on Shakespeare's Sonnets* (New Haven, 1969).

pointments, if all our expectations have been gratified, then the poem has been as predictable—and as interesting—as someone's reciting the alphabet. Art inhabits the country between chaos and cliché. [p. 14]

We may think of *integrity* as, in one sense, the property of a system of which the parts are more obviously related to each other than to anything outside that system. [pp. 23–24]

Closure . . . may be regarded as a modification of structure that makes *stasis*, or the absence of further continuation, the most probable succeeding event. Closure allows the reader to be satisfied by the failure of continuation or, put another way, it creates in the reader the expectation of nothing. [p. 34]

. . . this does not mean that our experience of the work ceases abruptly at the last word. On the contrary, at that point we should be able to re-experience the entire work, not now as a succession of events, but as an integral design. The point may be clarified if we consider that we cannot speak of the "end" of a painting or a piece of sculpture. [p. 36]

How shall we describe or locate this unpretentiously lucid and persuasive idiom of generalization about poems? It is of course Mrs. Smith's own idiom—an achievement which has helped to earn her book at least two prizes and a number of encomiastic reviews. At the same time, we can identify it with some exactitude, I believe, as a judicious blend of *Gestalt* psychology, which Mrs. Smith acknowledges, and of Aristotelian common sense, which strangely she is silent about. We might ascribe this silence to a prudent strategy by which the author is taking care not to look in the least old-fashioned. I incline rather to ascribe it to absentmindedness—and the fairly close resemblance in some of the phrasing simply to the principle that very good ideas, classically simple, essential, and true ideas, are likely to crop up spontaneously in any age, even in the midst of crowding rival fantasies and fads. Aristotle, as we have noted, does, in his account of the literary object, make a momentary appeal to the analogy of biological organism.[52] But for him it is indeed a momentary analogy and no more. A wholesome lesson that we can derive from this juncture in critical history—both from Aristotle and from Mrs. Smith and others like her who are these days raising their voices—is that neither the organicism of the extreme biological analogy nor that of the *a priori* or transcendental absolute assertion is likely to encourage superior readings

52. Aristotle, *Poetics*, XXIII. 1.

of poetry, but rather that homelier and humbler sort of organ-
icism, in the middle, which I have been trying to describe—
empirical, tentative, analytic, psychological, grammatical,
lexicographic. This, I believe, was in effect the kind of organ-
icism which was the preoccupation of the American critics who
were chronologically "new" a third of a century ago but who
were, or are indeed, both as old and as new as mankind's literate
ambition to make as much sense as possible of the perennially
experienced muddled shape of things.

                                                           1971

"JAM NUNC DEBENTIA DICI"
ANSWERS TO A QUESTIONNAIRE
ARION 9 (Summer & Autumn 1970)

1. and 2. Am I interested in Horace, and have I translated him or written anything that but for him I should not have written? As a young man I translated about two dozen odes of Horace (in stanzaic verse, but I guess not significantly) and even one of the Satires, "Ibam forte" (badly, and published in the college journal). Obviously, without Horace, I should not have written "Roman Classicism: Horace," chapter 5 of *Literary Criticism: A Short History* (W. K. Wimsatt and Cleanth Brooks, 1957). The index to this book and the indexes to my two collections of critical essays (1954 and 1965) suggest that Horace keeps coming up in my mind. As 1965 contains essays more closely related to the *History*, the index count shows an increase from three (1954) to eleven (1965). I did not remember this and would not have guessed it. Among works of the English poet Alexander Pope that I have been especially interested in are his Horatian *Essay on Criticism* and his Imitations of the Satires and Epistles of Horace. The three indexes I have just mentioned suggest Horace getting in via Pope even more often than directly. Without Horace, furthermore, Pope would not have been painted by Kneller in 1721, in an unmistakably medallic and Horatian image, profile, wearing a toga, gazing aloft ("sublimi feriam sidera vertice"), his locks crowned with the "critics's ivy" (*Essay* III, 706), and the whole enclosed in an oval frame of immortality, the uroboros. And without that I could not have written entries 6.1-6.13, pp. 50-59, of my *Portraits of Alexander Pope*, 1965.

3. and 4. The decline of Horace's fame since the romantic period, his suffering by contrast with Catullus, and Eliot's meaning in the essay on Marvell. "A whole civilization resides in these lines." It is not apparent in what you quote, but the phrase "these lines" refers to four lines from Marvell's "Coy Mistress," "At my back I always hear," etc., quoted by Eliot immediately before. Eliot then quotes Horace, "Pallida Mors . . .," and Catullus, "Nox est perpetua. . . ." Eliot thinks of Catullus as a poet of "grand reverberation" and a kind of "intense levity." I interpret the latter phrase as meaning a levity allied with seriousness and intensifying that. This makes Catullus a poet superior to Horace, who presumably entertained no seriousness which his levity could intensify. It seems that Eliot grades the three poets (at least in the three passages quoted) in this order: Catullus, Marvell, Horace. This essay of course could be adduced to illustrate the now familiar idea that the neoclassicism of Eliot is deeply warped or colored by a neo-

romanticism which, living and writing when he did, he could
hardly have avoided. Frank Kermode's book *The Romantic
Image* (1957) was I believe the first to push this thesis res-
olutely. As Eliot himself said, I suppose several times, nothing
in literary history ever repeats itself precisely. This answer to
question 4 is inevitably more a comment on Eliot than on
Horace.

Yet even Horace has his romantic turn, and so does all classi-
cism, deep or shallow. The presence of "Pallida Mors" in your
quotation kicking "aequo . . . pede" at the door of hut and castle,
carries me back, in spite of myself, to the Horatian excuses of a
young schoolteacher who in the early 1930's walked the cliffs
of Narragansett Bay in churchyard elegiac and Rubaiyatical
mood. "Solvitur acris hiems. . . ." "So one more wakening, while
livid Death/Still finds the homes of rich men and of poor,/While
you and I draw but a little breath,/A whiff of life, time but to
dream of more."

5. and 6. Horace boring? Too self-controlled? We have Mar-
vell, and Pope. Why read Horace? I cannot take these questions
seriously. I don't know whether he was "self-controlled." He
had artistic control. We might as well say: "We have Milton. Why
read Homer and Virgil?"

7. The artistic delight which Nietzsche found in the Horatian
odes. Beyond doubt I do not experience the same degree of de-
light Nietzsche did. You have to have nearly perfect immersion
in a language and literature, and much more also in native wealth,
to get the supreme delight. Still, what does give me delight in
Horace is, I think, the artistry, the control, his talent in keeping
cool, keeping the rhythm going at the right speed, saying the
right thing in the right place, with just the right winks and asides.

To those answers, let me add something that is probably not
weighty enough to be written up into an article and will not
have enough philology to win respect from the hard-core men,
but which you will perhaps take as an appendix written in the
spirit invited by your questionnaire and accompanying letter. I
should very much like to have a place to say a few things about
the structure of the *Ad Pisones* (*Ars Poetica*).

> Horace still charms with graceful negligence
> And without method talks us into sense.

That was a graceful thing for Pope to say, perhaps partly disin-
genuous (in the manner of Horace himself, professing[1] to ques-

---

1. Cf. note 2, below.

tion, *Satire* 1.4, whether satire and comedy should be considered
poetry at all). This specious opinion of Pope has been repeated
in later days by more earnest persons. But "without method"
and "negligence" will not do for Horace ("ut sibi quivis speret
idem,/sudet multum frustraque laboret/ausus idem"), any more
than rearranging parts of the *Ad Pisones*, as Heinsius and others
have tried, will do. I do not mean to make an intentionalistic
appeal to such places in the poem itself as the one I have just
quoted or that which follows it, "tantum series juncturaque
pollet" (242), or the "callida junctura" (46–47), or, best of all,
"ut jam nunc dicat jam nunc debentia dici" (43). These asser-
tions in themselves do not prove that Horace himself could write
that way or even that he tried to. Still they may serve as re-
minders of what we are actually witnessing and as rallying points
for exposition. Let me hazard the generalization that there is
no such thing as a famous and successful poem, a classic, which
turns out on study to be disorderly. I can't think there is even
any which can be called, as the present vogue of "sensibility"
would have it, "open-ended." (A recent book by Barbara
Herrnstein Smith, *Poetic Closure*, Chicago, 1968, says some
marvelously good things on this subject.)

At the same time, it may be well if we remember that the
"lucidus ordo," the "ordinis virtus et venus" (41–42) of
poetry is not necessarily, perhaps not even possibly, as tight and
univocal as that of a chess problem or a reasoning in symbolic
logic. Poetic order moves by bundles of associations, simulta-
neous progressions, local degrees of dense affinity. There is
satisfactory order, highly satisfactory, and yet a margin, not of
error, but of indeterminacy—in the sense that it is not really
possible to say that this and only this magic phrase or sequence
of paragraphs is conceivable here. Probably the epistolary disqui-
sition and the conversation (*sermo*) show some degrees or kinds
of this poetic freedom that are peculiar to them. But I do not
have to prove that here. All I need or wish to do is keep my eye
on the poem in question. The name "epistolary disquisition" or
"epistolary *ars poetica*," if the poem needs some such name,
seems to me to fit as well as any other. There has been some de-
bate as to whether the poem is (was conceived as?) a formal
treatise (*ars*), an *isagoge* (introductory manual), or an epistle.
Debate over a question like that seems to me empty, and espe-
cially if we think that answering the question correctly will
settle, or even help to settle, the problem where the major divi-
sions of the poem come, or what its sequence of topics is. It is
the topics and the sequence, as observable in the poem, that we
ought to be interested in.

If we are willing to make a list (and it is probably well to be-gin in this way) of the topics *de arte poetica* (the items of crit-ical subject matter at an easy and usual level of naming and definition), running in one linear sequence through the poem, we can distinguish, or I do distinguish, thirty-two in all. These are glossy, pregnant units, or capsules, extending from a few lines each to more than thirty here and there. As I have already suggested, they are bound together and smoothed into one an-other by multiple simultaneous associations (sometimes called, in the scholarship, "gliding transitions"). They are highly am-bivalent, and they link to their immediate neighbors with greater and lesser degrees of intensity or necessity. They have sometimes local connections, end on end like dominoes, or in some places they stand in a kind of parallel co-ordinate regional order. They are starred with little bursts of wit, formulations of right prin-ciple or censures of carelessness and ignorance, each appropriate where it occurs, but each so memorable in itself that it readily detaches from context in our memory and haunts us as simply a bright place in the poem. "Descriptas servare vices operumque colores/cur ego si nequeo ignoroque poeta salutor?" (86-87).

At the same time there is an overall trend of the poem from a first major category of topics to a second, and then to a third. There are thus two major divides or transition points. While nearly everybody, or perhaps everybody, agrees that the first of these must be present somewhere, there is a very wide dif-ference of opinion about where—in itself a curious testimony to the kind of series and juncture Horace has contrived. My own view of this problem is perhaps the only thing I shall say that is likely to be seriously disputed by anyone. I will defend it in due course. It is in fact integral with all the rest. Using numbers and some key Latin phrases which ought not to be very cryptic, let me first offer a compressed outline of the whole poem.

I. (1) "simplex et unum," 23; (2) "in vitium . . . fuga," 31; (3) "infelix summa," 37; (4) "sumite materiam," 41; (5) "ut jam nunc dicat," 45; (6) "callida junctura," 48; (7) "si volet usus," 72.

      Summary: PRINCIPLES (or Composition, Writing)—unity, measure, whole, choice, order, language (orig-inality, development, usage)—in short, GEN-ERAL DECORUM.

II. (8) "quo scribi numero," 92; (9) "singula sortita," 118; (10) "si forte reponis Achillem," 127; (11) "nec verbum verbo," 135; (12) "parturient montes," 145; (13) "in medias res," 152; (14) "notandi mores," 178; (15) "incredulus odi," 188; (16)

"nec deus intersit," 192; (17) "chorus," 201; (18) "tibia non ut nunc," 219; (19) "conveniet satyros," 250; (20) "syllaba longa brevi," 274; (21) "Thespis . . . nostri poetae," 294.

Summary: POEMS, i.e. kinds of poems, GENRES, especially the DRAMATIC—verse, dramatic characters (types and mythic persons), narrative problems (Homeric instances), characters again (ages of man), further rules of drama, historical dramatic topics—in short, SPECIAL DECORUMS, especially the DRAMATIC.

III. (22) "balnea vitat . . . docebo," 308; (23) "Socraticae chartae," 332; (24) "utile dulci," 346; (25) "ubi plura nitent," 360; (26) "ut pictura poesis," 365; (27) "mediocribus," 384; (28) "nihil invita Minerva . . . nonumque prematur," 390; (29) "silvestris homines," 407; (30) "natura an arte," 418; (31) "Quintilio . . . Aristarchus," 452; (32) "fanaticus error," 476.

Summary: THE POET—discipline, wisdom, purpose, excellence, sincerity, patience, humility, nature and art, taking criticism, sanity.

Somebody might wish to draw some of the local divisions a little differently. It would not matter much. Some slippery places appear, for instance, in section III. No. 22 is not a simple topic but uses a brief satiric sketch of the disheveled poet to lead (in the *middle* of line 301) to the mock-modest proposition that Horace himself will give up being a poet (of the crazy successful kind) and will be content merely to teach the poet's office and duty ("ergo fungar vice cotis . . .munus et officium . . . docebo"). Thus he asserts the theme, or at least the accent, of the whole third main part. This has a unity more by accent than by strictly cognitive theme. For example, "natura fieret . . . an arte," no. 30, is a typical genetic antithesis, but the other main Peripatetic antithesis, "aut prodesse aut delectare," no. 24, refers rather to the poem itself or even the audience. No. 23 might easily be divided into a first part (309–22) telling the kind of Socratic wisdom needed by the poet, and a second part (323–32) comparing Greek idealism to the commercial arithmetic of Roman education. Nos. 25 and 26, on beauties and faults, are separately memorable, yet together they lead very closely into no. 27 ("mediocribus esse poetis, non homines, non di . . ."), the rule that the luxury of aesthetic value is nothing if not perfect. No. 28, though only six lines long, requires two clue phrases in my scheme. Coming about half way in the whole third section, it compresses two principles that might be said to be the complementary themes of the whole section: You will write nothing contrary to your nature or inspiration—but remember to be duly mistrustful of that inspiration.

The satiric mode, seen briefly at the beginning of section III, occurs also memorably, grotesquely, in the first 37 lines of the poem—the fishtail woman and other monstrosities—and at the close of the poem, the last 24 lines—the Juvenalian ferocity of the assault upon the poet who is a poet only because he is sick and crazy. And thus this highly colored, conspicuous mode does something both to frame and divide the poem.[2]

The location of the first major division of the poem has been, as I have already suggested, the chief debate among the scholars. Opinions about where it comes range from line 41 (end of "subject matter," as some say, followed by "form") to line 130 (or 127) (end of *de partibus artis poeticae*, followed by *de generibus artis poeticae*) or line 118 (or 152) (end of miscellaneous considerations, followed by the dramatic genre). Fairly good reasons might be advanced for saying that a first major division of the poem does occur at some juncture such as any one of these three (subject-forms, parts-genres, miscellaneous-dramatic). Though it may perhaps be argued whether such junctures actually occur where they are supposed to, these all do represent thematic sequences that appear in the poem. I am concerned to argue only that the sequence I urge (Principles, 72; Genres, 294; Poet, 476) is in fact the most solidly coherent and deeply established of the several that run through the poem.

I avoid the major triadic terms *poema, poesis, poeta*. These are plausibly enough supposed to be the frame of reference in the lost early third-century work of Neoptolemus of Parium, which the Horatian commentator Porphyrio long ago said had been used by Horace. True, these terms make an inviting biographical suggestion in that Neoptolemus is preserved for us

2. The point has been made by Norman J. DeWitt, *Drama Survey*, Minneapolis, Fall 1961; cf. C. O. Brink, *Horace on Poetry: Prolegomena to the Literary Epistles* (Cambridge, 1963), p. 269, on the "humour and wit" of Horace. Brink (pp. 161–62) takes the sober view of Horace's profession of doubt (*Satire* 1.4) whether satire and comedy are real poetry. And so too does G.M.A. Grube, *The Greek and Roman Critics* (London, 1965), p. 232: "Horace is quite sincere in this disclaimer." For some good reasons in favor of taking it as a joke, see W. S. Anderson, "The Roman Socrates: Horace and His Satires," in *Satire: Critical Essays on Roman Literature*, ed. J. P. Sullivan (Bloomington, Indiana, 1963), pp. 1–37. It is a comfort to find that in his great new book, *Horace on Poetry: The "Ars Poetica"* (Cambridge, 1971), Brink (e.g., p. 445) has changed his mind. "An occasional colloquialism . . . cannot invalidate the consistently poetic language that H. employs. What can be invalidated is the poet's own paradox in calling the hexameter poems 'prosaic'."

through Philodemus, Epicurean philosopher and teacher of
Augustan poets, whose charred pages were found preserved in a
Herculanean villa which may have been that of the father of the
Piso who with his sons is addressed in the Epistle of Horace. Yet
other, more internal, considerations tell heavily, I believe, against
this inviting biography.

Poiēma apparently was associated by Neoptolemus very closely
with style (*sunthesis*), and *poiēsis* with the subject matter
(*hupothesis*). With this external support C. O. Brink[3] has not
implausibly argued for a division of the poem into an introduc-
tion on unity (1–40), and three major divisions:

I.   Order and style (41–118)
II. Subject matter, genres (119–294)
III. The Poet, general critical questions (295–476)

Brink's layout is clearly in a sense present—along with the others.
Yet the categories "style" and "subject matter" are thin enough
envelopes for the sequences he would contain by means of them
—and "subject matter" especially, for a sequence where "style,"
as he observes, does keep coming back in.

Horace may well have adapted precepts from Neoptolemus,
but we can hardly be sure that he had any use for the somewhat
specially slanted emphasis on *poiēma* and *poiēsis* that Neop-
tolemus seems to have intended. Brink himself performs a very
useful service in pointing out that during about a century before
the time of Horace (in Lucilius, in Varro, in Philodemus) *poiēma*
had meant something like a short poem or a passage of poetry,
poiēsis had meant a long poem. Horace uses these terms in a
casual enough way: "ego mira poemata pango" (416); "ut pic-
tura poesis: erit quae . . . et quaedam . . ." (316–62), some
smaller, some larger.

What is important is not the shifty meaning of two terms
which are not actually present as key or head terms in this
poem. What is important is the central and unavoidable classic
doctrine of the poetic genres. Horace is not Brooks and Warren.

---

3. *Horace on Poetry* (1963), pp. 13, 247. I would confess a consider-
able debt to the very formidable learning of this book. I have consulted
the same author's *Horace on Poetry: The "Ars Poetica,"* only as my own
essay is in galley proof. The elaborately supported outline of the poem in
the new book seems to differ from the earlier mainly in the addition of
one more major division, between poetic subject-matter and drama, at
lines 152–53. See esp. pp. 459, 468, 476, 486, 490, 499. As before, there
is perhaps little that I should venture to quarrel with except what seems to
me the oversight concerning the importance of the topic of genre, intro-
duced in the poem at line 73. Cf. pp. 160–63.

He quotes the opening of the *Odyssey*, but he undertakes no analysis of individual poems. Poems, if they come into the *Ad Pisones* at all, must be poems conceived precisely as belonging to certain specific genres. Even an individual poem must always be conceived in the Peripatetic tradition as belonging properly to some specific genre—for the reason implicit in the whole classic conception of an entity, and asserted with special clarity by Aristotle, that we do not have an entity, or at least we do not know that we have an entity, unless we can say what *kind* of entity it is. "When we say *what* it is, we do not say 'white' or 'hot,' or 'three cubits long,' but 'a man' or 'a god'" (*Metaphysics* VI [Z]. 1). "Nothing . . . which is not a species of a genus will have an essence" (*Metaphysics*, VII [H]. 4). We can assert with perfect assurance that for Horace the only way of locating a poem was to be able to say here is one of a given species —ode, epode, elegy, epic, comedy, tragedy. Even more clearly the only way of talking about poems in general was to talk about genres. And clearly too the first mention of genres in the *Ad Pisones* is at line 73, where he begins to talk about the union of certain kinds of meter with certain kinds of subject matter, producing certain kinds of poems, each with a name. He names *elegy* directly, touches epic and lyric with "Homerus" and "fidibus," and after the anticipation of "socci" and "coturni" gives us "versibus tragicis res comica . . . Comoedia . . . Tragicus." He is now launched into his central discussion of dramatic problems— problems arising in part from the fact that characters and certain other dramatic features are in part drawn from epic. Later comes the somewhat mistaken history of Satyr plays ("conveniet satyros"). Horace does not take the genres solemnly. He angles around them, in and out of them as he pleases, as in a Play Skool or Jungle Gym of the great tradition. He casts many a sly glance aside to the reader who will notice. The "operis lex," the only time he alludes to it (135), is a wry joke, a hobble for the plodders. The Neo-Aristotelians of the Chicago school (c. 1952) would have said that the American "new critics," who tended to think of all poems primarily and mainly as *poems*, and only incidentally as certain kinds of poems, could be summed up in the first 72 lines of Horace's *Ars*. After that, they were entirely in contempt of court. And there is a certain sense in which this would have been just.

Why has this very plainly important juncture, lines 72–73, been so largely[4] overlooked by the scholars? Perhaps in part

4. J. Wright Duff, *A Literary History of Rome* (1909), ed. A. M. Duff (New York, 1953), p. 390, seems the exception in taking this juncture for

through their not remembering or understanding the Aristotelian doctrine. But in large part too, I think, because Horace has in fact very skillfully shaded and graded his junctures in this part of the poem, so that we pass through several of them, to leave behind unity, order, measure, and vocabulary and arrive full in the field of genres and hence poems, and soon dramatic poems, without fully noting the precise transition point. That very substantive transition to the genres is covered and in part concealed by an arrangement that we might call layering or sheathing. Four successive paragraphs (or topical segments as I have distinguished them above), nos. 6, 7, 8, 9, two on each side of the important juncture, deal with words, words, verse, and styles, "singula sortita"—all these coming under the head of what today we should consider in a general sense "style." We cross the important divide while preoccupied with the theme of style. If anybody wishes to argue that only sixteen lines (73-88) deal with the broad issue of genres and verse, that after this, until 295, dramatic genres (with a few related epic questions) are steadily in view, and that hence the first major divide of the poem comes at line 89, this can scarcely be rejected out of hand. I would answer only that the step from language to verse and genres (72-73) is a wider and more theoretically significant one (for the reasons I have been giving) than that from verse and genre to style and dramatic characters (88-89). Lines 73-88, on verse and genres, read more like a proem to what follows than a tail to what has preceded.[5] Or, let us say: Lines 73-89 execute an emphatic, closely interlocked, double progression, from the boundless to the bounded and to a specific area of boundary, the comic and the tragic.

A similar sort of stepping, or sheathing, or envelopment appears at lines 251-308, nos. 20, 21, 22, on both sides of the second major juncture of the poem (294-95), where a continuous accent on craft[6] or on the rules, at the expense of laziness and of license, runs concurrently with the shift from dramatic topics to the character and role of the serious poet. Another thing that helps to ease the way for this major juncture is the fact that lines 202-94, paragraphs 18 ("tibia non ut

granted: lines 1-72, "precepts of style"; lines 73-288, "a special treatment of drama among different kinds of poetry"; lines 289-476, "essentials of literary success."

5. The transition at lines 89-92—"*versibus . . . carminibus . . . sortita*"—is well worth study.

6. Brink, *Prolegomena* (pp. 251, 261, 266), observes at various places throughout the poem a kind of structural repetition of a number of main theoretical motifs such as character, decorum, unity, craft.

nunc"), 19 ("conveniet satyros"), 20 ("syllaba longa . . . Plau-
tinos et numeros"), and 21 ("Thespis . . . nostri poetae"), sus-
tain almost continuously the mode of historical retrospect,
ending with the inclusion of *our poets*, those of today, who
might make Rome as great in letters as in arms if only they had
a little patience for the "limae labor et mora." Thus history
merges with the motif of craft. What is the value of these over-
lapping and simultaneous progressions? Well, at least they have
the character (and I should say it is a value) of softening, while
not deleting or deranging, the main dividing lines, and thus
lending to an argument which is orderly enough for its own
purposes the feel of a conversational ease and unforced, gentle-
manly flow of thought. "Horace still charms. . . ." Are we say-
ing something much different from what Pope said? Perhaps not.
But we are explaining it better. Is it likely that Horace himself
thought of such things, or would have admitted that he wrote
this way, or even would have put his stylus down at the points
of division we have chosen? We have no way of saying. It is
scarcely necessary that we should be able to.

1970

I.A.R.: WHAT TO SAY ABOUT A POEM

I

About ten years ago I wrote an essay entitled "What to Say about a Poem." It was published in a typescript offset conference report, as a chap-book with the contentious commentary of some of my friends, and in a volume of my collected essays. I have no reason to think that I. A. R. ever read it, or that if he did he approved of it. It was not directly derived from him nor even written with the benefit of any recent restudy of his writings. Yet I will venture that there is probably more of Richards than of any other critic in the funded antecedents, the essential substrate, of the essay.

"What to Say about a Poem" I conceived as a teacher's concern about a poem. As I asked the question and as I tried to answer it, I had in mind the kind of things that a teacher of poetry has to say—analytic, interpretive, explicatory (celebratory perhaps, rhapsodic—at the same time, more or less sober), reliable, internally oriented to the poem itself—and in these ways distinguishable from the various kinds of things that other kinds of writers, journal essayists, reviewers, historians, biographers, might legitimately say. If now I foist my title upon Richards, I commit perhaps a degree of aggression and perhaps too casually co-opt his ideas for my own aim; yet as he is, by his own profession and in his conspicuous achievement, a critic of and for teachers of poetry, the injustice cannot be very great.

I take as a starting point one of his more recent expressions—his long *TLS* middle article (28 May 1970) on the analyses of grammatical structure in poems being performed nowadays by Roman Jakobson. An opening accolade greets "what may very likely prove a landmark in the long-awaited approach of descriptive linguistics to the account of poetry." Then on a second page Richards moves into a series of observations and questions that we may well think more characteristic of this shrewd, skeptical intelligence. "There are bound to be dangers. . . . There is little profit in noting that strophes I and II here present nine diphthongs /ai/ . . . if the words in which they occur don't transfix the reader." "Probably only some, not all, of the features consciously discerned and included in the *account* will be actually operative in shaping the *response*. The machinery of distinctions used in the account has developed to meet general linguistic needs and purposes. . . . It may therefore distort, may invite attention to features not essential to the poetic process."

It cannot be a large exaggeration if I say that the whole of

234

Richards' career in poetic theory, from *The Foundations of Aesthetics*, 1922, to *So Much Nearer*, 1968, and *Poetries and Sciences*, 1970, has been an effort, canny, partly baffled yet resolute, and for his audience uniquely instructive, to describe and promote, and on occasion, with caution, to practice a certain kind of critical discourse. A discourse as nearly "positive" and reliable as such discourse can be—yet not neutral and dead; or, to reverse the emphasis, a rhapsode's explication, yet one that soberly avoids an escape into the boundless.

As a practical critic and as a promoter of practical criticism Richards has repeatedly worked to unify, to coalesce, two things (object and response) which the terms of his affective methodology have tended to separate. (I say "methodology" because I mean talk about method, rather than method itself in action.) Let me introduce here a snatch from a little-known, or at least, so far as I know, little-quoted, document, his College English Association Chap-Book, *A Certain Sort of Interest in Language*, October 1941. It was written in an hour when the pragmatic politics of World War II were afoot in the world—widely threatening all the "values" (wherever these resided, in our hearths or in our hearts).

A certain "influential teacher" had written to Richards deploring some of the current rallying cries: "Whenever business is seriously threatened, it appears that truth, justice, freedom, religion, democracy, ethics, and everything else are all crumbling." No doubt he had expected a response of warm sympathy. Instead:

> These great words, *justice*, *freedom*, and the others, it seems, mean primarily . . . that someone is getting at him. Interpretation and understanding mean debunking. . . . I have to remember how I and my friends were apt to talk some ten years back. And to recall the dreams of a Heaven on Earth . . . which then seemed to need this sort of blasphemy as their defense. . . . What simplicity in the heart and feebleness in the head made us think so? Because some scamps and villains misused them, did we have to turn against the very watchwords of all our political and moral faith, against the bearers of the truths which alone make men free?

On an earlier page he had said more succinctly: "I do not know how we separate ideas from feelings. I suspect that this division derives from a disastrous schism in the modern mind."[1]

---

1. *Mencius on the Mind: Experiments in Multiple Definition* (London, 1932) touches on the undeveloped state of anything like the Western log-

Yet it is not as if we can detect any great divide, a pronounced change in his views on objectivity, values, and language—signaled, as some have thought, by his books of the mid-1930's, *Coleridge on Imagination* (1934) and *The Philosophy of Rhetoric* (1936). The titles "Emotive Meaning Again" and "Emotive Language Still" appear in 1948 and 1949, and I take them to be characteristic and loyal to his most persistent thinking. Perhaps the economy of the present essay is best served if I say simply that I am a partisan of Richards' practical criticism (his immense talent for reading and talking about poems), but not of his affective methodology. And in this essay I will try not to dispute with him (as I have done now and then in the past, without his ever knowing it, I guess) about the *locus* of values—whether in objects (or verbal objects) or only in our experience of objects (and "projected"speciously by us or our language onto objects). (No doubt *some* implication or reflection of these issues will occur in any account of his views on how practical criticism is, or ought to be, written.) Polysemism, ambiguity, irony or inclusiveness, the poem's verbal independence of author's plans and motives, the multiple (yet coalescing) relations of language to emotion—these are matters all more or less sagely, even triumphantly, expounded by Richards in various places. They too must be assumed if the present argument is to proceed.

The essentials of the problem are delineated vigorously (in such a way as to stress the aspect of the problematic) in the two early and basic books *Principles of Literary Criticism* (1924) and *Practical Criticism* (1929). Richards is ruthless (chapter 3 of *Principles*) against two opposite kinds of critical abuse:—on the one hand, inflated terms of appreciation, our own emotive "projections," "bogus entities" (*beauty*, for instance, even *poetry— inspiration, rhythm*), and on the other, the tight, secure little poetic instruments (*rhyme*, for instance, or *meter*) when these, as so often, are naively promoted to poetic *ends*. What is the critic to do? Let it be understood that when he praises or damns a poem, he is talking about effects, experiences, "caused" in his own mind. Often he "goes further and affirms that the effect in his mind is due to special particular features of the object." And "this fuller kind of criticism is what we desire." Apparently not quite the same distinction is uppermost when Richards says

---

ical apparatus in ancient Chinese thought (pp. 88–90). The topic merges here with Richards' characteristic concern for the question whether "feeling" does not often largely dominate when we believe we are "thinking." "Mencius Through the Looking Glass," *So Much Nearer* (New York, 1968), says more emphatically that Mencius made no division between "thought" and "feeling" (pp. 204–05).

in the next paragraph that the critic's remarks about the object, the ways and means, are all merely *technical*; they are not to be confused with *critical* remarks, which are "about the values of experiences and the reasons for regarding them as valuable."

Two kinds of remarks about poems (technical and critical) correspond to two complementary aspects of poems themselves —the communicative and the experiential, and thus (it might well seem) not to neutrality and value, but to two kinds of value, or at least to two kinds of merit. Indeed there *are* two kinds of "badness" in poetry (expounded in chapter 25 of *Principles*), one a failure through meagerness or inefficacy of communication, the other an offense of inferior (stereotyped) values even where (or just because) communication is highly successful. Another chapter of *Principles*, however, chapter 4, on "Communication," observes that "the very process of getting the work 'right' has itself, so far as the artist is normal, immense communicative consequences." In *Coleridge on Imagination* this recognition will exhibit a phase of almost Crocean monism. "In an examination of poetic structure the distinction [between means and ends] prevents all advance by destroying the specimens we would examine" (chapter 9). And beginning at least as early as *How to Read a Page* (1942), Richards entertains a fully developed doctrine of the poem as autonomous linguistic artifact. Here are coils, irresolutions, and shifts of meaning which trace patterns in the puzzling dialogue of our own commonly experienced poetic speculation—but patterns which before reading Richards we may well have been aware of far less keenly.

In *Practical Criticism*, he had long since achieved a kind of maximum confrontation with the difficult implications of such dialectic for critical discourse. Two passages, on pages 11 and 302, are crucial. The earlier is the more circumstantial.

That the one and only goal of all critical endeavours, of all interpretation, appreciation, exhortation, praise or abuse, is improvement in communication may seem an exaggeration. But in practice it is so. The whole apparatus of critical rules and principles is a means to the attainment of finer, more precise, more discriminating communication. There is, it is true, a valuation side to criticism. When we have solved, completely, the communication problem, when we have got, perfectly, the experience, *the mental condition* relevant to the poem, we have still to judge it, still to decide upon its worth. But the later question nearly always settles itself; or rather, our own inmost nature and the nature of the world in which

we live decide it for us. Our prime endeavour must be to get
the relevant mental condition and then see what happens.

II

What kind of critical discourse will correspond to this high ideal
of understanding? What kind will cope with the paradoxical ten-
sions of a triple fidelity to poetic objects, to "experiences"
(themselves charged with emotions and hence with local values),
and to the ultimate poetic evaluation? What kind of critical dis-
course does Richards, in the fullest and clearest moment of his
vision, desire or approve? This question, perhaps unfair, no
doubt insusceptible of any neat answer, is the topic of my essay.

Richards himself has written critical essays on Hopkins, on
Eliot, on a cluster of Georgian poets, Hardy, De la Mare, Yeats,
Lawrence, on Dostoevsky, on Forster, on Shakespeare's "The
Phoenix and the Turtle" and on his *Troilus and Cressida*, on
Coleridge (1950, 1959, 1960), and on Shelley. And in chapters
of his books and in various detached essays there are shorter
passages of similar tenor—on Denham, on Donne, on Keats, on
Shakespeare, on Coleridge. But it may be said that his own
orientation as a deliberate practical critic has been very largely
doctrinal. That is, he characteristically adduces literary works
(in a way that the title "The God of Dostoevsky" will suggest)
as either statements or illustrations of literary, epistemological,
or ethical doctrine. The *Living Age* essay on T. S. Eliot (1926,
printed also in the same year as an appendix to the second edi-
tion of *Principles*) is mostly devoted to arguing that the coher-
ence of *The Waste Land* is emotive rather than intellectual. The
essay is methodological. A short passage on *A Cooking Egg* (in
the version in *Principles*) is the main place where he says any-
thing specific about any poem or its values. ("The reader who
appreciates the emotional relevance of the title has the key to
the later poems in his hand. I take Pipit to be the retired nurse
of the hero of the poem, and *Views of the Oxford Colleges* to
be the, still treasured, present which he sent her when he went
up to the University. The middle section of the poem I read as a
specimen of the rather withered pleasantry in which contem-
porary culture has culminated. . . . The final section gives the
contrast which is pressed home by the title. Even the most ma-
ture egg was new laid once.")[2] Two essays, that which explicates
The Windhover of Hopkins and that on *The Phoenix and the*

2. The correctness of this reading is not a relevant question here. For a
later report by Richards on this poem, see "Poetic Process and Literary

Turtle, are analytic exceptions to the main tendency. But the poems are difficult, and the conclusions, to my mind, in one way or another, obscure.

Clearly a manageable exposition of what Richards likes in practical criticism will have to center upon some fairly compressed and close criticisms of some fairly compressed (small and rich) poetic instances. It is not necessary that these criticisms be the work of Richards himself. Perhaps it is in some ways better if they are not. We can learn something from what a critic thinks about the work of other critics—and perhaps all the more if these critics are relatively artless and unprofessional. When *Practical Criticism* appeared in 1929 and for perhaps a decade thereafter, a very startling feature was the decimally graded assemblage of student "protocols," concerning thirteen undated and anonymous short poems which Richards had set before his Cambridge classes: five clearly bad poems (1, 4, 5, 7, 9), five clearly good poems (2, 3, 6, 8, 11), three problematics (10, better; 12, more dubious; and 13, I think, the occasion for a strange pronouncement by Richards himself).[3]

From the protocols themselves and from page 3 of Richards' Introductory, it is clear that evaluative opinion was a strongly invited part of the exercise. It is a main point of the method and of the book that most of the protocols (both positive and negative critiques of good and bad poems) are bad criticism—sheer ineptitudes, crashing bungles of one sort or another. Yet here and there in the crowded galleries of this modern *Dunciad*, amid all the stock responses, the sentimentalities and the inhibitions, the technical presuppositions, the doctrinal adhesions, the gauche intrusive images, the mnemonic irrelevancies, appear a certain few opinions (fewer than twenty, I should say, in the total of about 385 protocols) for which Richards deftly, almost slyly, hints a measure of approval.[4]

Certain good poems (the deceptively "sentimental" 8, Lawrence's *Piano*; the austerely mythic elegy 11, Hardy's *George Meredith*) elicited not a single criticism which met the master's approval. And so for the two middling poems, both cloudscapes, 10 and 12, by G. H. Luce[5] and Wilfrid Rowland Childe.

Analysis," in *Style in Language*, ed. Thomas A. Sebeok (New York and London, 1968), p. 21.

3. See below, note 7.

4. These are 1.63, 2.7, 2.71, 3.8, 3.81, 3.82, 4.1 (?), 4.23, 4.25, 5.8, 5.81, 6.13 (?), 6.2, 6.8, 7.43 (?), 9.74, 9.75, 12.6 (?), 13.64. (The verdict on 9.74 and 9.75 appears on pp. 193–98, at a remove from the page where they are quoted. That on 4.23 and 4.25 is assisted by p. 264. See note 5.)

5. This poem elicited a good instance of Richards' own gift for posing critical problems and for delicately suggesting solutions (pp. 143–44,

In more than a few bad criticisms, a conspicuously reiterated feature was the attempt to employ the raw idiom of the Richards methodology:

I find it impossible to recreate the poet's experience (6.33); Unimportant, as the experience is capable of excitation at will by normal people (7.55);[6] Perfect communication (7.56); Please do not think, because I consider hymns sordid, that I have an inhibition (8.2); I don't find this poem at all helpful nor does it express any feelings I have ever had or want to have (8.22); I feel myself responding to it and don't like responding (8.11); The communication is excellent (8.7); The whole poem leaves me with a sense of complete satisfaction (11.53); I feel someone is trying to play with my emotions (12.7); The impression that the author is deeply moved . . . showing in a small degree the author's attitude to life (12.7); This one seems to me a successful communication of an experience whose value is dubious (13.1); The underlying emotion is not of sufficient value (13.31); This form of stimulation to the mind can do it no good and may do it harm. The poem is therefore bad (13.8).

Richards indicated no pleasure in any of these responses.

We scan the small handful of more or less approved protocols for a plenary illustration of critical merit. If we have read *Principles* and the Introductory to *Practical Criticism* with any care, we are prepared to find that mere clarification of a certain level of sense, what *we* might call seeing the plot of a poem, is not enough. Thus, with Hopkins' *Spring and Fall, to a Young Child*, we are merely grateful for a "paraphrase kindly supplied by one writer."

An elderly man, experienced in such matters, has found a girl grieving at the falling of leaves in autumn. . . . Even now in weeping at the transience of the things she enjoys in autumn, she is really weeping for the transience of all things. She is

---

198–204, 214–16). Those pages together with his analysis (pp. 193–98) of objections to the incoherence of sea-harp imagery in poem 9, Alfred Noyes's carnival on the eightieth birthday of George Meredith, add up to a keen disquisition on the general problem of mixed metaphor. Several writers (not only the approved 4.23 and 4.25, but 4.1, 4.12, 4.14, 4.31, and 4.4) registered a certain disgust for the drafty sentimentalism of poem 4, Woodbine Willy's ". . . rapture of spring in the morning." But Richards, pp. 53–60 and 264, seems especially concerned, with this group, to distinguish merely forceful expressions of distaste from critiques that have a care for reasons.

6. Cf. *Practical Criticism*, p. 266.

set of motions, together with *panting* and, in another
motions, together with *dangerous draught* and *feverish*
The influence is thirst-arousing, perhaps, salt, intox-
alterative. (These motions bring in a very mixed and
g throng of feelings.)
it is impossible, not allowed (feeling of injustice suf-
or of regret alone . . .) to me . . . to
    Perform the "orphic" function of the Poet.
    Write in the spirit or purpose or manner, and on the
    subjects, of Homer, Virgil, Dante, Shakespeare.
specific form of the metaphor here loads the statement
feelings of loss and inevitability—the vanishing of a possi-
of the mind.
act in human history is over, it comes to an end like a
. . .

araphrase-exposition seems pregnant with intimations of
Yet the inquiring (the pestering) theoretical intelligence
t let us have such kinds of "profit" easily. After all, as we
to remember if we have read *Practical Criticism* with any
ion, "a judgment seemingly about a poem is primarily evi-
about a reading of it." And now he adds: "There are ways
ding almost any poem so as to make it magnificent or lu-
us." *Valid* ways of reading it as either magnificent or ludi-
? We might have thought in studying *Practical Criticism*
criticism was to permit us to get "perfectly, the experi-
the mental condition, relevant to the poem,"—and thus
d that there *was* a mental condition relevant to *the* poem.
now: the poem is magnificent (or it is ludicrous) only *if* I
en to be reading with "a mind of a certain sort," brought
his moment of experience in certain ways. This may sound
lling. We may recoil from this apparent rejection of all the
fit" we just thought we had found in the magisterial demon-
ion of a reading so far superior to the student naïvetés.
hether such a reader is likely to benefit from a university,
how he came there, are questions for another occasion.")
sumably Richards' way of reading the passage comes closer
making it magnificent than to making it ludicrous. (For pur-
es of the present argument, one need not feel sure that it *is*
te magnificent—a certain tumidity, a quality of straining
tho-poeticalness in the idiom—may have been left out of
ount.) But are we to think that the reading by the master is
nearer to being a good one than the miserable confessions of
ny of the students? This is not what he means. Reassurance
immediate—in the shape of this vigorous assertion:

mourning among other things, for the fleetingness of her own
youth. (6.1)

What does this lack? Something very important, which is found,
as it happens, in the next protocol quoted—"an admirable power
of analysis."

> . . . the accenting of the seventh line is particularly important
> —the accent falls on "will weep" and on "know why". . . . I
> like the simple opening and closing couplet, the one answering
> the other. The first six lines begin at a low pitch and then rise
> at "Ah! as the heart grows colder," only to fall again in the
> sixth line. I like the even accentuation of the sixth line. Then
> there is great control of vowel music. . . . (6.2)

"Very detailed analyses of correspondences between sound and
sense are perhaps always open to suspicion." Still, in the chapter
on Poem 2, "Spring Quiet," by Christina Rossetti, we encounter
protocol 2.7, "persuasive as well as subtle." And 2.71 "does
seem to be recording rather than inventing."

> In its own rather tiny way, it is quite exquisite. One feels the
> delicate movement of the rhythm as it changes from the clear
> fine tone of the 3rd and 4th verses to the gravity and stead-
> iness of the last two. The corresponding shift in vowel values
> might be noticed—the deepening effect given by the long "a's"
> and "o's." The adjectives are chosen with a full regard for their
> emotive value—in particular, "mossy stone" which at once
> produces the intended atmosphere of quietness and uninter-
> rupted peace.[7] (2.71)

A more smashing illustration of the right way was achieved by
two writers in response to one of Richards' bad poems, 5,
Edna St. Vincent Millay's preposterous sonnet. "What's this of

7. Poem 13. "In the Churchyard at Cambridge," which Richards had
discovered among the works of Longfellow, evokes the curious instance of
a vigorous negative upon its movement (13.64), "as subtly observed," says
the monitor, "as it is surprisingly expressed"—"showing an altogether
superior understanding of rhythm"—yet a mistake! For it depends entirely
upon a misapprehension of *sense* and *tone*. A sort of Augustan urbanity
and temperate social wit is mistaken for a stock exercise in provincial sanc-
timony. It is difficult to resist the genetic speculation that Richards prized
this poem in proportion to his own success in reading certain cryptographic
features, or provincial oddities, in the story of the lady buried in her family
plot, with a slave at her head and another at her feet. His essay on "Gerard
Hopkins" (*Dial* 81 [September 1926]: 196) opens with an account of the
"heightened attention," the "peculiar intellectual thrill," the "awakening
of other mental faculties" experienced by the reader who successfully en-
counters difficult poetry.

death. . . ?" Several readers were troubled by a suspicion that all was not right behind a "flashy façade." "Only two, however, coupled these suspicions with detailed observation of the matter and manner of the poem and it is these observations which we seek in criticism."

> This one offers cheap reassurance in what is to most men a matter of deep and intimate concern. It opens with Browning's brisk no-nonsense-about-me directness and goes on with a cocksure movement and hearty alliteration. It contains (along with the appropriate "dust to dust") echoes of all the best people. It is full of vacuous resonances ("its essential self in its own season") and the unctuously poetic. (5.8)

> This is a studied orgasm from a "Shakespeare–R. Brooke" complex. . . . A sort of thermos vacuum, "the very thing" for a dignified picnic in this sort of Two-Seater sonnet. The "Heroic" hectoring of line 1, the hearty quasi-stoical button-holing of the unimpeachably-equipped beloved, the magisterial finger-wagging of "I tell you this"!! Via such conduits magnanimity may soon be laid on as an indispensable, if not obligatory, modern convenience. (5.81)

The closely observant celebration of poetic value which Richards prescribed, the detailed account of objects reaching out somehow to encompass also not only experiences caused by objects but the "reasons" for value in such experiences, was clearly not conceived as any very severely measured description or rigorously ordered argument. There is feeling here, manifold feeling and emotion, and overall value, poetic value—directly imputed. And nearly everywhere the main descriptive technique is metaphor. (This should not surprise readers of *Coleridge on Imagination*, *The Philosophy of Rhetoric*, and *Interpretation in Teaching*.) There is wit. There is, I think we may say in brief, imagination.

III

Not much later than the Cambridge experiments reported in *Practical Criticism*, Richards, at work again with men and women students at Cambridge, Harvard, and Radcliffe, found that the responses to a passage from Walter Savage Landor's *Gebir* (III. 4–18) supplied a wide range of instructive aberrations. He expounded this collection of "facts of natural science," specimens of "medical" history, in *The Criterion* (April 1933), adding some

instances of critical blundering by Coleridg[e] Brooke, and then, "under shelter of these his own "paraphrase exposition" of the [L] bold and interesting departure from the res of *Practical Criticism*. Another difference set in the explanation: "It is best . . . to eli sible, the question 'Is the passage good or invite answers only to the question 'What instruction (likely enough to promote the ur in the passage I have quoted above from *Practical Criticism*) does much also, I conjec the fact that now the student testimonies s cious (either for good or ill) than the men rampaging in *Practical Criticism*. On the o doubt the real difficulty of the Landor pa "heightened," as Richards confesses, by his 1–3 of *Gebir* III) which mainly accounts for really *good* student expositions—though the papers in short excerpts, to accommodate a c of the poetry into three sections, may have d conceal any medium virtues that were present. feature of this essay is Richards' own virtuos manifold "paraphrase exposition"—or in "para sition," as he phrases it in his preliminary expl he asked the students to do. The distinction b activities is difficult to align either with the c ception of means, experience, and value expo *ciples* or with the more severely unified poeti Introductory to *Practical Criticism*. But I would much of this. The essential Richards seems to through very strongly in the mingled expositior and *feeling* which I am soon to quote.

The fifteen lines from *Gebir* are a congenial eno vehicle, a modern bard's richly blended reflection about his youthful infection with the poetry of Sh drank of Avon") and his subsequent frustrated re great poetic past of magic and myth (". . . can any v ping voice / The parting sun's gigantic strides recall an Iberian-Egyptian costume epic in blank verse. personal profession in III. 1–18 corresponds in *Paradise Lost* III. 1–55, and in its ejaculatory ope 1–8; in content it is a reversal of Milton's rejection romance in IX. 1–47.

Drank of Avon is a "wheel within wheel" metaphor

in one set of *thirst.* icant, fleetir Yet fered 1 2

The with bility A day.

This value. will n ought atten dence of re dicro crous that ence inde But happ to t app "pr stra ("V or Pre to po qu my ac n m is

It may seem that . . . the difference between good and bad reading is gone; that there is no sense left for "correct" as applied to interpretations. This would be a mistake. . . . the *tests*, we should ordinarily say, for the correctness of any interpretation of a set of complex signs are its internal coherence and its coherence with all else that is relevant . . . this inner and outer coherence *is* the correctness. When an interpretation hangs together (without conflicting with anything else: history, literary tradition, etc.) we call it correct.[8]

How these dual assertions are to be managed in the logical part of our minds may be less than clear. But the second emphasis, I will take it upon myself to assert, is the operative, the athletic and militant Richards—what he is earning, by indirections, all the time. The maneuver is like the strategy spread broadly throughout *Principles*, where in some chapters we read that customs, mores, tastes, judgments do differ widely among men, but in other chapters that some kinds of experience and judgment are more "normal," more adequate to the human capacity than others, and hence better.

IV

Having in earlier years so amply and so often demonstrated his extraordinary and sometimes bewildering faculty for seeing multiples, alternatives, ambiguities, Richards in later phases of his career, while reiterating the initial insight, seems also to have been especially concerned to assert that counter-conception of the real and important difference between correct and incorrect readings of poetry—or, more simply, the possibility (even the always imminent danger) of incorrect readings. In his volume of 1955, *Speculative Instruments*, he reached back, seven years earlier (1933) than for any other piece in the collection, to reprint "Fifteen Lines from Landor."

A few years later, or in the spring of 1958, during an "interdisciplinary conference" held at Indiana University on "verbal style and the literary process," interest in the "process" "reached its high point" at an evening public lecture, "Poetic Process and

8. "Correct interpretation of bad and good writing will not hang together in the same specific ways." This may send us back to the good protocols concerning both good and bad poems in *Practical Criticism* and to chapter 25 in *Principles*, "Badness in Poetry." The problem is a nice one. See perhaps my own effort in "Explication as Criticism," *English Institute Essays*, 1951, ed. Alan S. Downer (New York, 1952).

Literary Analysis," in which Richards narrated the stages of
composition of a poem written by himself and now thrown upon
a screen, "Harvard Yard in April / April in Harvard Yard." The
main theoretical concern was the authoritative exploitation of a
healthy doctrine that Richards had already asserted with em-
phasis as early as 1942, in *How to Read a Page*:—that a poem
has a kind of internal, linguistic life of its own, independent of
things its author may have intended, or thought of, or not
thought of, during the process. Richards was in a commanding
position to say: "This I did not think of, but consulting the dic-
tionary now shows it is indeed in the poem; or, this choice I
made in part because of certain antecedent associations, but
clearly a reader does not have to know these to understand the
relevance in the poem." The argument was full of witty ex-
plosions. And then, abruptly, near the end, he turned to a
complementary, or postscript, doctrine—once more concerning
correctness and incorrectness. If a poem has a life of its own,
even a capacity for self-defense, it is the important job of critics
and educators to assist that defense by correct interpretation.
Reaching yet again into files of student reports (presumably
recent or current) he produced a medley of incredible readings
—of Eliot, of Donne, of Coleridge, of Marvell.

> "Pipit sate upright. . . ." Pipit has obviously satisfied the
> "I" . . . ; a state of satiation has occurred.

"Some essential control over interpretation" seemed to have
been "relaxed." (At the same time, it remained "an interesting
point in *linguistics* to consider why we are sure that words in
such an instance do not work like that.")

A second, somewhat more technical piece by Richards, his
"work paper" for the conference, bore the title "Variant Read-
ings and Misreading." The obligingly obtuse student testimony
was of course once more at hand. And once more the refining
theoretical conscience was not easily appeased. "What can we
allege . . . to confirm our opinion (in which I, for one, am un-
shakable) that we have here a *misreading*—and not an allowable
variant?"[9] Later in the same year he published a volume entitled
Goodbye Earth and Other Poems—including "Harvard Yard in
April/April in Harvard Yard." A brief "Proem" contains echoes

9. Both this paper and the evening address may be found in the pro-
ceedings of the conference, *Style in Language*, ed. Thomas A. Sebeok
(New York and London, 1960). See especially pp. 23, 245, 246, 250,
251. A note to "Variant Readings . . ." confesses his awareness of the rise
("within my lifetime") of a school of extravagant explicatory "squeezing."
Cf. his remark on Eliot's rebuke to the "lemon-squeezer school of crit-
icism" ("On TSE," *Sewanee Review* 74 [Winter 1966]: 28).

of "Poetic Process and Literary Analysis" and one more swing of the pendulum in the issue between freedom and correctness.

> When is any interpretation ... complete? ... Whatever accounts are offered to the reader must leave him—in a very deep sense—free to choose, though they may supply wherewithal for exercise of choice.
>
> This is not—dare I note?—any general license to readers to differ as they please or in other ways and over other points than they must. For this deep freedom in reading is made possible only by the widest surface conformities: as to how the words in a poem are recognized, as to how the surface (plain sense) meanings are ascribed, as to how rhythms are followed, allusions caught. . . .

Does the surface determine any demarcations in the depths? The epistemology of this account of deep freedom may remind us of a much earlier statement, in the essay "The Interactions of Words" (1942), something perhaps even closer to a reconcilable, transcending truth.

> Understanding is not a preparation. . . . It is itself the poem . . . it is a constructive, hazardous, free creative process, a process of conception through which a new being is growing in the mind.[10]

We ponder the deep principle that human understanding is *always* more than a reflex. The mind *acts*. It has this dignity, even in error.[11]

10. In *The Language of Poetry* ed. Allen Tate (*Princeton*, 1942), p. 76.
11. I conceive the year 1958 as a climax of Richards' speculations on the issue of incorrectness. "Variant Readings and Misreading" is republished in his collection of 1968, *So Much Nearer: Essays toward a World English.* As the Preface indicates, "Variant Readings . . ." carries the precise issue of incorrect reading further than other essays, all of the 1960's, included in this volume. A second volume of Richards' poems, *Screens*, 1960, contains an essay, "The Future of Poetry," apparently delivered at some time as a lecture at Victoria College, Toronto; this too reappears in *So Much Nearer*; it contains an excellent assertion of the way in which *poems*, for interpreters and critics, are superior to *poets*. Another relevant essay (containing an explication of a difficult poem by Empson) is "How Does a Poem Know When It Is Finished?" appearing in *Parts and Wholes*, ed. Daniel Lerner (New York, 1963), and also in Richards' revision of *Science and Poetry* (1926) under the new title *Poetries and Sciences* (New York, 1970). His appreciation of Shelley's *Prometheus Unbound*, in *Major British Writers*, ed. G. B. Harrison, vol. 2 (New York, 1959), is a complicated blend of practical criticism with some other features.
Both in "Variant Readings . . ." and in "The Future of Poetry" Richards performs for criticism the valuable service of defusing the term "encode" with which mathematical "information" engineers are currently threatening the field of literary study. The Code Napoleon as an analogue of poetic

V

One other date, and the chronicle aspect of my paper is completed. In 1963 I edited for the English Institute a small collection of essays from its earlier years, under a title taken from one of my own in the *Essays* of 1951: *Explication as Criticism*. In a Foreword, looking back to the *floruit* of American explicatory criticism in the 1940's, and thinking of the free orientation within which it had operated, I invoked the five boundary forms of human awareness which Richards in *Practical Criticism* (p. 290) had seen as the conditions of "sincere" (i.e., adequate) "feeling" in the confrontation of poems:—man's fundamental loneliness, the "inexplicable oddity" of his birth and death, the "inconceivable immensity of the Universe," the vast perspective of time, the enormity of man's ignorance. These ideas seemed to me a better (a more objective, yet more flexible) frame of reference for literary criticism than the fantastically pigeon-holed neo-Aristotelian categories of the then-prevalent school of mythopoeic vision. In a parallel way, I have here been celebrating the insistent, the unrelaxing or relentless, concern for *value* manifested by Richards over the many years of his career (in spite of his hypersensitivity to the difficulties), and, no less, his confidence in the integrity of poems, the difference between right and wrong readings (again in spite of his almost tortured awareness of the difficulties). The critical thinking of Richards has always cut close to the quick of poetic interest. It has been exciting. It has generated a world of ideas favorable to a general excitement with criticism. And for that reason I see it as a better kind of critical thinking than most of the now emergent vogues:—the boundless expansions of the school of "consciousness," the self-justifying apparatuses of transformational grammar, the neutralisms of historical hermeneutics, the despairs of the trope of "silence," the "aleatory" assemblage of *textes* from newspaper, dictionary, or telephone directory, the celebrations of the "death of literature," the various other attempts to play midwife to the "post-modern imagination."

Like the object of his recurrent study Coleridge, like Arnold and Eliot, Richards has always been a believer in the superior vision of the superior. He is an aristocrat of the intelligence: "Are we to think that what is thought by enough people thereby becomes what should be thought?"[12]

---

systems? Perhaps . . . with due caution. The Morse Code? One language translated into another? In the text of a poem, what is encoded into what?

12. "Variant Readings and Misreading," in *Style in Language*, ed. Sebeok, p. 251.

Those ultimate ideas framing "sincerity" which I have quoted above from *Practical Criticism* of course remind me of the large difference between sacramental religion and secular humanism. One might have thought the obstacle to any shared experience of or thinking about poetry was insurmountable. Early statements by Richards, his essays on Dostoevsky and Hopkins, might strengthen this misgiving. No doubt he would now reaffirm these. Yet there is also such a phenomenon as the assurance with which the Richards of *Practical Criticism* pronounces, on the one hand, upon a certain exercise in soft-focus nature piety ("Between the erect and solemn trees, I will go down upon my knees"—Poem 7) and, on the other, upon the clamor and the quiet of a sonnet which requires in its reader no less than an acquaintance "with the rules for attendance at the Day of Judgment" (Poem 3).[13] "It is in the nature of some performances that they leave the spectator feeling rather helpless." I have written this essay out of a happy conviction that poetry and even the criticism of poetry are places of subsumption and reconcilement (of imagination)—where the dialogues of our opposed minds can take place without rancor, and with enlightenment.

At the Indiana conference in the spring of 1958, we sat around a big table and, after hearing papers, engaged in open debates. In a corner of the room tape recorders were busy. In a final session we heard summary papers by Roman Jakobson, George A. Miller, and René Wellek. It happened that near the end of the ensuing conversation, I got the floor and spoke briefly, urging something about the identity of "ends" and "means" in poetry. "A poem is a verbal expression which has no end except to be known." I alluded to "Harvard Yard in April." As these impromptu speeches were edited for the proceedings of the conference, only one sentence follows my little sprint. Except for a bibliography and an index, these are the closing words of the volume:

RICHARDS: Mr. Wimsatt and I are not in disagreement.

It is my hope that, with the insertion of some such word as "substantially" at some point in this sentence, he will be able to repeat it on reading this essay.

1973

13. See Richards' reflections upon this situation in *Practical Criticism*, pp. 271-73.

INDEX

Abrams, Meyer, 88, 210-12 passim
Addison, Joseph: *Spectator*, 62, 155
Aims and Methods of Scholarship in Modern Languages and Literatures, 79
Akenside, Mark, 122
Aldenham, Lord: *The Game of Ombre*, 106
Aldridge, Alfred Owen, 36; "Biography in the Interpretation of Poetry," 13*n*, 16*n*
Amiel, Henri, 187
Apollinaire, Guillaume: *Calligrammes, Poèmes de la paix et de la guerre*, 62, 72-73
Arabian Nights, 155
Aristotle, 21, 46, 50, 55, 77 and *n*, 85, 88, 100; *Poetics*, 76-77, 90; and syllogisms, 81; and form, 213, 222; and entity, 231
Arne, Thomas, 125
Arnold, Matthew, 21*n*, 78, 217; "The Literary Influence of Academies," 167
Ausonius: *Technopaegnion*, 62*n*
Axelos, Kostas: *Vers la Pensée planetaire*, 99; *Le Jeu du monde*, 99

Babbitt, Irving, 45
Bachelard, Gaston, 193
Bailey, Nathan, 179; *Dictionarium*, 162, 164, 165
Baker, Sheridan: "*Rasselas:* Psychological Irony and Romance," 158*n*
Barthes, Roland: *Writing degree Zero*, 9*n*; "Criticism as Language," 198*n*
Bateson, F. W., 48, 220; "Linguistics and Literary Criticism," 202*n*
Baudelaire, Charles, 11, 221; *Les Chats*, 200-01 and *n*
Beardsley, Monroe, 14, 28*n*, 29; "Intention" (1944), 12, 23, 25, 26, 35-36; "The Intentional Fallacy" (1945), 12, 16*n*, 23, 24, 27, 30, 35-36 and *n*; *Aesthetics* (1958), 12-13, 23, 24 and *n*, 36 and *n*; "Textual Meaning and the Authorial Meaning," 38*n*
Beaujour, Michel: "Flight out of

Time: Poetic Language and the Revolution," 7
Beckett, Samuel: *Watt*, 85-86; *Murphy*, 105
Bentham, Jeremy, 69
Berger, Harry, 219
Berne, Eric: *Games People Play*, 113
Bernini, Giovanni, 52
Birch, Thomas, 165*n*
Blackstone, Bernard, 207
Blake, William, 26, 80, 86, 93-94, 221; *An ancient Proverb*, 31, 33; *Songs of Experience*, 31, 47, 138; *London*, 31-34, 47 and *n*; pictorial art of, 46-48, 63, 85, 207; *Jerusalem*, 47; *Songs of Innocence*, 47, 138; *The Blossom*, 48; *Infant Joy*, 48; *Infant Sorrow*, 63*n*; *Poetical Sketches*, 135-38; *To Spring*, 136-37; *To the Evening Star*, 137; *To Morning*, 137; *Song*, 137; *To the Muses*, 137; *Blind Man's Buff*, 137
Bloom, Harold, 137, 138
Bloomfield, Leonard, 198
Boleslavsky, Richard, 70
Bolingbroke, Lord, 169
Booth, Stephen: *Essay on Shakespeare's Sonnets*, 221
Booth, Wayne: *The Rhetoric of Fiction*, 19
Bossu, René le, 114; *Treatise*, 110
Boswell, James, 34, 156, 170; *The Life of Samuel Johnson*, 17; on *Rasselas*, 140, 147, 153; on Johnson's *Dictionary*, 164, 165, 168
Botticelli, Sandro, 49
Brady, Frank: "The History and Structure of Pope's *To a Lady*," 218*n*
Brink, C. O., 230; *Horace on Poetry: Prolegomena to the Literary Epistles*, 229*n*, 232*n*; *Horace on Poetry: The Ars Poetica*, 229*n*, 230*n*
Bronson, Bertrand H., 45, 124, 129
Brooks, Cleanth, 124, 125, 136; *William Faulkner*, 192; *Literary Criticism: A Short History*, 224
Brown, Mrs.: of Falkland, 129

251